Tolley's Ba
to Pens

by
Simon Cann
Towers Perrin

Philip Churchhill
GlaxoSmithKline plc

Lisa Gillespie
Eversheds

Simon Head
Aon Consulting

Members of the LexisNexis Group worldwide

United Kingdom	Butterworths Tolley, a Division of Reed Elsevier (UK) Ltd, 2 Addiscombe Road, CROYDON CR9 5AF
Argentina	Abeledo Perrot, Jurisprudencia Argentina and Depalma, BUENOS AIRES
Australia	Butterworths, a Division of Reed International Books Australia Pty Ltd, CHATSWOOD, New South Wales
Austria	ARD Betriebsdienst and Verlag Orac, VIENNA
Canada	Butterworths Canada Ltd, MARKHAM, Ontario
Chile	Publitecsa and Conosur Ltda, SANTIAGO DE CHILE
Czech Republic	Orac sro, PRAGUE
France	Editions du Juris-Classeur SA, PARIS
Hong Kong	Butterworths Asia (Hong Kong), HONG KONG
Hungary	Hvg Orac, BUDAPEST
India	Butterworths India, NEW DELHI
Ireland	Butterworths (Ireland) Ltd, DUBLIN
Italy	Giuffré, MILAN
Malaysia	Malayan Law Journal Sdn Bhd, KUALA LUMPUR
New Zealand	Butterworths of New Zealand, WELLINGTON
Poland	Wydawnictwa Prawnicze PWN, WARSAW
Singapore	Butterworths Asia, SINGAPORE
South Africa	Butterworths Publishers (Pty) Ltd, DURBAN
Switzerland	Stämpfli Verlag AG, BERNE
USA	LexisNexis, DAYTON, Ohio

© Reed Elsevier (UK) Ltd 2001

All rights reserved. No part of this publication may be reproduced in any material form (including photocopying or storing it in any medium by electronic means and whether or not transiently or incidentally to some other use of this publication) without the written permission of the copyright owner except in accordance with the provisions of the Copyright, Designs and Patents Act 1988 or under the terms of a licence issued by the Copyright Licensing Agency Ltd, 90 Tottenham Court Road, London, England W1P 0LP. Applications for the copyright owner's written permission to reproduce any part of this publication should be addressed to the publisher.

Warning: The doing of an unauthorised act in relation to a copyright work may result in both a civil claim for damages and criminal prosecution.

Any Crown copyright material is reproduced with the permission of the Controller of Her Majesty's Stationery Office. Any European material in this work which has been reproduced from EUR-lex, the official European Communities legislation website, is European Communities copyright.

A CIP Catalogue record for this book is available from the British Library.

ISBN 0 7545 0745 9

Typeset by Tradespools Ltd, Vallis House, Robins Lane, Frome, Somerset BA11 3EG
Printed by Antony Rowe Ltd, Chippenham, Wilts

Visit Butterworths LexisNexis *direct* at www.butterworths.com

Preface

The aim of this book is simple. Starting from a position of no prior knowledge whatsoever, the reader should be able to get a broad understanding of all the main concepts of pension provision in the UK, and be left with a useful reference guide to dip back into from time to time.

This seems a simple goal, and fifteen years ago would not even have needed a whole book - maybe just a few handouts. However, after a period of relative calm from the mid 1970s to the mid 1980s, the last fifteen years have seen constant change in the area of pensions.

Since 1988 we have had the introduction of personal pensions and now stakeholder pensions. We have seen successive rounds of legislation aimed to protect the benefits of pension scheme members, much of it in reaction to the disappearance of funds from the pension schemes controlled by Robert Maxwell. In addition, legislation has been enacted to deal with pension entitlements on divorce and to deal with equal treatment between men and women, full time and part time employees. The State pension system has been changed regularly, culminating with the introduction of the State Second Pension in April 2002.

Employers have been struggling to come to terms with the financial implications of running a pension scheme and many have been reviewing the way they provide pensions. At the same time pension schemes are growing in size and a number in the UK are now worth far more than the companies which run them.

At the same time millions of individuals are simply looking to ensure that, when they retire, they will have an adequate level of income. People are living longer, but wanting to retire earlier, and are looking at how best they can build on whatever they may get by way of a State pension.

For those of us who have been involved in pensions throughout this period, it has been difficult enough to keep up. For anyone entering the field for the first time, or for those who come across the subject and want to understand how it all works, the complications must be

Preface

daunting. That is where this book comes in. It is not meant for pension experts. It is meant for the newcomer, or for the pensions layman who, for whatever reason - job, business, personal interests - wants a basic understanding of UK pension arrangements. When it was written, there was very little on the market offering such a comprehensive basic guide, so we jumped at the chance to help shed some light on a subject which is complex and full of jargon but, at the end of the day, is vital to each and every one of us.

By the time you have read the book you should have a clear understanding of the different types of pension provision in the UK - State, occupational and personal. You should know how they are run, by whom, how they are paid for and the legal framework within which they operate. You should also understand how benefits are calculated and have a feel for the practicalities of running a pension scheme - dealing with members and reporting to the authorities.

For those of you who just wanted the background, we hope this book fulfils that purpose. For those of you embarking on a career in pensions, we hope to give you a good grounding in the subject.

Finally the authors would like to thank the many people who have helped in putting this book together - the staff at Butterworths Tolley who kept us on track, and the many people in our own firms who helped to write, review and produce the content. Their contribution has been invaluable.

Simon Cann, Towers Perrin

Philip Churchill, GlaxoSmithKline

Lisa Gillespie, Eversheds

Simon Head, Aon Consulting

Contents

	Page
Abbreviations	ix
1. Introduction - The Pension Scheme and its purpose	**1**
How to use this book	1
History	2
Historical overview of legislation	4
Where are we now?	4
Concept and purpose of pension schemes	5
Who can join pension schemes?	7
When do you retire?	8
Calculation of early retirement payments	9
Calculation of late retirement payments	10
Early retirement without penalty	10
Why have a pension scheme?	11
2. Types of Pension Provision	**13**
Introduction	13
State pensions	14
Basic State pension	14
State Earnings Related Pension (SERPS)	15
State Second Pension	16
Contributions	16
Occupational pensions	17
Types	17
Design methods	19
Design details	20
Personal pensions	26
Contribution limits	26
Income drawdown	27
Self-Invested Personal Pensions	27
Stakeholder pensions	28
Background	28
Contract based	30
Trust based	31
Unapproved pensions	31
Background	31
Funded	31
Unfunded	32
Comments	33
3. The Legal Framework	**34**
Introduction	34

Contents

Trust law	34
Statutes governing pensions	36
Secondary legislation	38
Decided cases	38
European law	39
Inland Revenue limits	40
Defined terms used by the Inland Revenue	41
Limits on contributions	43
Limits on benefits	43
Summary of Inland Revenue limits on benefits	44
Contracting out	49
Guaranteed minimum pensions	50
The reference scheme test	51
Money purchase schemes	52
Mixed benefit schemes	53
Transfers from contracted-out schemes	54
Useful addresses	55

4. Trustee Duties and Liabilities   56

Introduction	56
Duties of trustees	57
Duty to act in accordance with the trust deed and rules	57
Duty to act prudently, conscientiously and honestly	58
Duty to act in the best interests of scheme members	59
Duty to act impartially between scheme members	59
Duty to pay benefits	60
Duty to collect contributions	61
Duty to produce a schedule of contributions or a payment schedule	62
Duty to keep separate bank accounts and scheme records	63
Duty to obtain audited accounts	63
Duty to invest the fund	64
Duty to appoint professional advisers	66
Duty to disclose information	67
Duty to register	69
Duty to comply with the Data Protection Act 1998	70
Duty to comply with court orders relating to divorce	72
Duty to appoint member-nominated trustees	74
Duty to comply with the Disability Discrimination Act 1995	74
Duty to implement an internal dispute resolution procedure	74
Duty to provide equal treatment	75
Duty to comply with PA 1995 s 67 in amending scheme rules	77
Powers of trustees	77
Power to delegate	78
Power to amend	79
Power to augment	81
Power to distribute lump sum on death	81
Power to make or accept transfers	81
Trustee liabilities	83

Penalties under PA 1995	84
Table of penalties	84
Liability under trust law	93
Protection of trustees	96
Trust deed exclusion clauses	97
Indemnity clauses	98
Insurance	99
Trustee Act 1925, s 61	100
Exercise of trustee powers	100
Decision making	100
Trust deed and rules	101
Notice of meetings	101
Minutes of meetings	101
Useful addresses	102
Useful texts	102

5. People in Pensions — 103

Introduction	103
The employer	104
Trustees	107
Eligibility to be a trustee	107
Appointment and removal of trustees	108
Remuneration of trustees	109
Member-nominated trustees	110
Independent trustees	111
Professional trustees	112
Pensioneer trustees	112
Custodian trustees	113
The scheme actuary	113
Auditor	115
Administrator	116
Legal and other advisors	116
Fund managers	117
Pension consultants and administrators	118
Inland Revenue	118
OPRA	119
OPAS	120
Pensions Compensation Board	120
Pensions Ombudsman	121
Useful addresses	121

6. Scheme Documents — 122

Introduction	122
Documents establishing a scheme	122
Deeds of removal, retirement and appointment of trustees	124
Deeds of amendment	124
Deeds of adherence or participation	124
Scheme booklet	125
Statement of investment principles	128

Contents

Audited accounts	128
Company accounts	129
Actuarial valuation report	130
Trustees' annual report	131
Schedule of contributions and payment schedule	133
Contracting-out certificate	135
Internal dispute resolution procedure	136
Useful addresses	136

7. Information for Scheme Members — **137**

Information or communication?	137
Disclosure Regulations	137
Communication material	139
Scheme booklet	139
Trustees report and accounts	140
Benefit statements	141
Statements of entitlement	145
Presentations	146
Other forms of communication to members	147
Effective communication strategies	147

8. Benefit Calculations — **149**

Introduction	149
Structure of model plans	149
Defined benefit plan	150
Defined contribution plan	152
Retirement from the defined benefit plan	153
Member's details	153
Calculation of normal retirement pension	153
Calculation of normal retirement lump sum	155
Effect of lump sum on normal retirement pension	155
Calculation of early retirement pension	155
Calculation of early retirement lump sum and effect on pension	157
Calculation of late retirement pension and lump sum	158
Retirement from the defined contribution plan	158
Key factors affecting the amount of pension under the defined contribution plan	159
Calculation of retirement benefits under a defined contribution plan	161
Leaving the plan	164
Increases under the defined benefit plan between leaving and retirement	164
Increases under the defined contribution plan between leaving and retirement	167
Increases to pensions in payment	168
Benefits on death in service	169
Benefits on death in service under a defined benefit plan	169
Benefits on death in service under a defined contribution plan	171

Benefits on death after leaving service under a defined benefits plan	172
Benefits on death after leaving service under a defined contribution plan	173
Benefits on death in retirement under a defined benefit plan	174
Benefits on death in retirement under a defined contribution plan	175
Benefits on disability	175
Pension benefits on retirement on disability grounds from the defined benefit plan	175
Benefits on divorce: pension splitting	176
Calculating benefits on divorce under the defined benefit plan	177
Calculating benefits on divorce under the defined contribution plan	177
Record keeping	178
Member joins the plan	178
Ongoing/annual	179
Leaving service	179
Retirement	180
Death	180
Inland Revenue limits	180
9. Funding and Valuations	**186**
What is funding?	186
Why fund a pension scheme?	186
Money purchase schemes	187
Actuarial valuations	188
Timing of valuations	188
What the actuary does	188
What the actuary does not do	189
The ongoing valuation	192
Sample valuation result	195
The discontinuance valuation	195
The minimum funding requirement (MFR)	196
The surplus test	197
The valuation report	198
10. Investment	**199**
Trustees' investment duties	199
The prudent man	199
The best interests of the scheme members	199
Expert advice	201
Diversifying investments	201
Investments must be suitable	202
Self investment	202
Statement of investment principles	202
What do pension schemes invest in?	203
Investment strategy	205
Setting strategy in a final salary scheme	206
Setting strategy in a money purchase scheme	208

Contents

Investment structure	210
Insured, pooled or segregated	210
Approaches to investment management	212
Investment manager selection	213
Past performance	214
Other aspects	214
Performance targets	215
Monitoring the investment manager	215
11. Additional Voluntary Contributions	**216**
Introduction	216
Why AVCs?	217
Types of AVC	219
Occupational	219
Free-standing AVCs	219
Stakeholder	220
Personal pension	220
Types of benefit	221
Money purchase	221
Fixed pension	221
Added years	221
Advantages/disadvantages	222
Investment	222
Building society	222
With profits	223
Unit-linked	225
Scheme assets	226
Matching	227
AVC projections	227
Rough guide	228
Range of assumptions	228
Flexibility at retirement	229
Ability to take benefits other than at normal retirement	229
Drawdown as opposed to taking at retirement	229
What if there is too much benefit?	230
Appendix A	*232*
Appendix B	*237*
Glossary	*242*
Table of Statutes	*326*
Table of Statutory Instruments	*329*
Table of Cases	*330*
Table of European Legislation	*330*
Index	*331*

Abbreviations

AVC	Additional voluntary contributions
COEG	Contracted Out Employment Group
COMBS	Contracted Out Mixed Benefit Scheme
COMPS	Contracted Out Money Purchase Scheme
COSRS	Contracted Out Salary Related Scheme
CSPSSA 2000	Child Support, Pensions and Social Security Act 2000
DB	Defined benefit
DC	Defined contribution
DPA 1998	Data Protection Act 1998
DSS	Department of Social Security
DWP	Department for Work and Pensions
ECJ	European Court of Justice
ECON	Employer's contracting-out number
FA	Finance Act
FSAVC	Free-standing additional voluntary contributions
GMP	Guaranteed minimum pension
GPP	Group personal pension
ICTA 1988	Income and Corporation Taxes Act 1988
ISA	Individual savings account
LEL	Lower earnings limit
LPI	Limited price indexation
MFR	Minimum funding requirement
MNT	Member-nominated trustee
NAE	National average earnings
NAPF	National Association of Pension Funds
NICs	National Insurance Contributions
NRA	Normal retirement age
NRD	Normal retirement date
OPAS	Pensions Advisory Service
OPRA	Occupational Pensions Regulatory Authority
PA 1995	Pensions Act 1995
PSA 1993	Pension Schemes Act 1993
PSO	Pension Schemes Office
RSC	Rules of the Supreme Court
S2P	State Second Pension
SCON	Scheme contracting-out number
SERPS	State Earnings Related Pension

SIPPS	Self-Invested Personal Pension Scheme
SORP	Statement of Recommended Practice
SSAS	Small Self-Administered Scheme
TA 1925	Trustee Act 1925
TA 2000	Trustee Act 2000
UBE	Upper band earnings
UEL	Upper earnings limit
WRPA 1999	Welfare Reform and Pensions Act 1999

1 – Introduction – The Pension Scheme and its Purpose

> This chapter covers the following:
>
> - History of pensions in the UK.
> - A review of one hundred years of legislation.
> - The current position and its complexity.
> - What pension schemes are for, their concept and purpose.
> - Who can join pension schemes.
> - When you can retire including early and late retirement.
> - Why have pension schemes?

How to use this book [1.1]

This book is intended to be both a basic overview of the whole subject of privately provided pensions and also a text book which can be referred to for information on a specific subject. It will be most appreciated by professionals who are new to the subject or non-pensions professionals who have a little knowledge.

The book is not intended to be an exhaustive review of the whole subject. It would need to be at least ten times larger to be able to even start to approach that level. It covers mainly occupational pension schemes set up by employers, but does contain some information on personal plans taken out by individuals.

Basic Guide to Pensions

This book is so designed that you can read the whole book if you want a quick overview or dip into various sections if you want information on a specific subject using the Contents section and/or the Index.

The book covers a wide range of subjects which are outlined below.

- This Chapter – Introduction, background, history, what pensions are all about.
- Chapter 2 – Summary of types of scheme and their features.
- Chapter 3 – The legal background including trust law and social security.
- Chapter 4 – Trustees, their duties, powers, responsibilities and liabilities.
- Chapter 5 – Who does what, why and how. How it all works.
- Chapter 6 – Paperwork. The documents needed to run a scheme both legally and on a day to day basis.
- Chapter 7 – What the members must be told.
- Chapter 8 – How benefits are calculated, the record keeping and administration.
- Chapter 9 – Actuarial work, funding and valuations.
- Chapter 10 – Investment. Where the money goes and how to check it is working well.
- Chapter 11 – Additional voluntary contributions. How much can be saved and why it can be a good idea.

History

Pension schemes in the UK can be traced back to pre-Roman tribal times. When a member of the tribe became too old to contribute they were looked after from the tribal assets. This 'pay-as-you-go' system is effectively the same system that the government uses today

The Pension Scheme and its Purpose [1.2]

for the old age pension. Current income (National Insurance Contributions) is used to pay current expenditure (old age pension). There is no attempt to save for the future.

We know that some saving was made in Roman times and later because people with metal detectors dig up stores of coins originally hidden for use in the future. These stores are equivalent to today's pension schemes where savings are put on one side during a productive working life in order that an income can be enjoyed when work ceases. The disadvantage of saving coins is that their value is eroded by inflation, so what you store buys less when you spend it than it did when you stored it.

The need to encourage people to retire when they were no longer able to work effectively brought about the first more recognisable pension schemes. When taking up a job with the Admiralty, Samuel Pepys records on 17 July 1660 that he agreed to pay £50 p.a 'if my salary be not encreased and £100 per annum if it be encreased to £350'. This was part of the normal procedure on taking over a job from another. In fact Pepys had already been told on 7 July his salary was to be increased from £100 p.a. to £350 p.a. It is not recorded exactly how much he did pay.

It became normal for persons employing others to make provision for their retirement, but on an ad hoc basis. A farmer or landowner might permit a worker to retain the use of a cottage and small piece of land and also add a small stipend. A shop keeper or mill owner might ensure that there was a small payment made to old employees. Those that were not provided for in this way had to rely on their own savings or become a cost to the State, often in the form of the local parish poor house or similar institution.

The common thread through these individual arrangements is that they were set up when needed, i.e. when an employee became too old to work productively. It was very rare for any promise to be made in advance and so there was no saving for the event of retirement. The landowner or shopkeeper made what provision they could afford when the employee could no longer work. We are back to the pay-as-you-go system.

By extension of this type of ad hoc personal responsibility the Civil Service became the first organisation to establish a true pension scheme. It had to set up a scheme to cope with the relatively large number of people employed and to ensure some measure of consistency in the treatment of those people. Because certainty was introduced by way of a promise as to what the retirement benefit would be, it became possible to save for the event itself. Thus were pre-funded pension schemes developed.

Historical overview of legislation [1.3]

A whole series of legislation started from the early part of the 20th century. This gradually codified, and made more complex, the provision of pensions whether by government, employer or the individual. Outlines of the legislation passed are given in Appendix A. You will particularly notice the increasing frequency of legislation.

The main effect of all this legislation is to make more complex the whole system. No attempt has been made to review the system as a whole. The main reason for this lack of total review is that the whole area has traditionally been split between two government agencies, taxation and social security. The Inland Revenue has essentially been concentrating on keeping in check the tax reliefs and breaks available. The social security agency (under various names) has been concentrating on ensuring that the integration of State and private benefits is effective but not overly partial to the private sector.

The failure of all governments since the Second World War to combine the competing views of these two departments has led to the current excessive and costly complexity.

Where are we now? [1.4]

The UK has (arguably) the most comprehensive, effective and regulated pension systems in the world. There is a State basic pension as a safety net; a State Earnings Related Pension to provide a better level of provision based on employee and employer participation. Occupational pensions are encouraged both by tax breaks and the ability to (minimally) profitably replace the State Earnings Related Pension. Personal pensions for the self-employed are encouraged, as is additional provision by members of occupational schemes.

The investment of all of the contributions and accumulated fund is a major driver of the Stock Market and has placed UK investment managers at the leading edge of their business world wide.

The expertise of UK actuaries is universally acknowledged and the skills of UK pensions lawyers and administrators is the envy of many countries.

Against this background of success and achievement must be set the current confusion and complexity of the domestic scene. An individual may find themselves in up to eleven different types of pension scheme (or combinations of these):

- basic State;
- additional State;
- occupational;
- personal;
- group personal;
- additional voluntary contribution;
- stakeholder;
- small self-administered;
- self-invested personal;
- funded unapproved;
- unfunded unapproved,

and quite possibly there will be more introduced in the near future (the Treasury has ideas on this).

Individuals are able to take some qualified advice on this range, but in some areas advice is effectively forbidden by strict rules on costs.

The whole system cries out for comprehensive and all embracing review. Don't hold your breath!

Concept and purpose of pension schemes [1.5]

A paper produced by Charles Booth in 1899 stated:

> 'Everywhere a good deal is done for old servants. Their care is a recognised charge on all industrial or commercial undertakings of Character and long standing.'

This paternalistic view of pensions is typical of the establishment of schemes by employers up to and including the 1970s. Gradually, during the latter half of the 20th century this view became overtaken by a more commercial position. From 1959 the government offered a reduction in National Insurance Contributions (NICs) paid by both companies and their employees. In return the company pension scheme became responsible for replacing the State graduated pension. The reduction offered was greater than the cost of replacing the graduated pension forgone. It was possible therefore to make a small 'profit' on the deal. It is doubtful if any company took this course merely to obtain the profit, other considerations made this unlikely. However, a signal had been given that there could be good commercial reasons to set up a pension scheme.

From the 1960s matters such as the ability to acquire, retain and selectively remove staff had become considerations. These were reinforced by the government's action in 1978 when a new State pension system was brought in which encouraged greater provision by employers.

The influence of trades unions in pension provision should not be forgotten. Whilst they have never had the level of influence as in Australia or in France (where trades unions help to run the various State related pension schemes), they have encouraged the establishment and extension of pension arrangements, and often take a useful and responsible part in the trusteeship role.

Today pensions are normally seen as part of an employee's earnings. The total earnings are split, part to be paid immediately and part to be deferred and invested for the future. This is, again, reinforced by government action. Governments around the world are being faced by the fact that people are living longer, intending to retire earlier and thus becoming a greater drain upon pay-as-you-go State pensions. At the same time workers are spending longer in the education process and retiring earlier and thus reducing the period over which they contribute.

The end result is more to pay out and less being paid in. Pay-as-you-go systems are out of balance and cannot cope unless either contributions are increased or benefits reduced. An increase in contributions has an immediate effect on the electorate. A reduction in benefit at some time in the future does not have the same immediate effect. It is not surprising that politicians with an eye to the next election choose benefit reduction.

The Pension Scheme and its Purpose **[1.6]**

Although not seen so clearly, benefit reductions are noticed by the electorate. Various polls and surveys have shown that current workers do not expect to be able to rely on the state to provide them with an adequate pension in retirement. Today's workers therefore know they must look to either their employer or themselves to make provision for their future.

Paragraph [1.4] above gives an overview of the multitude of choices facing current employees, and the complexity they face.

Who can join pension schemes? [1.6]

Almost anyone can join a pension scheme of some type. Essentially pension schemes fall into two main groups:

- work-related provision; and
- personal provision.

If you are employed you may well be eligible to join a scheme set up by your employer, trade union or trade association. Some employers belong to multi-employer schemes run by an employer association; to the employee these often look like the employer's own scheme.

If you are not employed, or if your employer offers no scheme, you can make your own provision through a personal pension or a stakeholder pension.

Entry to an employment-based pension scheme is regulated by the eligibility conditions of each scheme. Employers will set limits on who can join and when to suit their particular company circumstances. An employer with a high labour turnover in the early years of employment may make it a condition of pension scheme membership that the employee has completed, say, two or three years of continuous employment before joining. An alternative may be to make the minimum age for joining the attainment of 30. Combinations of age and service are common conditions, with the objective of excluding people who would move quickly into and out of the scheme thus generating little or no benefit but increasing administration costs.

The result tends to be a set of conditions such as:

- at least age 25 and under age 60, and with two years' continuous service;
- over age 18 and under age 64, and with 12 months' continuous service.

An additional hurdle for prospective members to complete may be some form of grade or job description. Employees may have to be 'Grade 5 or higher' or 'permanent staff' or some other similar description.

When a job description is combined with age and service requirements the actual membership may become a remarkably small proportion of the total workforce.

An area of great difficulty for eligibility conditions is the matter of equality. There must be no hint of sex discrimination in the eligibility terms and this includes indirect discrimination. A practical (and genuine) example of this was found in lingerie manufacture. The eligibility conditions were: 'attained age 18 but not age 64 and earning at least standard base pay'; 'standard base pay' was defined as '£12,000 p.a. increasing at the same rate each year as the average increase awarded to all staff within the factory'.

At the time, the maximum earnings in the factory were about £11,000 p.a. and the staff in the factory were 95% female machinists. The minimum pay in the offices was about £11,500 p.a. and the vast majority of the staff was male.

This set of conditions was decided to be indirect discrimination as it excluded nearly all female staff but not males, and would continue to do so into the future. It is obvious that eligibility conditions must be set with care and with detailed knowledge of the particular circumstances of a given company and the likely effect of those conditions.

When do you retire? [1.7]

As an individual you can make your own decision on the date of your retirement, but the rules set by the Pension Schemes Office and the particular scheme of which you are a member will have a profound influence on your decision.

The Pension Scheme and its Purpose **[1.8]**

To obtain approval the rules of a pension scheme must set a normal retirement age (NRA). This must be non-discriminatory and is thus usually the same for males and females. There is an immediate conflict between this fixed and legal NRA and the State scheme where the retirement ages are 65 for males and 60 for females. This conflict may well be more in the legal terms than in reality. Many people choose to retire at ages other than the NRA. See paragraph [2.18] for a further discussion of this.

If you wish to retire earlier than the NRA the benefit paid will be reduced. The reason for a reduction is that both member and employer will have paid less than expected into the scheme and the member will draw a benefit for longer than expected, i.e. from early retirement to normal retirement date (NRD) plus the normal time after NRD. There is less money going in and a longer period to pay money out. A smaller amount must be stretched over a longer period and thus less paid out in each instalment.

Calculation of early retirement payments [1.8]

The exact method of calculation of the early retirement reduction will be set out in the rules of the scheme. The technically correct method will require actuarial calculations including consideration of altered mortality and morbidity, lost interest, etc. However, for practical purposes and for ease of communication it is not unusual for the exact calculation to be replaced by a simple formula along the lines of:

> 'a reduction of 5% in the accrued pension for each year (proportionate for part years) the member retires early'.

In this case the pension normally paid at NRD for service completed to date would be calculated and that amount reduced by 5% for each year early. Thus for a male with an NRD of 65 but actually retiring when aged 55 with 20 years' service the calculation would be:

(Pension at NRD for 20 years) less 50% (i.e. 10 years early times 5%).

It will be seen that the reduction is considerable. It should be noted that the pension is also based on the salary at age 55 and not on the salary at 65. Additionally the State pension will not be paid until 65 and it will be reduced below the normal level as the member has not worked from age 55 to age 65. Overall the loss of spending power is considerable.

Calculation of late retirement payments [1.9]

Late retirement also changes the pension payable, but the change is not as extreme. Normally both the member and the employer cease contributions at NRD. This means the only effects which will apply are those of interest for late payment and changes in mortality due to the late retirement. The result is usually shown as a simple rate of interest to be applied to the pension accrued at NRD, for instance:

> 'an increase of 5% applied to the pension accrued at NRD for each year after NRD (proportionate for part years) that the member defers drawing pension'.

In both the cases of late and early retirement the exact rate of interest may be replaced with a wording such as:

> 'at a rate of interest recommended from time to time by the appointed scheme actuary'.

This type of wording overcomes objections to out of date rates of interest particularly in times of fluctuating rates or unusually high rates.

Early retirement without penalty [1.10]

Many schemes now set a NRD of age 65 for both males and females, but allow all to retire at age 60 without penalty. This means females can retire when their old age pension is due without suffering additional loss under the employer-based scheme. Whilst this is stated to be 'without penalty' the service taken into account would be only that up to the date of retirement and they would not receive any additional amount for service uncompleted between ages 60 and 65. The 'without penalty' refers to the fact that there is no additional reduction to take account of the fact that the pension will be paid for a longer period. See paragraph [2.18] for a further discussion of this.

Pension ages in the range 60 to 65 are normal, there would have to be good reason for another age to gain approval of the Pension

Schemes Office. There are exceptions where it is obvious that earlier retirement is required. Obvious occupations such as footballer, jockey and airline pilot have lower retirement ages. It is most unusual to find retirement ages over age 65.

Why have a pension scheme? [1.11]

The standard reasons for an employer to take the trouble to have a pension scheme are based around the concepts of:

- competitive advantage;
- statutory requirement (local government, Quangos, etc.);
- staff attraction;
- staff retention;
- deferred pay (i.e. if some pay is not deferred more must be paid immediately raising other overhead costs such as NICs).

There are still some employers who will look upon the provision of a pension scheme as 'the right thing to do'. Paternalism is not dead.

A long-sighted view would be that if current saving for pensions is not instituted, future costs by way of taxation will be much higher as the State tries to cope with a failing pay-as-you-go system. Paying a 'voluntary tax' now is cheaper than paying a compulsory tax in the future.

Pensions should not be seen in isolation. Pensions are a part of the total reward which is paid to an employee for a given amount and level of work. The total package will be made up of:

- immediate basic items such as base pay;
- immediate incentive items such as annual bonus based upon short-term results;
- medium-term incentives, share save plans, etc.;
- long-term incentives, share options, long term bonus, etc.;
- deferred items, pensions, savings incentive plans, etc.

[1.11] *Basic Guide to Pensions*

The particular mix of total reward elements for any employment will be decided by the employer (perhaps in conjunction with employees, trades unions and the like) based upon perceived need, competitive advantage and (to a certain extent) tradition within the industry sector. Thus banks traditionally have a high non-pay benefits package whilst the building industry does not.

2 – Types of Pension Provision

> This chapter covers the following:
>
> - State pension provision (basic, earnings related, and projected methods) and the cost of these.
>
> - Occupational pensions showing the various types and covering many design considerations.
>
> - Personal pensions.
>
> - Stakeholder pensions.
>
> - Unapproved pensions.

Introduction [2.1]

Total income in retirement comes from a mixture of sources. Some people will have only the basic old age pension. They may never have worked to gain an occupational pension or saved to have a personal or stakeholder pension. But even these people will receive additional payments from the government in the form of income supplement or other payments which means that their total income comes from more than one source.

Most people will have at least two, and frequently three or more, sources of income in retirement. The sources can be thought of as the components of a wall of income.

Private provision through personal savings, additional voluntary contributions, personal pension, stakeholder etc.	
State Earnings Related Pension	Occupational pension
Basic State pension	

[2.2] *Basic Guide to Pensions*

The Basic State pension will be received by all. In addition employed persons will receive either the State Earnings Related Pension (SERPs) or an occupational pension. Above this level the individual has the opportunity to make personal provision in various ways. Because pension arrangements attract tax advantages there are limits and restrictions on their use. Some people will decide that all or part of their saving for retirement should be through a non-pensions route such as individual savings accounts (ISAs). Just because this is not the conventional pensions route it should not be ignored. Personal saving can be a valuable addition to formal pension provision.

State pensions [2.2]

State pensions are provided on a pay-as-you-go basis. Contributions collected from employees and employers via National Insurance Contributions are received by the government and immediately paid out as benefits. No fund is built up to ensure benefits in the future can be paid. There is total reliance on the electorate being willing to continue making contributions. There are notional calculations of a 'National Insurance Fund' but this Fund does not truly exist. National Insurance Contributions and pension payments are effectively part of the general taxation and benefits system, not a separately funded pension scheme.

The level of pension paid depends on whether the pensioner has been contracted in or out (see paragraph [2.14] below). When SERPS started in 1978 it was intended that the total possible State pension should increase from 24% of national average earnings (NAE) in 1978 to between 40% and 45% in 1998. The Basic State pension was about 24% of NAE in 1978 but only 12% in 2001, and is expected to reduce further as it is linked to the Retail Price Index and wages tend to rise faster than prices. By 2020 the maximum State provision is expected to be about 23% of NAE. This scaling down of benefit is common in many other countries.

Basic State pension [2.3]

The Basic State pension is paid to all workers with a full contribution record and from April 2001 amounts to £72.50 per week (£3,770.00 p.a.) for a single person and £115.90 per week (£6,026.80 p.a.) for a married couple.

Types of Pension Provision   [2.4]

The pension is paid weekly and many people collect the pension in cash from a Post Office. It is possible to elect to have the pension paid monthly or quarterly direct into a bank, building society or Post Office account.

A full contribution record requires that the person has contributed for a minimum of 90% of a working lifetime, i.e. between the ages of 16 and 64 (males) or 59 (females). Credits can be gained for periods of unemployment or acting as a full-time carer. Additional credits can be claimed for time spent in various countries, usually members of the Commonwealth. If credits for overseas working are to be claimed it is essential that the documentary evidence presented is strong. Taxation records or local social security payment records would be needed.

State Earnings Related Pension (SERPS)   [2.4]

The State Earnings Related Pension (or SERPS) is additional to the old age pension. The level of benefit is based on earnings over a period and it is possible to buy the pension either from the government (via increased National Insurance Contributions) or through an occupational or personal pension. If SERPS is bought from the government this is known as 'contracting in', if privately via occupational or personal pension it is known as 'contracting out'. More detail on contracting out is given in paragraph [2.14] below.

SERPS is calculated on an upper band earnings (UBE) which is a band of earnings between a lower earnings limit (LEL) of about 1 × Basic State pension, and an upper earnings limit (UEL) of about 7 × Basic State pension. As at April 2001 the LEL was £72 per week (£3,744 p.a.) and the UEL £575 per week (£29,900 p.a.).

The pension is 1% for each year of UBE with a maximum of 20 years to count. To attempt to 'inflation proof' the calculation the UBE is increased each year in line with national average earnings up to State pension age before the 1% calculation is applied. Pensions in payment are increased in line with the Retail Price Index. Higher accrual levels were in force in the past and there is a transitional period to April 2009 when these higher levels are being phased out.

The pension is paid from age 65 for males and 60 for females. The female age will be increased to 65 on a phased basis from April 2010 to April 2020.

State Second Pension [2.5]

From April 2002 SERPS will be replaced by the State Second Pension (S2P). The principles are very similar to SERPS except that:

- those earning below £9,500 annually will be treated as if they had earned £9,500, this includes carers of old people and young children who may not have earned at all;
- earnings between LEL and £9,500 p.a. will attract a 2% pension accrual;
- earnings between £9,500 and £21,600 (note below the current UEL) will attract a 0.5% accrual;
- the 'earnings thresholds' of £9,500 and £21,600 will grow in line with national average earnings.

Contributions [2.6]

The level of contributions to the State system depends on whether you are contracted in or out. There is a reduced level for contracted out persons as the State will pay a smaller benefit to them. The current percentage rates (April 2001) are:

	Employer			Employee	
	Contracted out		Contracted in	Contracted out	Contracted in
	COSR*	COMP*			
Under LEL	0.00	0.00	0.00	0.00	0.00
LEL–£86.99	0.00	0.00	0.00	8.40	10.00
£87.00–UEL	8.90	11.30	11.90	8.40	10.00
Above UEL	11.90	11.90	11.90	0.00	0.00

*COSR = Contracted-Out Salary Related
*COMP = Contracted-Out Money Purchase

Occupational pensions

Types

Large [2.7]

Here we are looking at the majority of occupational pension schemes. They are established by an employer, under trust and thus kept separate from the assets of the employer. A group of people are appointed as trustees to be responsible for the running of the scheme and they in turn appoint advisers to help them. The administration is often run by a specialist, as is investment. Advisers such as an actuary, lawyer, auditor, communications consultant, etc. are also appointed. The basic job of the trustees is to administer the trust as set up by the employer. They are not expected to be expert in every field required which is why the advisers are appointed.

The smaller the scheme the more likely it is to be dealt with by one adviser offering a bundle of services. As the scheme gains more and more members and value, the more likely it is that specialist advisers will be appointed to deal with different parts of the required duties. As happens in many fields it is unlikely that you will find one adviser that is best at all aspects of the job. However, it is more expensive to use separate advisers. A small scheme cannot afford the costs of having a group of advisers, but a large one can make use of the advantages of scale and purchase what is perceived as the best advice from whatever source seems appropriate. Specialist consultants may be made use of by the trustees to help select and monitor administration and investment managers. Some of the largest schemes will have their own administration team and, possibly, their own investment team, both more or less directly employed by the scheme itself.

Schemes with tens of thousands of members and billions of pounds of assets are like a medium to large company and require as much care and attention as a major company would. Some large schemes have effectively branched out and made use of their in-house expertise to set themselves up to assist smaller schemes by offering administration and investment services. By increasing the scale of their business even further they find they can reduce the per capita cost and thus provide cost advantages to both themselves and their new clients.

Small Self-Administered Schemes [2.8]

Small Self-Administered Schemes (SSAS) are a special type of scheme set up to look after a small group of members. The are usually employed for small companies where most of the members will be directors of the company. Not infrequently these companies will not have a lot of spare cash or liquid capital as most of the assets are tied up in the business. The normal rules on investment are relaxed to an extent to allow the scheme to carry assets used by the company as investments of the scheme. It is not unusual for these schemes to hold property used by the company as a pension asset. Although the investment rules may be a little relaxed, this is matched by more strict regulation of investments.

As a quid pro quo for the slightly relaxed rules there are restrictions in some areas. In particular one of the trustees must be a pensioneer trustee. This is a person approved by the Pension Schemes Office as being expert and responsible. They will ensure the rules are followed and that inappropriate investments are not made. When SSASs were first permitted there was a tendency on the part of a minority to use the SSAS to 'hide' assets in a tax efficient manner. A yacht or a holiday home is not considered an appropriate investment for a pensions scheme, particularly if they were previously owned by the managing director of the company concerned. Since August 2000 the pensioneer trustee must also be a party to the scheme bank accounts and a co-owner of the assets.

Members have to use their assets to buy an annuity by age 75. Before that age they can 'draw down' part of their assets each year as a pension. The amount withdrawn is limited to between 35% and 100% of rates set by the Government Actuary's Department. When the eventual annuity is purchased the benefit is still subject to overall benefit limits so it may be that the asset available is too great for the maximum benefit and the balance would have to be returned to the employer or distributed between the other SSAS scheme members. If we are dealing with a family company this option of distributing between scheme members may have considerable merit and could be a useful aid in inheritance planning.

Group personal pensions [2.9]

Personal pensions (see paragraphs [2.22]–[2.25] below) are a contract between the employee (or self-employed person) and a provider, usually an insurance company. They come under contract law not trust law. A group personal pension (GPP) is a set of personal pensions put in place by an employer instead of having an occupational scheme. It is a simplified system where exactly the same insurance contract from one provider is put in place for every individual. The employer may or may not contribute (they usually do). The perceived advantages are simplicity and uniformity.

Design methods [2.10]

Within the various types of pension scheme which can be put together there are various design possibilities.

Final salary [2.11]

In this type of scheme (also known as defined benefit (DB)) the pension payable is a function of service and salary. The formula for pension calculation is usually of the type:

(company service) × (final earnings just before retirement) × (factor)

= pension

The factor used can vary from scheme to scheme. It is often a fraction such as:

1/60 or 1/80 or 1/50

This type of scheme is common in the UK. It provides certainty for the member as the pension to be paid is a known function of final pay and can be shown as a percentage of final pay. The member knows what purchasing power they will have in retirement.

The problem for the employer is that the cost is unknown. The cost of a DB scheme is a function of the investment return achieved in future and the rate of pay inflation from now to retirement age. The higher the return, the lower the cost. The higher the pay inflation, the higher the cost. Effectively the employer underwrites the future rate of inflation. By skilled use of statistical and actuarial techniques an actuary will predict the most likely long-term cost with surprising accuracy. By being conservative in their assumptions actuaries tend to slightly overestimate future costs and the employer tends to pay slightly more than is actually required. At least long-term budgetary control can be established using these techniques.

Money purchase [2.12]

This is effectively the opposite of DB. A money purchase scheme (or defined contribution (DC)) does not calculate the final pension as a basis, but the cost. The employer promises to pay a given percentage of salary as a contribution and invest this along with the employee contributions. The result of these contributions after investment provides the eventual pension. The actual pension payable will depend upon the investment return achieved during the period of membership and the rate at which this capital amount can be converted to a pension. Thus we have a known cost and an unknown pension. There is security for the employer but not for the employees.

Hybrid [2.13]

As the name suggests, this type of scheme is a mixture of DB and DC. It provides "the best of both worlds". A frequent method of providing the pension is to run the scheme as a DC arrangement and, on retirement, apply a DB formula. The actual pension paid is the greater of the DC accumulation and the DB calculation. The cost will obviously be the greater of the normal DB and DC costs, as the benefit is the greater of the two.

Design details

Contracting out [2.14]

An early decision must be made as to whether to contract out or not. Pension schemes are simple in concept. For any given cost a level of benefit can be calculated. If the employer (who designs, sets up and pays the major cost) decides that the pension scheme should give maximum credit to the employer for its establishment and level of generosity then contracting out is likely to be the initial decision. By contracting out the State appears to pay a lower pension and the employer a higher. However, there is a greater level of administrative cost and the employer has linked the scheme to the State system. Bearing in mind that governments in general are seeking to reduce their pension costs, it follows that a scheme linked to the State is likely to automatically pick up any shortfall in government contribution.

A decision to contract out should no longer be automatic. The decision has been complicated by stakeholder pensions. The current government has already indicated that if insufficient employers contribute to stakeholders they are likely to bring in compulsion. If compulsory contributions to stakeholders occur, the concept of compulsory contracting out may not be far behind. Both are effectively an employer subsidy to State provision.

Contracting in [2.15]

The term 'contracting in' implies a definite action takes place. In fact 'contracting in' is what you do if you fail to contract out. The employer and all the employees remain in SERPS and in the occupational scheme at the same time. A deliberate decision may be made to follow this route. If this is done great care must be taken with the scheme design. The problem with contracting in is that the eventual pension could be too high. An occupational scheme giving 1/60th of final salary per year of service provides a maximum pension of 67% of final earnings. Add to this the State maximum of (currently) about 30% of final earnings and it can be seen the replacement income is near 100% of actual earnings.

Conventional wisdom is that pensioners can live more cheaply because they do not have costs associated with working, children or mortgages. It is, perhaps, time this conventional wisdom was challenged. Many pensioners are fit and active enough to undertake voluntary work (with associated costs), have grandchildren and pay rent. There is little reduction in financial need in these circumstances.

A third option is to integrate with the State scheme. This is becoming less attractive as State provision is reduced. Integration automatically increases the private benefit (and thus the private cost) as State benefits reduce.

Pensionable salary [2.16]

How much of earnings should attract a pension? If an employee is paid simply a basic salary the answer is fairly straightforward: all earnings can count towards pension. However, the higher the proportion of fluctuating earnings the more difficult becomes the decision on how much of earnings to pension.

Consider the case of a scaffolder. His earnings start off low, increase substantially by piece work, bonus, overtime, etc. from about age 20 to (say) age 45, and then reduce as advancing years mean he is not as agile about the construction site as he once was. A pensionable salary of 'all earnings' would see him paying contributions on high earnings in his thirties, but receiving a final salary pension on lower earnings in his sixties. A DC plan may be a fairer answer and perhaps a pensionable salary of 'basic pay' with an incentive to save from fluctuating earnings might prove to be the best overall solution.

Each different company must consider the differing needs of its workforce and competitive position to determine the best solution. It may well be that differing solutions are needed for different parts of the workforce who are remunerated on different bases.

Pensionable service [2.17]

This is another area where solutions will have a major effect on the eventual benefit level and cost. The normal wisdom is that a member should accrue benefit over the same period as they have contributed. So what about a non-contributory scheme? What about a scheme where there is a long waiting period before joining?

A long waiting period can mean that a person joining at age 50 and retiring at 60 may only have half their service counting for benefit. This will not attract many new employees with experience and deep knowledge of the job. One solution is to pension all service, not just contributory service.

Again the employer needs to decide what is right in their own specific circumstances, and to take advice on the cost equation. It can be absolutely right to exclude people with less than five years' service on cost of administration grounds, and then accept the extra cost of backdating their service to the date of joining the company.

Normal retirement age [2.18]

The State scheme currently uses age 65 for men and 60 for women. But this will change gradually for women until all retire at age 65 from April 2020 onwards.

Equality considerations must be taken into account. Work-related factors can be important. Are some of the employees likely to be unable to cope with the physical demands of the job after age 60, or after age 55? Is the job so onerous that a special agreement might be needed to allow very early retirement, say 50 or even 45? Is the normal span of working life in this specific occupation short, as in commodities trading, but the employee able to go on and enjoy another occupation after leaving?

Employees have been retiring more and more early over the last 20–30 years. The average age of retirement for males is now down to about age 60. At the same time the length of life has been extending. The combination of these two effects is that a pension which has been saved for over a shorter period now has to be paid out over a longer period. Inevitably the pension must be smaller or the cost higher. There are many who would argue that employees should be encouraged to stay longer at work, i.e. retire later. Unsurprisingly, the employees themselves are not amongst those putting forward this argument.

The annual survey of pension funds conducted by the National Association of Pension Funds shows that the most common normal retirement age is still 65 with 60 being the second most common. It is not uncommon for a scheme to have 65 as the NRA but to permit retirement at any age from 60 onwards without applying any penalty other than the inevitable one of shorter service counting.

Taking the benefits [2.19]

What does a pension scheme provide?

The answer seems obvious, you receive a pension. However, it is currently possible to exchange (commute) part of the pension for a tax-free cash sum. The maximum amount remaining must be at least as large as the replacement element for SERPS if contracted out, and there are limits to the commutable amount in any event. Apart from the attraction of a cash sum there can be advantages to taking part cash rather than all pension. If the cash is used to buy a purchased life annuity the Inland Revenue regards part of each annuity payment as a repayment from the insurance company of the capital paid to buy the annuity. As a repayment of capital this portion is not taxable, and only the balance is treated as taxable income. The proportion treated this way increases with age and can mean a substantially reduced tax bill.

Other advantages of taking the cash sum include the freedom to invest the money as required and the ability to pass it on down the generations.

The amount that can be commuted has been restricted over the years and varies dependent upon when the member originally joined the pension scheme:

- joined before 17 March 1987 – $1\frac{1}{2}$ × final remuneration if over 20 years' service with a reduced level for shorter service;
- joined 17 March 1987 to 31 May 1989 – increased lump sum proportional to any increased pension;
- all members of schemes started after 14 March 1989 and members of all schemes joining after 14 March 1989 who have elected these limits – $2\frac{1}{4}$ × the full annual actual pension (including any AVC pension).

The advice of an actuary, or tables created by an actuary, will be used to calculate how much pension is given up to secure the cash sum. The older the person the less pension is given up because it costs less money to buy a pension for an old person than a young one as the pension will not be paid for so long. A common factor for a male aged 65 used to be £1 p.a. pension given up for every £10 cash received. However lower interest rates and extended life expectancy have made it more common for specific scheme rates to be constructed and regularly reviewed by actuaries.

Pensions in payment can be increased, and often are. Increases can be either discretionary or fixed by the rules of the scheme. Discretionary increases are decided upon by the trustees from time to time and are limited to the rise in the Retail Price Index.

Dependant's benefits [2.20]

Employees are not the only possible beneficiaries of a pension scheme, their wives, children and other people financially dependent upon them can also benefit.

Almost all pension schemes provide a cash payment on the death of a member. About 50% provide four times basic salary (or pensionable salary) and a further 36% give between three and four times salary. This amount is payable to one or more of a class of people defined in the trust deed.

The trustees are responsible for deciding exactly to whom, and in what proportions the cash is paid. They can take into account the wishes of the deceased member, usually set out in a form letter provided by the administrator to all new members when they join. The reason for using this procedure is that, if the amount is payable at the discretion of the trustees it has never been the property of the member and thus cannot be part of the deceased member's estate. In this circumstance there is no inheritance tax payable on the cash paid out.

It is normal for a spouse to receive a pension on the death of a member whether before or after retirement. This may be augmented by payment of a pension for dependent children. Most schemes provide a spouse's pension of 50% of the pension a member would have received had they lived to normal retirement age on the salary they were earning at the date of death. The maximum benefits payable on death are:

- cash sum – four times final remuneration plus a refund of the employee's own contributions with interest;
- spouse's pension on death before retirement – two-thirds of the member's maximum pension assuming they had stayed to normal retirement age on the same earnings;
- spouse's pension on death after retirement – two-thirds of the maximum pension that could have been provided for the member at normal retirement age increased by reference to the growth in the Retail Price Index over the period;
- orphans' pensions – must not total more than two-thirds of the spouse's pension.

Contributions [2.21]

It is normal for members to contribute towards a pension scheme. About two-thirds of final salary schemes and half of money purchase schemes are contributory according to the NAPF Survey.

The maximum a member may contribute in any one year is 15% of earnings (plus P11D items) from that employment. About one third of members are in non-contributory schemes and about two-fifths contribute from 4% to 5%. This leaves less than one quarter of members in the private sector paying less than 4% or more than 6%.

If members are in a plan where contributions are less than 15% they can pay additional voluntary contributions (AVCs) making the total contribution up to 15%.

AVCs come in two types:

- additional voluntary contributions;
- free-standing additional voluntary contributions.

More detail on this subject will be found in Chapter 11.

Personal pensions [2.22]

Personal pensions are a contract between an individual and a provider. They are used by people without access to an occupational scheme, the self-employed, employed with access to an employer run scheme, the employed who decide not to join the employer's scheme.

The pension eventually payable is the amount which can be purchased at the date of retirement with capital available. This means the pension is a function of both the investment return achieved and the interest rate at the date of retirement.

Contribution limits [2.23]

Personal pensions are a defined contribution type of scheme and thus limits are placed on contribution rather than on benefit levels. The amount of contribution which can be approved increases by age, because the cost of buying £1 p.a. of pension increases with age. The current limits are:

Age at beginning of tax year	Maximum % of earnings
35 or below	17.5
36–45	20.0
46–50	25.0
51–55	30.0
56–60	35.0
61–74	40.0

It is possible for an employer to contribute to a personal pension for an employee but this is unusual except where the employer has set up a group personal pension for a class of (or all) employees.

Income drawdown [2.24]

In a low interest period the pension which can be bought with the proceeds of a personal pension is low. It is often regarded as 'unfair' that the vagaries of interest rates should restrict the purchasing power of a pensioner. The problem is that the purchase of an annuity sets the pension for the rest of the pensioner's life. The unhappy circumstance of reaching retirement age when interest rates are low forces the pensioner into a lower income for life.

In an attempt to rectify this 'income drawdown' was created.

The concept is simple but the application can be very complex. It is essential that any person considering this alternative should take expert advice from an expert who actually deals in the field.

Normally the owner of a personal pension must purchase an annuity on retirement. Income drawdown permits them to remove assets from the personal pension and treat them as income up to age 75. At this time an annuity must be purchased. The advantage is that the delay period allows time for interest rates (and thus annuity rates) to increase, creating a larger pension. However the capital has been eroded by the withdrawals and this may have reduced the amount available to the level where even the increase in annuity due to increasing age cannot replace the 'lost' income. The amount drawn down must lie in a range calculated from tables provided by the Government Actuary.

Self-Invested Personal Pensions [2.25]

Self-Invested Personal Pensions (SIPPS) are a special sub-set of personal pensions. Essentially the individual purchases a shell arrangement from a provider and then directs the investment of the assets themselves rather then leaving it to the provider. The type of investments permitted are unit trusts, stocks and shares. Residential property and personal items are expressly forbidden, but commercial property is allowed provided it is on commercial terms. None of the fund may be used for loans to the member or a connected person.

[2.26] *Basic Guide to Pensions*

This type of arrangement requires quite substantial assets (certainly over £100,000 and preferably £200,000+) and some sophistication is needed on the part of the individual as far as investment is concerned.

Stakeholder pensions

Background [2.26]

A stakeholder pension is a new State initiative to try to bring more people into the privately provided pensions arena. The State realises that the basic old age pension and SERPS is likely to prove inadequate without further government subsidies and is seeking to encourage people to provide for themselves. This private provision is mainly to be achieved by an extension of employer provided pensions on a defined contribution basis. The target market is a group of 5.3 million employees earning between £9,000 p.a. and £20,000 p.a., a field where private provision is thought to be low. Stakeholder schemes must have especially low charges and fees (stated to be not more than 1% of the fund p.a. but see below) and must be easy to transfer. There is no compulsion on employees to join, but there is compulsion on many employers to make a stakeholder pension available and to put in place the salary deduction systems that would be required.

The main details are:

- Set up – employers must consult (trades unions, employee representatives, etc.) and appoint at least one stakeholder provider by 8 October 2001. Failure to comply can lead to fines of £50,000. Only small employers, i.e. those with fewer than five relevant employees and those exempt because, for instance, they already provide occupational pensions as set out below are excused.
- Relevant employees – employees are 'relevant' if employed in the UK (or outside unless the employer is registered and resident outside the UK).
    - Employees are not 'relevant' if they:
        - qualify for an occupational scheme. This means if they are in a waiting period or have rejected membership they are not relevant and do not have to be counted;

Types of Pension Provision **[2.26]**

- have been employed for less than three months;
- have had earnings below the LEL within the past three months (£72 per week from 1 April 2000).

- Group personal pension – acceptable instead of a stakeholder, provided:
  - the employer matches at least the first 3% of employee contribution;
  - there are no transfer or exit charges;
  - employees can initially reject membership and still join later;
  - it is open to all relevant employees aged 18+.

- Member contributions – members may contribute up to £3,600 p.a. without reference to pay. Higher contributions based on pay and age can be made:

Age at start of tax year	% of net relevant earnings
35 or less	17.5
36–45	20.0
46–50	25.0
51–55	30.0
56–60	35.0
61–74	40.0

- Employer contributions – employers have no compulsion to contribute (except to replacement GPPs as above). However the Government have already indicated they intend to review the position in 2003–04 and there is the feeling that compulsion may come in if the take up by employees is low and/or if most employers do not contribute.

- Benefits – can be taken at any time from age 50 to 74 (inclusive) and may be of the "draw down" type up until age 75 when an annuity must be bought. Up to 25% of the benefit may be taken as tax-free cash.

- Fees are limited to 1% of the fund each year. This has been a headline promise and much is made of it. However, specifically excluded from this fee level are stamp duty and dealing costs on investments. The stakeholder provider accepts money from the investors and then invests it on their behalf. The cost of running these investments is excluded from the 1% limit which applies only to the administrative and marketing costs of running the plan. The result of this is that, according to some observers, the extra fee may be as high as 1.3% p.a. of the fund. The actual cost will vary according to the type of investment involved. Standard Life has estimated that a UK-based investment policy will attract fees of about 0.7% and a fund invested in Japan about 1.1%. Overall the fee may well be more than double the headline rate. The effect of this will be to reduce the fund available for investment at the retirement of the member and thus the eventual pension payments.

- Concurrency – there is a new concept known as 'concurrency' from 6 April 2001. Up until this date members of an occupational scheme were prevented from making additional pension provision via a personal pension. Now, members of an occupational plan who earn up to £30,000 p.a. are permitted to pay £3,600 p.a. into a personal pension or stakeholder pension in addition to their contributions to an occupational plan. (Controlling directors are excluded from this.)

- Provision for others – stakeholder pensions can be bought for others. A husband could provide a pension for his non-earning wife or even his children by going direct to a stakeholder provider.

- Contracting out – stakeholder schemes can be used for contracting out of SERPS. A new State Second Pension (S2P) will be brought in from April 2002. Stakeholders will be allowed to contract out of this as well. The Government has already indicated that if stakeholder pensions are successful they will cut back on S2P as stakeholder benefits accumulate, effectively making contracting out compulsory.

Contract based [2.27]

Stakeholder pensions will be based on one of two legal methods, contract law or trust law. A provider such as an insurance company will normally set up a stakeholder scheme based on contract law. It is anticipated that the majority of new Stakeholder schemes well be set up under the contract law basis. Providers are mainly the large institutions with experience in this or similar fields, i.e. that are used to dealing with large numbers of small contributions from a multitude of sources and reporting back to the members on a regular basis. The need for modern IT solutions is obvious. It is clear that some schemes will be set up totally online with a minimum of paperwork, employees accessing their record online, and the employer deducting contributions and remitting them totally electronically.

Trust based [2.28]

This type of stakeholder scheme is most likely to be used in conjunction with existing large occupational schemes, where an administration function is already in place and can be readily extended to cover the stakeholder needs.

Unapproved pensions

Background [2.29]

The vast majority of pension schemes are approved because this offers tax advantages. It also means there are restrictions on what can be provided and to whom. Particularly, there is a cap on earnings which can be taken into account for new members of an approved plan meaning that earnings over £95,400 (at April 2001) cannot be taken into account when calculating benefits.

In order to take all earnings into account an unapproved fund may be set up to cover earnings over the cap. There are essentially two types of unapproved fund, funded and unfunded.

Funded [2.30]

A funded arrangement provides greater security for the employee as assets are put on one side to ensure the benefits can be paid when the due date arrives. However there is a charge for tax if assets are put on one side. Provided the employee is not a director of the company the fund can be set up in such a way that they are not directly involved in the payment of income tax on the employer's contributions. The investments are usually directed to an accumulation fund so that there is no investment income and thus no tax on that income.

If benefits are taken as a cash lump sum there is no tax payable as the contributions have already been taxed as a benefit in kind. By using the tax-free cash to buy a purchased life annuity only the interest element of the annuity payments would be chargeable to the employee as income.

Unfunded [2.31]

No employer contributions are made so there is no charge to tax. However, the employee suffers a loss of certainty. A promise to pay may have been made but could be lost in cases of company failure or take over.

Various ways of attempting to ease this situation can be used, not all of them completely successful.

- Insolvency insurance – the employer may be able to arrange insurance to pay out the capital required if the company becomes insolvent. The problem here is that, like motor insurance, the policy is usually annually renewable and the insurance company may refuse to renew if it looks likely that the company will become insolvent.
- Bank guarantee – short-term cover may be available from such a guarantee but they are difficult to arrange and banks usually will only be willing to contemplate such a guarantee if there are arrangements in hand for long-term permanent cover.
- Charge on assets – provided the assets charged are not directly linked to the promise made and the charge can only be effected on the default of the employer, this charge will not be regarded as funding the arrangement. Thus no tax arises during the period of the promise. This is a difficult area and professional advice must be taken to ensure the agreement of the Inland Revenue to this type of arrangement.

Tax will be paid on any lump sum or pension paid at the end of the promise.

Comments [2.32]

Unapproved arrangements are useful but complex schemes which do not avoid taxation. If it is funded there will be tax on contributions but not on benefits. If unfunded there will be tax on benefits. The setting up of these arrangements tends to be complex and it is easy to fall into various tax traps. Specialist professional advice is needed.

3 – The Legal Framework

> This chapter covers the following:
>
> - The legal framework within which an occupational pension scheme must operate.
>
> - The sources of the rules and regulations by which it must abide.
>
> - How pensions law has evolved and where it can be found.

Introduction [3.1]

A pension forms part of an employee's remuneration package, and as such will be referred to in his contract of employment. It will be necessary to have regard to the employee's employment rights, particularly when changing pension terms, and these are discussed in paragraph [5.2].

In a tax-exempt scheme approved under the *Income and Corporation Taxes Act 1988 (ICTA 1988), s 591* the maximum benefits which a scheme can provide are limited by the Inland Revenue. The limits adopted by the Inland Revenue under its discretionary practice set out in its Practice Notes (IR 12 (2001)) are discussed in some detail in this chapter. A pension scheme may also be constrained in the minimum benefits it can provide if it is contracted out of the State Earnings Related Pension Scheme (SERPS), and details of these minimum benefits are also set out here.

Trust law [3.2]

Most occupational pension schemes are set up under trust. This is a legal device developed over the years originally to enable families to pass on property to future generations. It has long been used by pension schemes and further adapted over time to meet their needs.

The Legal Framework [3.2]

Under a trust the settlor (in the case of a pension scheme, the employer) sets aside assets (that is its contributions and those of its employees, and the investment return on them). These are then held by another person – here the trustees – for the benefit of specified people, the beneficiaries. As with family trusts, the trustees' first duty is to the beneficiaries. They must look to their interests, rather than to those of the original settlor (the employer), or of a trade union or of employees who are not scheme members.

The law of trusts has evolved through court cases over many years, and is not to be found in a single statute. The Maxwell affair in the early 1990s prompted a debate about its appropriateness for the modern pension scheme, and its main advantages and disadvantages can be summarised as follows:

Advantages	Disadvantages
• Security – the scheme's assets are separate from those of the employer.	• Lack of clear legal framework – trust law is evolutionary, dependent upon an understanding of many cases, and lacks the accessibility, structure, organisation and clarity of a statute.
• Tax approval – it is a useful vehicle for establishing the conditions on which the Inland Revenue will grant the scheme exempt approved status, affording it valuable tax reliefs.	• Lack of protection for members – the powers of employers and trustees were seen as too wide, and in need of limitation.
• Flexibility – case law shows the rights of beneficiaries and the duties of trustees can evolve to meet new situations.	• Complicated language – its aims may be laudable, but its language is difficult, especially for non-lawyers.
	• Solvency – trust law provides no rules to ensure the solvency of a pension scheme.

In the end, the best of both worlds was sought, and in 1995 the *Pensions Act 1995* (*PA 1995*) was passed to strengthen the trust framework. However trust law principles continue to govern pension schemes. The role of a pension scheme trustee encompasses duties which also apply to trustees of family and charitable trusts. Principles deriving from trust law include the duties of a trustee not to profit from his position, to act prudently in the conduct of the trust's affairs and to act impartially between different classes of beneficiaries.

From time to time there are trust law cases which impact upon pension schemes. A recent example is that of *CAS (Nominees) Ltd v Nottingham Forrest plc (2000) AER (D) 1115* which concerned minority shareholders of a football club and made it clear that beneficiaries are entitled to see legal advice obtained by trustees if the advice is not for the purpose of litigation involving the beneficiaries. Disclosure of information is only one area where trustees of pension schemes must have regard to developments in trust law as well as statutory requirements.

Statutes governing pensions [3.3]

Building on the foundations established by trust law, *PA 1995* imposed specific obligations on trustees and employers, and in many areas it codified the best practice of the pensions industry. It also sought to introduce a solvency standard in the form of the minimum funding requirement (MFR).

Another major statute is the *Pension Schemes Act 1993 (PSA 1993)* which gathered into one Act the various pieces of earlier legislation affecting pension schemes. It deals with such matters as contracting out of SERPS, the protection of early leavers by preserving their scheme benefits, and the functions and procedures of the Pensions Ombudsman.

More recently the *Welfare Reform and Pensions Act 1999 (WRPA 1999)* introduced pension sharing on divorce, as well as stakeholder pensions. It also contains provisions to ensure that on bankruptcy, the benefits of a member of an approved scheme (and in due course certain unapproved schemes) will be protected from his trustee in bankruptcy.

The *Child Support, Pensions and Social Security Act 2000 (CSPSSA 2000)* not only introduced the Second State Pension but also amended *PA 1995, PSA 1993* and *WRPA 1999* to strengthen the

The Legal Framework **[3.3]**

role of OPRA particularly in relation to the winding up of schemes, to extend the jurisdiction of the Pensions Ombudsman, and to change provisions relating to member-nominated trustees.

In addition there are many other statutes which, although not obviously and primarily concerned with pension schemes, do have an impact upon them. Examples include:

- *Contracts (Rights of Third Parties) Act 1999* – This gives powers to enforce terms in a contract to a person who is not a party to it.

- *Data Protection Act 1998* – This provides eight principles (governing disclosure accuracy and security) which must be observed in dealing with data (such as member records and information), and obliges the data controller (which may be both the sponsoring employer and the trustees of a pension scheme) to take responsibility for compliance. A new Information Commissioner is appointed to enforce this Act.

- *Disability Discrimination Act 1998* – This introduces measures to outlaw discrimination on the grounds of disability.

- *Employment Rights Act 1996* – This contains provisions dealing with the benefits of and contributions to an occupational pension scheme during periods of maternity, parental and paid family leave.

- *Financial Services Act 1986* – Authorisation under this Act is necessary for a person to carry on investment business or give investment advice, unless the Act specifically exempts him. Trustees require authorisation if they themselves make day-to-day investment decisions, rather than delegating to a fund manager, and should be wary of giving investment advice. This has been further strengthened by the *Financial Services and Markets Act 2000*.

- *Trustee Act 2000* – Although pension scheme trustees are not affected by the widening of investment powers contained in earlier legislation, this Act makes statutorily explicit the duty of a trustee to act as a prudent man of business, introducing a subjective test of this to allow for the particular skills of the trustee.

Secondary legislation [3.4]

The principles introduced by primary legislation, (that is Acts of Parliament), are often implemented by statutory instruments containing detailed regulations. A prime example is the regulations under *PA 1995*. Topics introduced by this Act are covered by more than 50 sets of regulations. These set out the rules and procedures to be followed in relation to such matters as member-nominated trustees, scheme administration, disclosure of information, fund investment, contracting out of SERPS and the winding up of pension schemes.

Decided cases [3.5]

Unlike court decisions, Pensions Ombudsman decisions are not legislative in nature, but they do serve to indicate how the Ombudsman is likely to view a similar complaint in the future. Full reports of his determinations are issued, and a website is now available. The Pensions Ombudsman can be appealed to the High Court on issues of law, and the last few years have seen many such cases.

Any decision of the High Court, whether on a matter started in that court or on appeal from the Ombudsman, may be appealed on a question of law or fact to the Court of Appeal, and then to House of Lords. The case of *National Grid (2001) 19 PBLR (21), (2001) UKHL 20* began life as a Pensions Ombudsman decision, and was ultimately decided in the employers' favour by the House of Lords, having previously been heard in the High Court and by the Court of Appeal. The case concerned the use of surplus to enable the employers to be released from the payment of special contributions used to fund early retirement pensions on redundancy. Whilst not answering the age-old question of who owns a pension scheme surplus, it did serve to recognise that an employer may have claim to it, and it does not automatically belong to the members.

OPRA also issues bulletins detailing its decisions. Again these are useful in showing how OPRA is likely to view a breach of *PA 1995*'s regulations, but are not legislative in nature.

European law [3.6]

European Union law has an increasing part to play in the development of pensions law in this country. Treaties may have direct effect in all Member States, and in doing so override UK law.

An example is Article 119 of the Treaty of Rome, later renumbered Article 141 by the Treaty of Amsterdam. This required all Member States to 'ensure the principle of equal pay for male or female workers for equal work or work of equal value is applied'. The case of *Defrenne v Sabena (No 2) (1976) ECR 455* confirmed that this Article had direct effect and did not need further legislation by each of the Member States to make it enforceable. As a result of the case of *Barber v GRE Assurance Group (1990) ECR I-1989* brought before the European Court of Justice it was established that pension was indeed pay for the purposes of the Article, and that men and women of the same age and doing similar jobs should be treated in the same way by their pension scheme. The principle of equal treatment had been confirmed, and logic dictated that this principle should be applied with effect at least from the date of the *Defrenne* case, if not from the date of the Treaty of Rome in 1960. The expense and difficulty this entailed was such that it was a matter of some relief when the Maastricht Protocol and the European Court of Justice in the case of *Coloroll Pension Trustees Ltd v Russell (1994) ECR I-4389* determined that it should only have effect from the date of the *Barber* case, that is 17 May 1990.

The Council of the European Union also issues Directives requiring to be implemented by Member States by the passing of national legislation. Recently the Council passed the *Part-time Workers Directive* dealing with all employment rights of part-time workers. This was followed by a statutory instrument, the *Part-time Workers (Prevention of Less Favourable Treatment) Regulations 2000 (SI 2000 No 1551)*, which came into force on 1 July 2000 and gave part-time workers the right to join their company pension scheme established for full-time workers (unless their continued exclusion could be objectively justified), and to be given the same benefits, but calculated on a pro-rata basis.

The European Court of Justice (ECJ) decides issues arising from European law, and in the pensions field the issue of equalisation of benefits for men and women has prompted a number of celebrated cases. Sometimes an issue will be referred back to the national courts by the ECJ, as happened recently in the case of *Preston v Wolverhampton Healthcare NHS Trust (2001) 09 PBLR (16), (2001) UKHL/5*. This concerned the question of part-time workers excluded from their pension scheme before the *Part-time Workers (Prevention of Less Favourable Treatment) Regulations 2000* came into force on 1 July 2000. They successfully claimed that this amounted to unlawful sexual discrimination as the exclusion affected more women than men and that their employer had no objective justification for such discrimination. In line with the *Occupational Pension Schemes (Equal Treatment) Regulations 1995 (SI 1995 No 3183)*, the UK courts had decided that a woman had the right to bring a claim of this nature before the courts within six months after her employment had come to an end, and that her backdated membership should be limited to two years from the date of the claim. The ECJ considered these limits in the light of the principles it had established in an earlier case (that of *Fisscher v Vorhuis Hengelo BV (1994) ECR I-4583*). These were that such time limits should be not less favourable than those for similar actions and should not serve to frustrate the enforcement of European law. It concluded that by this measure the six-month limit was acceptable, but the two-year period for backdating membership was not. It then fell to the House of Lords to determine an alternative period, and it decided that membership could be backdated as far as 8 April 1976, the date of the *Defrenne* case.

Inland Revenue limits [3.7]

Favourable tax treatment is available to occupational pension schemes if they meet the Inland Revenue's criteria. The employer and employee enjoy tax relief on their contributions, and the employee's contributions are not treated as benefits in kind. When a pension is paid it is treated as earned income and may in part be taken as a tax-free lump sum. Furthermore the fund itself is generally free from tax on its gains and investments. However income from trading, rather than investment, is subject to tax.

ICTA 1988 requires schemes to be approved by the Inland Revenue if they are to enjoy these advantages. Mandatory approval is granted when a scheme satisfies the strict provisions of *ICTA 1988, s 590(3)*. Most schemes however seek discretionary approval of the Inland Revenue under *ICTA 1988, s 591*.

To gain such approval a scheme must satisfy the criteria set out in the Inland Revenue's practice notes (IR 12 (2001)) and contributions

The Legal Framework **[3.9]**

and benefits must be subject to certain limits which must be incorporated in the scheme's rules. The limits are particularly stringent for high earners and controlling directors (that is those with more than a 20% shareholding in the employer at any time in the preceding ten years).

Withdrawal of approval will result in the removal of tax reliefs from the date of withdrawal. In the case of a small self-administered scheme (SSAS), the scheme's assets will be subject to a tax charge of 40%.

Defined terms used by the Inland Revenue **[3.8]**

Certain defined terms are used to determine the maximum contributions and benefits permitted by the Inland Revenue and are key to understanding its limits. They are not necessarily the same as terms used in calculating pension promised by a scheme. Further, the limits differ according to the tax regime of the member. If he joined the scheme before 17 March 1987 he will be a Class C member; if he joined between 17 March 1987 and 31 May 1989 he will be a Class B member, and if he joined after 1 June 1989 he will be a Class A member. It is, however, possible for a member to join a scheme after 1 June 1989 and still be a Class B or a Class C member. This can occur for example where a member is reinstated after the mis-selling of a personal pension plan or, more commonly, where a member joins the scheme from another scheme of the same employer. Also a Class C member can elect to be treated as a Class B member, and scheme rules can permit a Class B or C member to elect to be treated as a Class A member.

The important defined terms are briefly as follows.

Remuneration **[3.9]**

This is all pay subject to case 1 or case 2 of Schedule E tax (including profit-related pay) except 'golden handshakes' (subject to tax under *ICTA 1988, s 148*), payments on redundancy and gains and income from share options or incentive schemes where the rights were acquired after 17 March 1987.

For a Class A member remuneration is limited to the 'earnings cap' imposed by *ICTA 1988, s 590C*. This is increased each year in line with the increase in the Retail Prices Index, and for the tax year 2000–01 stands at £94,500.

Final remuneration [3.10]

This is either:

(a) basic remuneration plus fluctuating pay averaged over the previous three or more years, for any year in the five years before the member exits the scheme (through leaving the scheme or the employer, death or retirement); or

(b) the average total remuneration over any three or more consecutive years ending not more than ten years before the member exits the scheme. This second calculation must be used if the member's remuneration for any tax year after 5 April 1987 is more than £100,000, unless the member takes £100,000 as his pay and effects the calculation under paragraph (a) above.

Where a year is taken which is not the year immediately before the member exits the scheme, remuneration may be increased in line with the increase in the Retail Prices Index.

For a Class B or C member final remuneration is limited to £100,000 for the purposes of calculating the maximum tax-free cash sum which may be taken on retirement.

Normal retirement date [3.11]

This is the date specified in the scheme rules as the age at which members normally retire. Generally it must be between the ages of 60 and 75, and may differ between categories of member.

Retained benefits [3.12]

These are benefits from approved schemes of previous employers and section 32 buy-out policies, personal pension plans and free-standing additional voluntary contributions (FSAVCs) from earlier employment.

Service [3.13]

This is the total length of service of a member's employment by the current employer and any associated employer. It may not exceed 40 years.

Limits on contributions [3.14]

Employer contributions are allowable for income and corporation tax and are deducted in the accounting period in which they are paid. Other, or special contributions, may at the discretion of the Inland Revenue be spread for tax purposes.

The employee's contributions enjoy relief from income tax, but whether compulsory, voluntary or to a FSAVC must not exceed in total 15% of his remuneration. Greater contributions may be permissible if the employee is being reinstated in the pension scheme following the mis-selling of a personal pension, or if as a part-timer he or she is being retrospectively admitted to membership. However tax relief is restricted to 15% of remuneration in any tax year.

Limits on benefits [3.15]

The limits on benefits depend on when they are being taken and are briefly summarised as follows. Full details of the limits are contained in the Inland Revenue's Practice Notes (IR 12 (2001)).

[3.16] *Basic Guide to Pensions*

Summary of main Inland Revenue limits on benefits [3.16]

At normal retirement date

Pension

Class A, B and Class C members with more than 20 years' service	The greater of: (i) 1/60 × service × final remuneration; and (ii) 2/3 × final remuneration LESS retained benefits.
Class A and B members with less than 20 years' service	The greater of: (i) 1/60 × service × final remuneration; and (ii) 1/30 × service × final remuneration up to a maximum of 2/3 × final remuneration LESS retained benefits.
Class C members with less than 20 years' service	The greater of: (i) 1/60 × service × final remuneration; and (ii) the following fractions of final remuneration according to service:

Service years	No of 60ths
1–5	1 for each year
6	8
7	16
8	24
9	32
10 or more	40

up to a maximum of 2/3 × final remuneration LESS retained benefits.

Lump sum

Class A member	The greater of: (i) 3/80 × service × final remuneration; and (ii) $2^{1}/_{4}$ × initial rate of pre-commutation pension (including AVCs and FSAVCs).

Class B member	The greater of: (i) 3/80 × service × final remuneration; and (ii) $\frac{(A-B)}{(C-B)} \times (D-E) + E$ Where: A = pre-commutation pension (including AVCs and FSAVCs) B = pension calculated as 1/60 × service × final remuneration C = pensions calculated as 1/30 × service × final remuneration D = lump sum calculated as if Class C member E = 3/80 × service × final remuneration

NB: In this calculation final pensionable earnings under the scheme may be used instead of final remuneration.

Class C member	The greater of: (i) 3/80 × service × final remuneration; and (ii) the following fraction of final remuneration according to service:

Service years	No of 80ths
1–8	3 for each year
9	30
10	36
11	42
12	48
13	54
14	63
15	72
16	81
17	90
18	99
19	108
20 or more	120

up to a maximum of $1\frac{1}{2}$ × final remuneration LESS retained benefits.

On early retirement

Pension

Class A member	The greater of: (i) 1/60 × service × final remuneration; and (ii) 1/30 × service × final remuneration up to a maximum of 2/3 × final remuneration LESS retained benefits.
Class B and C members	The greater of: (i) 1/60 × service × final remuneration; and (ii) $\dfrac{\text{service}}{\text{total prospective service up to normal retirement date}} \times$ maximum pension member could have earned had he remained in service to normal retirement date but based on his final remuneration

NB: If the member is retiring due to ill health the maximum pension is that which he could have earned had he remained in service to normal retirement date subject to final remuneration being assessed on the basis of a Class A member.

Lump sum

Class A member	The greater of: (i) 3/80 × service × final remuneration; and (ii) $2^{1}/_{4}$ × initial rate of pre-commutation pension (including AVCs and FSAVCs).

Class B and Class C members	The greater of:
	(i) 3/80 × service × final remuneration; and
	(ii) either
	  (a) the lump sum formula applicable at normal retirement date but taken on service and final remuneration at actual retirement; or
	  (b) a lump sum calculated as:

(ii)	service / total prospective service up to normal retirement date	× lump sum member could have taken at normal retirement date based on final remuneration at actual retirement

On late retirement

Pension

Class A member	Maximum pension member could have received if actual retirement date were substituted for his normal retirement date, and service and final remuneration are as at actual retirement.
Class B member	The higher of: (i) the calculation for Class A member; (ii) the calculation for Class A member but adding 1/60 × final remuneration for any year (up to five years) of service in excess of 40 years; and (iii) the maximum pension which the member could have received at normal retirement date increased by the greater of the increase in the cost of living between normal retirement date and retirement and an actuarial increase. **NB**: (a) (i) and (ii) only are available to a controlling director in respect of service over the age of 70; and (b) scheme rules may permit this alternative method of calculation for a Class B or C member: 1/30 × service × final remuneration (assessed as if Class A member) up to a maximum of 2/3 × final remuneration (assessed as if a Class A member) LESS retained benefits.

Lump sum

Class A member	The greater of: (i) 3/80 × service × final remuneration; and (ii) $2^{1}/_{4}$ × initial rate of pre-commutation pension (including AVCs and FSAVCs).
Class B and C member	Either: (i) the maximum lump sum the member could have received if actual retirement had been his normal retirement date adding 3/80 × final remuneration for any year (up to five years) of service in excess of 40 years; or (ii) the maximum lump sum that could have been paid at normal retirement date increased for late payment in line with the return on the scheme's investments.

On death before normal retirement date

Lump sum

All members	The greater of: (i) £5,000; and (ii) 4 × final remuneration + refund of member's contributions LESS retained benefits. **NB**: (a) for this purpose final remuneration includes 'golden handshakes' and share option gains. It may also be taken as total earnings over the 12-month period in the three years before death. (b) retained benefits need not be taken into account if rules provide for a death benefit of less than 2 × final remuneration.

Pension for spouse

All members	2/3 × maximum pension which could have been paid to the member had he retired due to ill health immediately before his death and disregarding retained benefits.
Deferred members on death under 50	A lump sum and spouse's pension may be provided based on member's maximum approved deferred pension.

Pension increases

All members	Any pension in payment may be increased up to the level of the member's pre-commutation pension and further increased by the increase in the Retail Prices Index or 3% per annum if greater.

Contracting out [3.17]

In order to minimise the cost of SERPS, the Government allows employers to contract out of it. It reduces employer and employee National Insurance contributions and in return requires contributions to be paid to a suitable exempt-approved pension scheme. Until 1988 this meant a final salary scheme. At first such a scheme had to provide benefits which met certain basic criteria (the requisite benefit test), and had to provide a guaranteed minimum pension (GMP) roughly equal to the pension which would otherwise have been provided by SERPS.

The requisite benefit test was abolished in 1986. In 1997 GMPs were also abolished, and from 6 April 1997 a final salary scheme has once again to meet a test of quality or statutory standard (the reference scheme test). GMPs cannot be ignored, however, as any GMPs earned by service before 6 April 1997 still have to be provided.

From 1988 it has been possible to contract out also using a money purchase scheme, a FSAVC or personal pension. In the case of a company money purchase scheme the employer's contributions are required to be at least equal to the reduction in National Insurance contributions. These are called 'minimum payments' and must be used to provide benefits (protected rights benefits) for the member and any widow or widower.

A contracted-out scheme must comply with the restriction set out in *PA 1995, s 40*, namely that not more than 5% of the market value of its assets are invested in employer-related investments. Thus SSASs which are not subject to this restriction may not contract out.

If a scheme is contracted out of SERPS, its contracting-out provisions determine the minimum benefits it may provide. The Department for Work and Pensions (DWP) (formerly the Department of Social Security (DSS)) oversees contracting out and the Contracted-out Employment Group (COEG), a sub-division of the Inland Revenue, deals with day-to-day administration, including the issue of the contracting-out certificate needed to obtain the reduction in National Insurance contributions.

Guaranteed minimum pensions [3.18]

The GMP does not reflect accurately the SERPS entitlement which has been relinquished. It is based on earnings factors derived from a member's earnings between the lower and upper earnings limits, and the formula for its complicated calculation is set out in *PSA 1993*. It will generally start to be paid at State pension age, which for these purposes remains at 60 for women and 65 for men. If its commencement is delayed it must be appropriately increased. It is then payable for life, and, if it has been earned by service after 6 April 1988, it must be increased in payment by the lower of the increase in the Retail Prices Index and 3% per annum.

If a member receiving a GMP dies, a GMP is payable to any widow or widower for life or, if so provided in the scheme's rules, until the spouse remarries. In the case of a widow this is half the member's GMP, and in the case of a widower this is half of the member's GMP attributable to service between 6 April 1988 and 5 April 1997.

Although GMPs may not accrue after 6 April 1997, those which are held in a scheme must continue to satisfy legislative requirements, and once every three years the scheme actuary is required to sign a certificate that this is the case. Before 1997 it was possible to buy back into the State scheme; upon the payment of a premium, the State would resume responsibility for paying SERPS benefits, and the scheme would no longer have to pay GMPs. Today this is only possible for schemes which ceased to be contracted out before 6 April 1997.

While a GMP is being held by a scheme for a member who will retire after 6 April 1997, it must be revalued in line with inflation. Schemes can either provide for it to be revalued at 6.25% per annum (reducing to 5.5% after April 2002), or in line with wage inflation, which is disclosed in government orders each year.

As the GMP is designed to reflect State benefits with different pension ages for men and women, it inevitably is not the same for men and women. Article 119 (now Article 141) of the Treaty of Rome is apparently breached, and it was only a matter of time before a complaint against trustees of a pension scheme was brought.

The case of *Marsh Mercer Pension Scheme v Pensions Ombudsman (2001) 16 PBLR (28)* is the result. Mr Williamson, an actuary, complained to the Pensions Ombudsman that the transfer value with which his scheme's trustees had supplied him showed that he had suffered sex discrimination. His GMP was not the same as it would have been had he been a woman; it was not payable until he was 65 (rather than 60) and pension increases between his normal retiring age of 60 and the State pension age of 65 were offset against the need to provide revaluation of his GMP up to the age of 65. The Ombudsman's determination contained a cogent review of the law, concluding that GMPs should be equal for men and women. The matter was referred to the High Court where Mr Justice Rimer declined to decide this substantive issue of the case, but instead made his decision in favour of the trustees of the scheme and the sponsoring employer on the grounds that the case fell outside the Ombudsman's jurisdiction; other members were affected by any decision of the Ombudsman and should therefore have been given the opportunity to be heard.

The reference scheme test [3.19]

For service after 6 April 1997, a contracted-out final salary scheme must satisfy the statutory standard set out in *PSA 1993, s 12B*. It must provide for active and deferred members and their widows and widowers pensions which are broadly equivalent to, or better than those provided by a hypothetical reference scheme. It is for the scheme's actuary to decide whether a scheme meets this standard, and he is required to give a certificate that the pensions the scheme offers are equivalent or better than the pensions under the reference scheme for at least 90% of members and their spouses.

The benefits provided by the hypothetical reference scheme are briefly as follows:

- a pension for the member payable from age 65 calculated as 1/80th of average qualifying earnings for each year of service up to a maximum of 40 years. Qualifying earnings here means 90% of his earnings between the upper and lower earnings limits averaged over the preceding three years.

- a pension for a widow or widower equal to half the member's pension (calculated by reference to the member's actual service where the member dies before the age of 65). Such a pension may not be payable however if:

    - the member and the spouse married after he started to receive his pension from the scheme;

    - the spouse remarries or lives with a person as husband and wife, or indeed is so cohabiting when the member dies.

- annual pension increases in line with the increase in the Retail Prices Index up to 5% per annum.

- revaluation on benefits preserved for deferred members at least in line with the minimum level imposed by *PSA 1993*.

Money purchase schemes [3.20]

An exempt-approved money purchase scheme may contract out of SERPS by using minimum payments to provide protected rights. Minimum payments correspond to the minimum contributions which an employer must make to the scheme, that is amounts equal to the flat rate rebate of National Insurance contributions applicable to the member. They must be paid to the scheme's trustees within 14 days of the income tax month to which they relate and invested within one month of the end of that tax month.

Protected rights are rights to money purchase benefits deriving from:

- minimum payments;
- additional compulsory members' contributions;

The Legal Framework **[3.21]**

- age-related rebates (payments made by the DSS (now the DWP) after April 1997 on behalf of the employee after the end of each tax year, varying according to age and currently ranging from nil for a 15-year-old to 6.8% for an employee over the age of 48);
- any so-called 'incentive' payments from the DSS (now the DWP) of 2% of the difference between the upper and lower earnings limit received in respect of those contracting out for the first time between 1 January 1986 and 5 April 1993;
- a transfer into the scheme of a GMP, or post-1997 contracted-out rights from a final salary scheme; and
- protected rights transferred into the scheme from another scheme.

Under *PSA 1993*, ss 28 and 29, protected rights must be used either to provide a pension, or, more commonly, an annuity from an insurance company of the member's choice. In either case payment must start between the member's 60th and 65th birthdays (unless he agrees a later date), and continue for life. The factors used to calculate the pension or annuity must not be sex discriminatory.

In addition, a pension or annuity must be provided for a widow or widower unless an unmarried member so agrees. The widow or widower must be at least 45 years old when the member dies, entitled to child benefit in respect of a qualifying child under 18 or living with a qualifying child under the age of 16. A qualifying child is a child of the member and his or her spouse, or any other child in respect of whom they were entitled to child benefit. The spouse's pension is to be payable for life or at least until the spouse remarries while under State pension age. If there is no surviving spouse, or if he or she dies while receiving the pension, the scheme's rules may allow the pension to be paid to a qualifying child until he or she reaches the age of 18.

Mixed benefit schemes **[3.21]**

Until 1997 it was not possible for a single scheme to contract out on the GMP basis and the protected rights basis. However from 6 April 1997 it has been possible to have both a contracted-out final salary section and money purchase section within the same scheme, if the scheme contracts out on a mixed benefits basis. Such a scheme is called a COMBS – a Contracted-Out Mixed Benefit Scheme.

A COMBS must satisfy the following criteria:

- benefits under the final salary section must meet the reference scheme test and comply with provisions relating to GMPs for benefits accrued before 6 April 1997;
- benefits under the money purchase section must meet all the requirements relating to protected rights;
- the whole scheme must meet the funding requirements of a final salary scheme, that is, it must meet the MFR; and
- no member may be contracted-out under the final salary section and the money purchase section at the same time.

A COMBS may close down one of its sections, without discharging its current contracting-out liabilities, and COEG will continue to supervise the inactive section.

Between 6 April 1997 and 31 January 1998 final salary schemes could change from being contracted out on the GMP basis to being contracted out on the money purchase basis. Strictly speaking this is not a COMBS but a money purchase scheme in which the GMPs will continue to be supervised by COEG.

Transfers from contracted-out schemes [3.22]

With the member's consent a transfer of the following may be made to a contracted-out final salary scheme, provided that the member's employer contributes to the receiving scheme or the member has previously been a member of that scheme:

- GMP;
- post-1997 contracted-out rights under a final salary scheme. The transfer must be at least equal to the cash equivalent of those rights, and be used to provide the normal benefits under the receiving scheme; and
- protected rights. Again the transfer must be at least equal to the cash equivalent of the benefits transferred, and pre-1997 protected rights must be used to provide a GMP. Post-1997 protected rights must be used to provide the normal benefits under the receiving scheme.

If it is proposed to effect a transfer from a final salary scheme without the member's consent, then the transferring trustees must obtain an actuarial certificate (GN16) confirming that the value of the rights in the receiving scheme are broadly no less valuable than those being transferred.

With the member's consent a transfer of the following may be made to a contracted-out money purchase scheme. In each case the transfer must be used to provide protected rights in the receiving scheme, and the member's employer must contribute to the receiving scheme or the member must previously have been a member of that scheme. Further, the transfer must be of an amount at least equal to the cash equivalent of the rights being transferred.

- GMP;
- post-1997 contracted-out rights under a final salary scheme before the pension comes into payment; and
- protected rights.

Useful addresses [3.23]

COEG
Chillingham House
Benton Park View
Benton Park Road
Longbenton
Newcastle upon Tyne
NE98 1ZZ

Inland Revenue
IR Savings, Pension Share Schemes
Yorke House
PO Box 62
Castle Meadow Road
Nottingham
NG2 1BG

4 – Trustee Duties and Liabilities

> This chapter covers the following:
>
> - The duties of trustees.
>
> - Powers of trustees.
>
> - Liabilities of trustees if their duties are breached.
>
> - How powers are exercised in practice: in trustee meetings.

Introduction [4.1]

Where an employer establishes a pension scheme under trust, it will appoint trustees to control the assets of the scheme, and to be responsible for its administration and operation. The trustees may be individuals or corporations, or a mixture of the two. Details of eligibility to be a trustee can be found in Chapter 5, para [5.4].

The trustees control the assets of the scheme on behalf of the scheme members, who are the beneficiaries under the scheme. The trustees will have legal title to the scheme assets, which means they have power over those assets. However, they also have duties to hold the assets for the benefit of the scheme members, who have beneficial interests in the scheme assets. This means that they have interests in and rights to the scheme assets that can be enforced against the trustees.

The duties of the trustees are usually set out in a formal trust deed establishing the scheme, as described in Chapter 6. Under trust law (the common law as it applies to trustees), the trustees have a legal duty to comply with the rules set out in the trust deed. Trust law also imposes other duties on trustees, and additional specific duties are imposed by statute.

Where a pension scheme is established under contract, there are no trustees. Instead, the employer will appoint managers who are not subject to trust law, but to the terms of the contract establishing the scheme and governing their appointment. However, many of the statutory duties and liabilities that apply to pension scheme trustees also apply to managers.

Duties of trustees [4.2]

The trustees of a pension scheme established under trust are subject to the duties applying to all trustees under trust law. These duties are set out in judgements made by the courts. More recently, legislation such as the *Pensions Act 1995 (PA 1995)* has more clearly defined particular duties, while also creating new obligations. The following is not intended to be a comprehensive guide to all of these duties, but an examination of the main principles.

Duty to act in accordance with the trust deed and rules [4.3]

Trust law requires trustees to comply with the rules of the trust, and act in the manner directed by the trust. In practice, this normally involves operating within the framework laid down by the trust deed and rules. This will contain details of the powers and duties of the trustees, how they are required to exercise their powers, and the limits on their powers. The trust will also be subject to overriding legislation, which may vary the scheme rules (for example, see paras [4.24] and [4.26] below). In this case, the duty is to comply with the scheme rules as varied by the legislation.

Trustees have a duty to familiarise themselves with the trust deed and rules, and with other relevant documentation such as amending deeds, or undertakings given to the Inland Revenue in connection with the scheme. This should be the first priority for a newly appointed trustee, and extends to taking legal advice on the meaning of the trust deed and the implications of relevant legislation if necessary.

If trustees find themselves unable to solve a particular problem under the terms of the trust deed, or cannot determine its meaning, they may need to seek directions from the court. Trustees may apply to the court for determination of any question arising in the execution of a trust under *RSC Order 85 rule 2*. This may be a request for a determination of whether a particular course of action is in breach of trust, or alternatively the trustees can surrender their powers to the court and ask the court to direct them on how to proceed. Trustees may also make complaints about each other to the Pensions Ombudsman, who will investigate disputes of fact and law and complaints of biased, negligent, incompetent or arbitrary conduct.

Duty to act prudently, conscientiously, and honestly [4.4]

Trust law requires a pension scheme trustee to look after the scheme assets, and to act prudently, conscientiously, and honestly in relation to them. This duty has a number of implications:

- A trustee has a duty to administer the scheme. This must be done in accordance with the scheme rules (see para [4.3] above).

- A trustee must act in good faith, and must not make any personal profit at the expense of the scheme. As a result, a trustee cannot be remunerated out of scheme funds unless the trust deed so allows. However, under s 31 of the *Trustee Act 2000* a trustee is entitled to be reimbursed expenses out of the trust fund.

- A trustee should avoid any conflicts of interest between himself and the trust. He should not personally buy or sell fund assets, and should avoid contracts between the trust and his family members. This rule has never, however, prevented a trustee from being a member of the scheme. Problems of conflicts of interest caused by scheme membership of trustees have now been solved by *PA 1995 s 39*. This provides that the rule of law against conflicts shall not apply to a trustee of a trust scheme who is also a member of the scheme merely because, in exercising his powers, he benefits himself as a member of the scheme.

- If a trustee has interests which conflict with those of the trust, or which may cause him to be biased in the exercise of discretions under the trust, he has a duty to disclose those interests to his fellow trustees on appointment. For example, a trustee might disclose that he has relatives who are members of the scheme, as the relationship could influence his exercise of discretions in relation to those members.

- A trustee has a duty to act prudently when dealing with the scheme assets. For an individual trustee, this means treating them as carefully as a prudent person would treat their own assets. This involves considering risks, obtaining professional advice, and diversifying investments (see para [4.12] below on the duty to invest). Provided that a trustee does act honestly and with ordinary care and prudence, he will not be in breach of trust, and so will not be liable for accidental loss. However, a higher standard of diligence and knowledge is expected of a professional trustee who is paid for acting as a trustee. Professional trustees are expected to exercise professional knowledge and expertise when dealing with trust property.

- A trustee is expected to take professional advice when needed, and also to go to the court if required, for example to obtain clarification if the rules of the scheme are unclear.

Duty to act in the best interests of scheme members [4.5]

Pension scheme trustees have a duty to exercise their powers under the scheme rules in the interests of the scheme's beneficiaries, and in particular the scheme members. For example, trustees should only exercise any power they might have to allow an employer to have a "holiday" from paying contributions to the scheme if there would still be enough money in the scheme to pay benefits to the scheme members.

Duty to act impartially between scheme members [4.6]

Trustees must not favour one scheme member at the expense of another, and must be even-handed in their dealings with different classes of members. However, this does not mean that all scheme members must be treated the same. It is common for trust deeds and rules to specify that different classes of scheme members are to be treated differently, and in addition to give the trustees discretions allowing them to differentiate between members, e.g. to waive contributions from a scheme member who is on long-term sick leave. However, the trustees must consider all scheme members when deciding whether to exercise such a discretion, and ensure that favourable treatment for one or more members will not adversely affect other members of the scheme.

Duty to pay benefits [4.7]

Trustees of a pension scheme have a duty to pay benefits to those members who are entitled to benefits under the scheme. The trust deed and rules will specify who is entitled to benefits and the level of their entitlement. The trustees must ensure that the correct persons receive the correct amounts at the times specified in the scheme rules.

The trust deed and rules may give the trustees discretion to enhance benefits in particular circumstances. If so, the trustees have a duty to consider whether to exercise such discretions when these circumstances arise.

Trustees also have duties under legislation such as the *Pension Schemes Act 1993* (*PSA 1993*) to preserve benefits earned by members who leave the scheme early. The member must remain entitled to at least an appropriate proportion of the benefits to which he would have been entitled on retirement. Death in service benefits do not have to be continued. In addition, the pension rights of early leavers must be increased from time to time to take account of inflation. These requirements apply once a member has two years' pensionable service under the scheme. Pensionable service under a previous scheme will be included if there has been a transfer payment into the scheme (see [4.33] below). The Trustees have a duty to ensure that the scheme rules comply with the preservation requirements.

Rights under a pension scheme are not usually assignable, so any benefits must be paid to the beneficiary specified under the scheme. In the case of occupational pension schemes, this is because *PA 1995 s 91* does not allow the assignment of rights under a pension scheme, and because a scheme cannot be approved by the Inland Revenue for tax-exempt status if the benefits can be assigned. However, both *PA 1995 s 91* and the Inland Revenue requirements allow assignment in a few limited circumstances, for example assignments to widows, widowers, other dependants, or in order to comply with a pension-sharing order in relation to an ex-spouse. Pension schemes may therefore allow assignment in these circumstances. If a pension scheme does give the trustees discretion to pay benefits to a person other than the individual member (for example, on the member's death in service), it is the trustees' duty to ensure that the discretion is correctly exercised, and that the correct recipient is identified. It is worth noting that trustees must be careful where a member becomes bankrupt, as under the *Welfare Reform and Pensions Act 1999 (WRPA 1999) s 11* an individual's rights under a pension scheme approved by the Inland Revenue do not transfer to a trustee in bankruptcy.

Duty to collect contributions [4.8]

The rules of a pension scheme will set out how it is to be funded. Occupational pension schemes will be funded by contributions from the employer and the scheme members. A trustee's obligations to comply with the rules of the scheme, and to act prudently in relation to it, effectively require a trustee to ensure that these contributions are paid. They also oblige a trustee to pursue unpaid contributions.

The duty to collect contributions on time has been reinforced by statutory provisions:

- *PA 1995 s 49(8)* and regulations made under it require an employer who has an occupational pension scheme to hand employee pension contributions deducted from pay over to the trustees within 19 days of the end of the month in which they are deducted. If the employer fails to do so, and the failure is either the third in one period of 12 months, or is not corrected within 10 days, the trustees will have to report the failure to the Occupational Pensions Regulatory Authority (OPRA). If the failure is not corrected within 60 days the trustees will also have to inform scheme members. The failure is also an offence by the employer. Where an employer is required to pay minimum contributions in respect of a contracted-out scheme, the payments must be made within 14 days of the end of the income tax month to which they relate.
- *PA 1995 s 56* provides that the assets of most salary-related occupational pension schemes must not exceed their liabilities. This is known as the minimum funding requirement (MFR). It does not apply to money purchase schemes. The removal of the MFR was recommended in the Myners report, published in March 2001, which recommendation was accepted by the Chancellor in his 2001 Budget speech. If Parliament implements the report, the MFR will be replaced with a long term funding

standard. However, for the time being, where the MFR applies to a scheme, *PA 1995 s 57* requires the trustees to:

- obtain actuarial valuations of the scheme at least once every three years;
- draw up a schedule of contributions (see para [4.9] below);
- obtain a yearly certificate from the scheme actuary confirming that the contributions are sufficient to meet the MFR;
- where the schedule is inadequate, obtain a fresh valuation or revise the schedule;
- prepare a report for members if a valuation shows that the scheme is underfunded;
- report any failures to pay contributions to OPRA and/or scheme members (see para [4.9] below); and
- report to OPRA and the scheme members if the employer fails to make up shortfalls in scheme funding.

In addition, both shortfalls and unpaid contributions may become debts due from the employer to the trustees, giving the trustees the option of taking enforcement proceedings.

- *PSA 1993 s 111* requires trustees of occupational pension schemes to ensure that the scheme rules allow members to pay voluntary contributions in return for additional benefits. However, where a scheme has been approved for tax-exempt status by the Inland Revenue, trustees can impose limits on the amount of voluntary contributions that can be paid in order to comply with Inland Revenue requirements.

Duty to produce a schedule of contributions or a payment schedule [4.9]

Where an occupational pension scheme is subject to the MFR (see para [4.8] above), the trustees of the scheme have a duty to maintain a schedule of contributions (*PA 1995 s 58*). For information about this schedule, please see Chapter 6, para [6.12].

Occupational pension schemes that are money purchase schemes do not require a schedule of contributions. Instead *PA 1995 s 87–89* requires the trustees to maintain a payment schedule containing similar information. As with a schedule of contributions, the payment schedule must be agreed with the employer or, in default of agreement, determined by the trustees. Equally, failure to make the contributions must be reported OPRA and the members of the scheme.

Duty to keep separate bank accounts and scheme records [4.10]

Trustees of all trust schemes have a statutory duty to keep any money received by them in a separate account with a bank, building society or other institution authorised under the *Banking Act 1987 (PA 1995 s 49(1))*. However, regulations allow payment into an account held by a third party in certain circumstances.

In addition, the *Occupational Pension Schemes (Scheme Administration) Regulations 1996 (SI 1715)* require trustees to keep proper written records, including:

- details of past and present scheme members;
- the date each member joined the scheme;
- details of contributions received;
- records of all payments to and from the scheme;
- details of movements of assets;
- records of transfers of members' benefits to and from the scheme; and
- records of trustee meetings (see para [4.57] below).

Records must be kept for at least six years from the end of the scheme year to which they relate. Trustees must also make the records available on request to the scheme's professional advisers, to OPRA, to the Pensions Ombudsman or the Pensions Compensation Board. Trustees also have duties to provide information to scheme members (see para [4.14] below and Chapter 7).

Duty to obtain audited accounts [4.11]

With a few exceptions, pension scheme trustees have a statutory duty to produce audited accounts within seven months of the end of each scheme year (*Occupational Pension Schemes (Requirement to Obtain Audited Accounts and a Statement from the Auditor) Regulations 1996 (SI 1975)*). For further details see Chapter 6, para [6.8].

Duty to invest the fund [4.12]

A trustee of a pension scheme has a duty to invest the scheme assets prudently on behalf of the scheme members, and as directed by the trust deed and rules. To take the requirement to comply with the trust deed and rules first, this implies that provisions in the trust deed and rules can impose limitations on the trustees' power to invest. However, this principle is limited by *PA 1995 s 35(4)*, which specifically prohibits any requirement in the trust deed and rules for trustees to obtain the consent of the employer before exercising their powers of investment. In practice it is common for trustees to be given wide discretion to invest the scheme assets as they think fit.

However, the duty to act prudently and in the interests of members also restricts trustees' powers to invest. This duty involves the following:

- The duty to act prudently is a duty to manage the scheme assets with as much care as an ordinary prudent man of business would take in making investments for persons for whom he felt morally obliged to provide. This is a higher duty of care than the general duty to act prudently (see para [4.4] above). It involves taking greater care than the trustee would with his own investments, for example ignoring speculative investments which he might be tempted to make on his own account.

- Trustees must invest the scheme assets in order to obtain the best possible returns for the members, without taking unnecessary risks.

- Ethical considerations are not strictly relevant to the duty to invest. To settle for a lower return for ethical reasons alone is likely to be a breach of trust, although in practice trustees will often be able to find other justifications. If the trustees do adopt a policy of socially responsible investment, they have a duty to disclose this policy in their statement of investment principles (see Chapter 6, para [6.7]).

- Usually the trust deed and rules will allow trustees to delegate the duty to invest to an agent or fund manager.

Trustee Duties and Liabilities **[4.12]**

This is, in fact, obligatory for an occupational pension scheme if its assets include investments within the meaning of the *Financial Services Act 1986 (PA 1995 s 47)*. Trustees should, however, take care to ensure that they delegate their investment powers to a responsible and reputable body, or they could be liable for the bad decisions of their chosen manager. *PA 1995 s 34(2)* reinforces this by only allowing delegation of investment duties to a fund manager if the manager is either authorised under the *Financial Services Act 1986* or exempted from its requirements. *PA 1995 s 34(4)* provides that trustees will not be responsible for the acts or defaults of their fund manager, but only if they have taken all reasonable steps to satisfy themselves that the manager has the appropriate knowledge and experience, and is carrying out his work competently and in accordance with *PA 1995 s 36* (please see below).

- If the trustees are inexperienced in investment, delegation of investment decisions to a fund manager may even be a necessary result of their duty to act prudently, conscientiously, and honestly (which involves taking professional advice when needed) even where appointment of a fund manager is not obligatory (see [4.4] above). However, the Myners report recommended that trustees should be required to have enough expertise to understand and critically evaluate the investment advice they receive, possibly appointing a sub-committee to deal specifically with investment. The report suggested that trustees should draw up a business plan, set an overall objective for their scheme, and should consider all major investment classes and the relative benefits of active and passive investment management for each class. An explicit written mandate should also be agreed with investment managers. The recommendations of the Myners report have been accepted by the Government, but have not been implemented at the date of writing.

- Trustees should carefully consider the suitability of investments, and should take into account the need for diversification to avoid an unacceptable level of risk. This is not only part of the requirement to act prudently when investing, but is a statutory duty imposed by *PA 1995 s 36*. The duty does not preclude investing all the assets of the fund in an insurance policy.

- A similar duty is to look for balanced investments, some long-term and some short-term. Trustees should ensure that the spread of investment is appropriate to the fund, so that it can meet calls on its assets as and when necessary. Failure to do so is a breach of trust.

- Under *PA 1995 s 35*, trustees are obliged to ensure that a written statement of investment principles governing their decisions about investments for the purposes of the scheme is prepared and maintained. For details see Chapter 6, para [6.7]. It is likely that further information on subjects such as investment performance and risk controls will be included in the statement of investment principles when the Myners report is implemented (please see above).

- Under *PA 1995 s 36(3)*, pension scheme trustees are required both to obtain written advice on whether an investment is satisfactory from a qualified person (as specified in *PA 1995 s 36(6)*), and to consult the employer, before any investments are made. Under *PA 1995 s 36(4)* they must similarly obtain advice and consult about existing investments from time to time.

- *PA 1995 s 40* restricts the extent to which trustees may make investments connected with the employer who established the pension scheme, or any other participating employer that employs persons who are members of the scheme. Such investments would include the purchase of shares in the employer's business. Currently trustees may only invest 5% of the market value of the assets of the scheme in employer-related investments. However, there is an exception for small self-administered schemes.

Duty to appoint professional advisers [4.13]

As discussed above, the duty of a trustee to act prudently, conscientiously and honestly includes a duty to take professional advice when needed. This will necessarily involve appointing advisers. A trustee must be careful to ensure that the persons appointed have the necessary experience and expertise to advise, or they may be held liable for the adviser's mistakes under trust law.

These general duties have now been added to by statute. For details of advisers that must be appointed under statute, see Chapter 5. In addition, *PA 1995 s 47* provides that trustees can only rely on advice from professional advisers if they have properly appointed the advisers themselves, in accordance with the provisions of *PA 1995 s 47*.

Duty to disclose information [4.14]

Under trust law, trustees must on request give a scheme member all reasonable information on the administration of the pension scheme, and on its assets. They must also provide copies of the scheme's governing documents (*Re Londonderry's Settlement (1965) Ch 918*). These obligations are wide, and may on occasion give members the right to see minutes of trustee meetings, advice from the scheme actuary, and even legal advice and counsel's opinions (unless relating to a dispute with the member concerned). However, there is no duty to prepare specific information or to put together additional documents that are not already in existence. In addition, trustees have no obligation to give reasons for the exercise of their discretionary powers (*Wilson v Law Debenture Trust Corporation plc (1995) Pensions Law Reports 141*).

Statute also imposes specific duties of disclosure on trustees:

Disclosure to Members and Potential Members [4.15]

Under *PSA 1993 s 113, PA 1995 s 41*, and accompanying regulations, trustees of occupational pension schemes (with a few exceptions, for example trustees of schemes with fewer than 2 members) have a duty to make information about the scheme available to:

- members;
- prospective members;
- spouses of members and prospective members;
- other people entitled to benefits under the scheme;
- independent trades unions recognised in respect of members or prospective members; and
- personal representatives of members.

Members and prospective members should be given information about the scheme and the benefits it provides automatically where possible, and in any event on joining the scheme (*Occupational Pension Schemes (Disclosure of Information) Regulations 1996 (SI No 1655) reg 4(1)*). Usually this information is provided by way of the scheme booklet, which is described in detail in Chapter 6, para [6.6]. The other categories of persons listed above are entitled to this information on request, and all of them, as well as members and prospective members, can also ask to see:

- the scheme's trust deed and rules;
- actuarial valuations and statements;
- the scheme's schedule of contributions or payment schedule (see para [4.9] above);
- the auditor's statement about contributions to the scheme (see para [4.8] above);
- any report prepared by the trustees concerning failure to meet the minimum funding requirement (see para [4.8] above);
- the scheme's statement of investment principles (see para [4.12] above); and
- the trustees' annual report and accounts.

The trustees must notify all members of material alterations to the scheme. They must also provide specific information on an individual's entitlements in certain circumstances, for example if a member takes early retirement.

The exact information that must be provided to members is set out in detail in regulations such as the *Occupational Pension Schemes (Disclosure of Information) Regulations 1996*. For further details of the information which must be provided please see Chapter 7. Further information on the annual report and the information that must be included within it can be found in Chapter 6.

Disclosure to Professional Advisers and OPRA [4.16]

PA 1995 also imposes the following duties of disclosure on trustees:

- To disclose information to the scheme's professional advisers (*PA 1995 s 47(9)b*). The extent of this duty is set out in *The Occupational Pension Schemes (Scheme Administration) Regulations 1996*, which provide that:
    - trustees must disclose to their professional advisers such information as may reasonably be required for the performance of their duties; and
    - trustees must also make available to their professional advisers such of the scheme's books, accounts, and records as they may reasonably require for the performance of their duties.

Trustee Duties and Liabilities **[4.17]**

- To produce to OPRA any documents requested by OPRA which are relevant to the discharge of OPRA's functions (*PA 1995 s 98*).

Duty to register [4.17]

There is a statutory requirement for trustees to register pension schemes with the Registrar of Occupational and Personal Pension Schemes (the Registrar), which is currently OPRA. This can be found in *PSA 1993 s 6*, and the *Register of Occupational and Personal Pension Schemes Regulations 1997 (SI No 371)*.

A pension scheme must be registered if:

- it is a personal or an occupational pension scheme;
- it is established in the UK, is managed in the UK, or has a representative carrying out the functions of a trustee in the UK;
- it is a scheme approved by the Inland Revenue, an application has been made for approval, or it is a public service scheme;
- it has more than one member; and
- it provides benefits other than benefits payable on the death of a member.

A trustee of a registrable scheme must provide the following information to OPRA within three months of the scheme becoming registrable:

- name and address of scheme;
- names and addresses of trustees;
- addresses for communicating with trustees;
- whether the scheme is open, closed (i.e. no new members may be admitted), or frozen (i.e. no new members may be admitted, and benefits have ceased to accrue);
- name, any previous name, and address of each employer of earners to which the scheme relates or has related at any time since 6 April 1975;
- number of members;

- whether the scheme provides money purchase benefits, benefits other than money purchase benefits, or a combination of the two;
- whether benefits are secured by an insurance or annuity contract, and if so the name of the insurers;
- date on which the scheme became registrable; and
- scheme's Inland Revenue reference number.

Changes in information (other than a change in the total number of members) must be notified to OPRA within 12 months.

Duty to comply with the Data Protection Act 1998 [4.18]

Trustees invariably hold the personal details of scheme members. As a result, the *Data Protection Act 1998 (DPA 1988)* imposes a number of duties on them in connection with handling this data. The main duties are as follows:

- Trustees must notify the Information Commissioner that they are 'Data Controllers' under the *DPA 1998*. The notification must include specific details such as the purpose for which the data is used, the intended recipients of the data, and any security measures taken to protect it.
- Trustees must obtain the consent of scheme members to processing their personal data. 'Processing' data basically includes any type of data handling, including data storage and retrieval, even if done through a third party. A suitable consent could be included in each member's application form to join the scheme. There are some exceptions to the requirement for consent, and it has been argued that pension scheme trustees may be able to avail themselves of these.
- If trustees are dealing with sensitive personal data, such as information on physical or mental health, they must obtain the member's explicit consent (a routine consent in an application form is unlikely to be sufficient for these purposes). Again, there are limited exceptions, the scope of which remains unclear.
- Trustees have a duty to ensure that any personal data they hold is accurate and up-to-date. This includes destroying

information when it is no longer needed. However, before destroying information, trustees should consider their statutory obligation to keep certain records for at least six years (see para [4.10]).

- Trustees must provide information to members about their personal data within 40 days of request and the payment of a £10 fee. Members are entitled to know whether their personal data is being processed by the trustees, and if so:
    - the description of the data;
    - the purposes for which it is being used;
    - the intended recipients of the data;
    - the information comprising the data; and
    - any information about the source of the data.

    Members are also entitled to have inaccurate information corrected or removed.

- Trustees have a duty to put measures in place to prevent unauthorised or unlawful processing of personal data, and its accidental loss, damage or destruction. This includes ensuring that external advisers and administrators have sufficient security guarantees. The Information Commissioner should be informed of key changes in security measures (such as improvements) within 28 days.

- Trustees must not transfer personal data relating to a member to a country which is outside the European Economic Area unless the country in question has 'adequate protection' for the rights and freedoms of data subjects. For example, an organisation in the USA will have the required adequate protection if it has signed up to the 'safe harbour principles', as shown in a register maintained by the US Department of Commerce.

The *Data Protection Act 1998* applies to manually held personal data 'held in a relevant filing system' as well as data held electronically. A 'relevant filing system' is one where personal data is readily accessible and filed by reference to the individual. It is likely that member files held by trustees will fall within the statutory provisions, and correspondence files will also do so if filed by reference to the members' names. However, there are transitional provisions that apply until 2007.

Duty to comply with court orders relating to divorce [4.19]

Pensions form part of the matrimonial property that may be split on divorce. The courts are therefore entitled to make orders relating to pensions in a divorce situation, and the trustees have a duty to comply with these.

The powers of the courts to make orders relating to pension schemes on divorce are complex, and are contained in a number of statutes. The main types of court order are considered below.

Variations of Settlements [4.20]

Under the *Matrimonial Causes Act 1973*, s 23–4, a divorce court has the power to order the transfer or settlement of property, or the variation of an existing settlement. It has been decided in court that a pension scheme which provides for a wife or widow amounts to a post-nuptial settlement, so can be varied by the courts under this power to provide a pension for a divorced spouse (*Brooks v Brooks (1996) 1 AC 375*). However, this only applies in very limited circumstances: where it does not affect third party rights, the scheme is in surplus, the scheme is established under trust, and the spouse is employed by the same employer as the member.

Earmarking Orders [4.21]

A much more important power for divorce courts was introduced by *PA 1995 s 166*, which amended the *Matrimonial Causes Act 1973* by inserting *ss 24B–24D*. These sections allow a court to make an attachment order on pensions once they start to be paid. This is usually called an 'earmarking' order. Under such an order, the court may require trustees to pay all or part of a pension to the ex-spouse rather than to the member. Payment will commence once the member retires and the pension becomes payable, and the payments will cease on the death of the ex-spouse or of the member. Also, the court has power to order that any lump sum (or part of it) which becomes payable by a pension scheme (including death-in-service benefit) may be paid to the former spouse. Where the rules of a scheme allow commutation into a lump sum of part of the pension at the time of retirement, the member can be required to ask for the maximum commutation possible.

In practice earmarking orders have rarely be used by the courts. This is because they can often be inappropriate, as the payment of the pension depends on the member's circumstances, rather than the circumstances of the spouse. In addition, earmarking orders prevent the 'clean break' favoured by divorce courts and divorcing couples.

Pension Sharing on Divorce [4.22]

The *WRPA 1999* gives the court the power to order pension sharing on divorce for all pension schemes except for certain excepted public service schemes. Such an order compels the trustees to assign all or part of a member's pension to his (or her) ex-spouse. In essence, a percentage of the value of the member's benefits under the scheme is debited from his pension, and credited to the ex-spouse. The statutory provisions override the provisions of pensions schemes to which they apply, so pension sharing can take place even if the trust deed and rules prohibit assignment of benefits. However, the Inland Revenue requires the deeds of approved schemes to be amended as soon as possible, and in any event when any other changes are made.

Trustees' duties under the statute include:

- Supplying information to a member on request, including a transfer value. Where a transfer value is requested, trustees have three months to supply the information unless divorce proceedings are in progress, in which case the time limit is six weeks. If no transfer value is requested, the information must be supplied within a month.

- Supply a member's spouse with a summary of how benefits are calculated under the scheme on request. The time limit for providing this information is one month.

- If trustees wish to charge for the provision of information or the implementation of a pension sharing order, they must give notice before a sharing order is made or they cannot recover the charges. Charging for information is only allowed in limited circumstances, for instance if a transfer value has already been supplied within the previous 12 months, or if a court orders a transfer value to be provided within less than three months.

- Once an order has been made, the trustees are entitled to receive relevant matrimonial documents and personal details from the parties to enable them to implement the order.

They must generally implement the order within four months of the order or receipt of this information.

Trustees may implement a pension sharing order either by making arrangements to allow the ex-spouse to become a member of the scheme, or by arranging for a transfer to another scheme in accordance with the provisions of the *WRPA 1999* and its regulations.

Duty to appoint member-nominated trustees [4.23]

The duty to appoint member-nominated trustees is a statutory duty introduced by *PA 1995 ss 16–21*. For details see Chapter 5, para [5.7].

Duty to comply with the Disability Discrimination Act 1995 [4.24]

The *Disability Discrimination Act 1995 s 17* provides that the rules of all occupational pension schemes shall be taken to include a rule against disability discrimination. This rule requires trustees of a pension scheme not to discriminate on the grounds of disability. The duty applies to the terms of admission of the scheme, and to how members are treated under the scheme.

There is an exception to this rule in the *Disability Discrimination (Employment) Regulations 1996, (SI No 1456) reg 4*. This permits discrimination where the cost of providing benefits to a disabled person under an occupational pension scheme would be substantially greater than for a comparable person without the disability. This exception applies to the following benefits when provided under an occupational pension scheme:

- termination of service benefit;
- retirement, old age or death benefits; and
- accident, injury, sickness or invalidity benefits.

Duty to implement an internal dispute resolution procedure [4.25]

PA 1995 s 50 requires trustees of occupational pension schemes to introduce an internal dispute resolution procedure (IDRP). This must

Trustee Duties and Liabilities **[4.26]**

provide for a designated person to make decisions on disagreements, and must also allow an appeal to the trustees. On appeal, the trustees must reconsider the matter and may either confirm the original decision or make a new decision. The requirement for an IDRP does not apply to schemes in which all the members are trustees, or which have only one member.

The IDRP adopted by the trustees must include matters set out in the *Occupational Pension Schemes (Internal Dispute Resolution Procedures) Regulations 1996*. For details please see Chapter 6.

Duty to provide equal treatment [4.26]

Although historically UK pension schemes have discriminated between men and women, it is now accepted that trustees have a duty to ensure that there is equal treatment. This requirement was introduced by the *Treaty of Rome, Article 119* (later renumbered Article 141 by the *Treaty of Amsterdam*), which provides that there shall be equal pay for men and women (see Chapter 3, para [3.6]).

UK statutes relevant to a trustee's duty to provide equal treatment include:

- *Equal Pay Act 1970 s 1* and *6*. This provides that an employer cannot make the terms of access to and membership of an occupational pension scheme more favourable to men than to women, or vice versa. There is an exception if an employer can show the discrimination is due to a material factor other than gender. This would allow for different classes of benefits for different classes of employees, e.g. executives as opposed to other employees. These duties have now been extended to trustees by *PA 1995* (see below). Part-time employees must not be treated differently from full-time employees under the *Part-time Workers (Prevention of Less Favourable Treatment) Regulations 2000 (SI No 1551)*, and in any event doing so might constitute indirect sex discrimination if more people of one sex are affected.

- *Sex Discrimination Act 1975 s 6(4)*. This makes it unlawful for an employer to discriminate on grounds of sex when offering access to benefits.

- *Social Security Act 1989 s 23*. This introduced a requirement for equal treatment during paid maternity absence. For the purposes of pension entitlement, a woman on paid maternity leave must be treated as if she was working normally and being remunerated accordingly during a period of maternity absence, but can only be required to pay contributions on the amount of remuneration or statutory maternity pay actually paid to her during the maternity leave. Any paid family leave offered to employees (whether male or female) must be treated in the same way as maternity leave for the purposes of pension provision.

- *PA 1995 s 62–66.* These provisions are intended to implement *Article 141* of the *Treaty of Rome.* They only apply to pensionable service on or after 17 May 1990. The sections provide that:
    - All pension schemes are deemed to contain an equal treatment rule relating to admission and to the treatment of members once admitted. The equal treatment rule amends any provisions less favourable to members of one sex so that they are not less favourable. For example, if women can take a full unreduced pension at 60 but men not until they are 65, men will also be given the right at 60. It extends to provisions made for dependants of members, and also to the exercise of discretions by trustees.
    - The equal treatment rule does not operate if the trustees can prove that the difference is genuinely due to a material factor which is not the difference of sex, but is a material difference between a woman's case and a man's case, for example the fact that women live longer than men.
    - Trustees are given equivalent duties in relation to members as those imposed on employers in respect of employees under the *Equal Pay Act 1970 s 1* (see above).
    - Different benefits under State retirement pensions are permitted.
    - Differences between contributions paid and benefits received by men and women are permitted in some cases, provided they are based on the different life expectations of men and women. The rules are set out in the *Occupational Pension Schemes (Equal Treatment) Regulations 1995 (SI No 3183).*

Trustees are expected to amend the scheme rules to comply with these provisions, and can do so retrospectively. If trustees do not have the power under the trust deed to amend the scheme, or the procedure for doing so is unduly complex, protracted, or subject to unavailable consents, *PA 1995 s 65* gives the trustees the power to amend the scheme by resolution in order to comply.

It is also worth noting that the *Race Relations Act 1976* makes discrimination on grounds of race unlawful, including discrimination in the terms on which someone is offered employment or access to employment benefits.

Duty to comply with PA 1995 s 67 in amending scheme rules [4.27]

The power of trustees to amend the trust deed and rules of a pension scheme is often subject to the consent of the employer under the scheme rules. In the case of an occupational pension scheme (other than a public service scheme) the power to amend is also restricted by *PA 1995 s 67(2)*, as explained in Chapter 6, para [6.4]. Even if the power to amend is exercisable by the employer alone, the trustees are bound to ensure that the requirements of *s 67 PA 1995* are met before any amendment is affected. For further discussion of the power to amend, see para [4.30] below.

Powers of trustees [4.28]

The trust deed and rules will set out the powers of the trustees, and how these powers are to be exercised. These will vary from scheme to scheme. In many cases the powers will be necessary for the trustees to exercise their duties. For example, trustees have a duty to invest the trust fund, and will be given the power under the trust deed to do so.

The trust deed and rules may also give discretionary powers to the trustees. For example, the trustees may have the power to admit members who would not normally be eligible to join the scheme. They do not have to exercise this power, but can choose to do so if they wish. However, trustees do have a duty to consider whether to exercise discretionary powers in appropriate circumstances. They must also exercise discretionary powers promptly if they are not subject to specified time limits. If there is a time limit in the deed and rules of the scheme, the duty is to exercise the power within that time limit.

Trustees must also be careful to comply with their other duties when exercising discretions. In particular they should be careful to act prudently, conscientiously, and honestly in the exercise of discretions, to use them in the best interests of all scheme members, and to act impartially between different classes of members when exercising discretions (see paras [4.4], [4.5] and [4.6] above).

The following section discusses some of the main discretionary powers often found in pension scheme trust deeds and rules.

Power to delegate [4.29]

As a general principle of trust law, a trustee cannot delegate his duty. However, this has been changed by a number of statutes. In particular, the *Trustee Delegation Act 1999 s 5* provides that 'notwithstanding any rule of law or equity to the contrary, a trustee may, by power of attorney, delegate the execution or exercise of all or any of the trust powers and discretions vested in him as trustee . . .'. However, the delegation can only be for a maximum period of 12 months. The trustee will also remain responsible for the actions of the person to whom he has delegated his powers as if the actions of that person were his own actions.

Delegation of the duty to invest is dealt with separately, in *PA 1995 s 34(2)*. This specifically allows delegation of the duty to invest to a fund manager, though only if an appropriate person is appointed (see para [4.12] above). It is logical that delegation to a fund manager should not be time-limited, as it is compulsory for many pension schemes under *PA 1995 s 47* (see para [4.12] above).

Trustee Act 2000 (TA 2000) s 11 allows trustees to employ agents for specified 'delegable functions'. Delegable functions include all functions which cannot otherwise be delegated under statute or the trust deed and rules, but exclude functions relating to the distribution of assets, decisions on making payments out of income or capital, and the appointment of new trustees. However, pension scheme trustees may not appoint scheme members as agents. They are also subject to a statutory duty to exercise such care and skill as is reasonable in the circumstances when appointing agents (taking into account any special knowledge or experience they may have) unless this duty is specifically excluded in the trust deed and rules. There are further limits on trustees of occupational pension schemes, who are not permitted to appoint agents to perform investment functions i.e. to take decisions about investments and investment strategy, rather than performing the role of an investment manager who simply implements the trustees' investment strategy (*TA 2000 s 36*). This section also provides that a trustee of an occupational pension scheme must not appoint as agent a person who is an employer in relation to the scheme or anyone connected with such an employer.

Even where a trustee is permitted to delegate by the trust deed and rules or under statute, a trustee who wishes to delegate must take care that the power concerned is suitable for delegation. He also has a duty to ensure that the persons to whom the delegation is made are suitable, and have sufficient knowledge and experience to be able to perform the duty on the trustee's behalf.

Power to amend [4.30]

As a general principle, neither an employer nor a trustee has the power to amend a scheme unless the trust deed so provides. The trust deed and rules of most pension schemes therefore include express provisions stating how they can be amended. Usually amendments require the consent of both the trustees and the employer, though sometimes one or the other alone will be given the power to amend.

The trust deed and rules may include an express power to make retrospective amendments, as it is doubtful whether this power can be implied. The power to amend may also be expressly limited, for example there may be no power to alter the main purpose of the scheme.

In all cases, when amending the trust deed and rules, the trustees and/or the employer must consider the power of amendment carefully and determine whether they are acting within its limits. Any exercise of an express power of amendment in the trust deed and rules is also limited by both case law and statutory provisions, including the following:

- *PA 1995 s 67* (see para [4.27] above);
- *Income and Corporation Taxes Act 1988 (ICTA 1988) s 591B(2)*, which provides that amendments will cause

[4.30] *Basic Guide to Pensions*

Inland Revenue approval of a scheme to lapse unless the alteration is also approved by the Inland Revenue;

- *ICTA 1988, s 590(2)*, which requires, as a condition of approval, that all employees who are members, or have a right to be members, of the scheme are given written particulars of the key features of the scheme (which will include any amendments that affect them);

- *Occupational Pension Schemes (Disclosure of Information) Regulations 1996 (SI No 1655) reg 4(5)*, which requires pension trustees to notify all members of any changes to the scheme that will materially affect the information provided to them under *s4(1)* (see para. [4.15] and Chapter 6, para [6.6]);

- *PSA 1993 s 72*, which prevents any amendments that would result in a member who left the scheme early having reduced benefits, or in a member being treated less favourably on leaving the scheme early than if they retired from the scheme at normal retirement age;

- *PSA 1993 s 37*, which restricts alterations that can be made to a contracted-out pension scheme;

- case law suggesting that there are implied limits on the most widely-framed powers of amendment in that they may not be used to amend the fundamental nature or purpose of a pension scheme as it applies to any particular member without the consent of that member *(Hole v Garnsey (1930) AC 472, Hillsdown Holdings plc v Pensions Ombudsman (1997) 1 All ER 862)*; and

- case law providing that trustees may not bind themselves to exercise a power in a particular way at a future time, so cannot undertake to make an amendment on a future occasion *(re Vestey's Settlement (1950) 2 All ER 891 at 895)*. No such restriction applies to an employer in relation to a pension scheme.

There are, however, specific statutory powers of amendment that are not limited by the above restrictions. *PA 1995 s 68* allows trustees of an occupational pension scheme to amend the scheme by resolution in order to achieve certain specified purposes, such as introducing member-nominated trustees and extending death benefits to a new class of members (though this also requires the consent of the employer). *PA 1995* also permits alterations to comply with certain statutory requirements, such as the equal treatment rule *(PA 1995 s 65)* (see para [4.26] above).

Power to augment [4.31]

Pension scheme trust deeds and rules often give trustees the power to increase or augment benefits for scheme members in certain circumstances, for example if the scheme has surplus funds. Any such power to augment will be discretionary. For discussion of how trustees should approach the exercise of such a power, see para [4.28] above.

Power to distribute lump sum on death [4.32]

Many pension schemes provide that lump sums will be payable on the death of a member while he is still an employee. It is possible for the scheme rules to provide that this lump sum will be paid to someone nominated by the member, such as a relative. However, this is unusual, as if a specific individual is nominated, the money will be subject to inheritance tax. This tax charge is avoided by providing that the money will not be payable to a specific individual, but will be held on trust by the trustees who will have discretion to pay it to one or more of a wide class of potential recipients. If this route is followed, the Inland Revenue requires the money to be paid within a period of 2 years or less.

If a scheme provides that a lump sum is to be payable at the discretion of the trustees, this can create difficulties for the trustees in deciding who should receive the benefit of the payment. It is therefore common for trustees to request scheme members to complete 'expression of wish' forms specifying who they would like to receive the money. These forms will only be suggestions by the members and will not be binding on the trustees. Trustees therefore have the power to decide to ignore a wish form if they consider it inappropriate to comply with it in the particular circumstances.

Power to make or accept transfers [4.33]

Under *PSA 1993*, where members of an employer's occupational pension scheme cease employment with that employer, they have the right for the cash equivalent of all or part of their benefits to be paid as a transfer value to another occupational pension scheme approved by the Inland Revenue. This right only applies where the pension scheme is funded at least partly by contributions from the employer or members, and is subject to there being a period of at least one

[4.33] *Basic Guide to Pensions*

year between the termination of the member's pensionable service and their normal pensionable age. Similar rights apply to members of personal pension schemes on leaving the scheme.

Members who opt out of an occupational pension scheme without leaving employment only have the right to transfer a partial cash equivalent relating to service after 5 April 1988 (*Occupational Pension Schemes (Transfer Values) Regulations 1996 reg 3*). This is the date when members generally first had the right to opt out. In practice, the deed and rules may give wider powers than the legislation, for example trustees of an occupational scheme may have the discretion to transfer a full cash equivalent to members who opt out of the pension scheme without leaving employment.

It is also common practice for trust deeds and rules to allow trustees of pension schemes to accept incoming transfer payments from other schemes, although there is no requirement for schemes or trustees to do so. Legislation does, however, prescribe the types of transfer that may be accepted, for example an occupational pension scheme may accept transfers from:

- another occupational pension scheme;
- a personal pension;
- a retirement annuity, where the policy has been endorsed to permit the transfer;
- a deferred annuity contract, or buy-out annuity; or
- a freestanding additional voluntary contribution scheme.

There are detailed regulations governing the calculation of transfer values. In the case of a final salary occupational pension scheme, the basis of calculation must be approved by an actuary, and be consistent with various criteria set out in the *Occupational Pension Schemes (Transfer Values) Regulations 1996*. These criteria provide, for example, that discretionary benefits must be taken into account when calculating the transfer value if the trustees have established a practice of granting the discretionary benefits.

Transfer values must be calculated in the same way as pension benefits on retirement. In the case of a money purchase occupational scheme, it is therefore usual for the transfer value to be the realisable value of assets earmarked for that individual under the scheme. In the case of a final salary occupational scheme, by contrast, the transfer value will be a proportion of the final benefits the member would have been entitled to under the scheme, and will be calculated by reference to factors such as period of service, salary on leaving the scheme, and anticipated salary had the individual remained a member of the scheme. Under *PSA 1993 s 93A*, the trustees of a salary-related occupational pension scheme are obliged, on request, to provide a member with a 'statement of entitlement' setting out the cash equivalent of his benefits under the scheme on a stated 'guarantee date'. Under *PSA 1993 s 94(1)*, this level of entitlement must then be guaranteed for three months.

Trustees cannot refuse to pay a transfer value. However, if a scheme which is subject to the MFR (see para [4.8] above) is underfunded according to the last actuarial valuation, the trustees can reduce the transfer value to take account of the underfunding. Under *PSA 1993 s 99* a transfer request must be implemented within six months of the request, or of the guarantee date in the case of a salary-related occupational scheme.

Trustee liabilities [4.34]

If trustees breach their duties, complaints can be made against them by anyone who suffers as a result. Such complaints are usually made to the Pensions Ombudsman, or to the courts. In addition, OPRA has the power to impose penalties on trustees for breaches of *PA 1995*. For details of the powers of OPRA and the Pensions Ombudsman, see Chapter 5, paras [5.19] and [5.22].

This section aims to give an indication of some of the liabilities and penalties that can be imposed on trustees for breach of duty by considering statutory penalties under *PA 1995*, and discussing trustee liability under trust law. It is not intended to be a comprehensive guide to trustee liabilities. In particular, there are many liabilities imposed by statues other than *PA 1995* that are not considered below, and this section does not consider the role of the Pensions Ombudsman further. Trustees should, however, be aware that there are additional statutory liabilities, and that many breaches of duty can be referred to the Pensions Ombudsman as an alternative to the courts.

Penalties under PA 1995 [4.35]

PA 1995 gives OPRA the power to impose civil penalties on trustees who breach its provisions. In some cases, criminal penalties also apply. The table below summarises the main statutory offences and penalties that apply for breach of the statutory duties discussed above. However, this is not a comprehensive guide, and for exact details of the relevant penalties reference should be made to *PA 1995*.

As well as imposing penalties, *PA 1995* and legislation passed under it provide statutory remedies for members of pension schemes against trustees. For example, *PA 1995 s 11* provides that members who claim to have been discriminated against in contravention of the equal treatment principle may take trustees to an employment tribunal. These remedies are not included in the table below.

Penalties are listed in the table below by reference to trustee duties, in the order in which they are considered above. Sections marked with an asterix have criminal penalties. Other sections impose only civil penalties on trustees. All section references refer to *PA 1995* unless stated otherwise, in which case the reference is to subordinate legislation made under that statute.

Table of penalties [4.36]

Section of PA 1995	Offence	Penalty
Duty to collect contributions		
s 49(10)	Failure to take all reasonable steps to give notice to OPRA and the members concerned that the employer has not paid over employee contributions deducted from salary within 19 days of the end of the month in which they are deducted.	• A fine of up to £5,000 for an individual, or £50,000 for a corporation. • Prohibition from acting as a trustee.

Trustee Duties and Liabilities **[4.36]**

★s 49(12)	Being knowingly concerned in the fraudulent evasion of the requirement for an employer to pay over employee contributions within 19 days of the end of the month in which they are deducted.	• On summary conviction, a fine not exceeding the statutory maximum (currently £5,000). • On conviction on indictment, up to 7 years imprisonment and/or an unlimited fine.
s 57(7), 59(4) & 60(8)	Failure to take all reasonable steps to: • obtain actuarial valuations; • obtain actuarial certificates; • make such valuations or certificates available to the employer within 7 days; • prepare a report for members if a valuation shows that the scheme is underfunded; • notify OPRA and members that the employer has failed to make up shortfalls in scheme funding.	• Fine of up to £5,000 for an individual, or £50,000 for a corporation. • Prohibition from acting as a trustee.

Duty to produce a schedule of contributions or a payment schedule

s 58(8) & 87(5)	Failure to take all reasonable steps to maintain a schedule of contributions or payment schedule.	• Fine of up to £5,000 for an individual, or £50,000 for a corporation.

[4.36] *Basic Guide to Pensions*

		• Prohibition from acting as a trustee.
s 59(4) & 88(4)	Failure to take all reasonable steps to notify OPRA and members that contributions/payments have not be paid by the due date.	• Fine of up to £5,000 for an individual, or £50,000 for a corporation. • Prohibition from acting as a trustee.

Duty to keep separate bank accounts and scheme records

s 49(6)	Failure to take all reasonable steps to: • keep trust money in a separate bank account; • keep records of meetings and transactions.	• Fine of up to £5,000 for an individual, or £50,000 for a corporation. • Prohibition from acting as a trustee.

Duty to obtain audited accounts

Reg 2(3), Occupational Pension Schemes (Requirement to obtain Audited Accounts and a Statement from the Auditor) Regulations 1996	Failure to take all steps necessary to: • obtain audited accounts; • obtain an auditor's statement.	• Fine of up to £5,000 for an individual, or £50,000 for a corporation. • Prohibition from acting as a trustee.

Duty to invest the fund

s 35(6)	Failure to take all reasonable steps to: • maintain a statement of investment	• Fine of up to £5,000 for an individual, or £50,000 for a corporation.

Trustee Duties and Liabilities [4.36]

	principles;
	• when preparing or revising the statement, consult:
	  • the employer;
	  • a person with knowledge of financial matters and the management of pension scheme investments.
		• Prohibition from acting as a trustee.

s 36(8)	Failure to take all reasonable steps to obtain and consider written advice on the question of whether an investment is satisfactory, having regard to suitability and diversification: • before making the investment; • periodically in relation to retained investments.	• Fine of up to £5,000 for an individual, or £50,000 for a corporation. • Prohibition from acting as a trustee.
s 40(4)	Failing to take all reasonable steps to comply with the limits on employer-related investments.	• Fine of up to £5,000 for an individual, or £50,000 for a corporation. • Prohibition from acting as a trustee.
★s 40(5)	Making prohibited employer-related investments (the offence is only committed by a trustee who agrees to	• On summary conviction, a fine not exceeding the statutory

	make the investment, not by a trustee who objects to it).	maximum (currently £5,000). • On conviction on indictment, imprisonment and/or an unlimited fine.

Duty to appoint professional advisers

s 47(3)	Relying on the skill or judgement of a person appointed to exercise any prescribed functions in relation to the scheme, or appointed as legal adviser or fund manager, which person is not appointed in writing by the trustees.	• Fine of up to £5,000 for an individual, or £50,000 for a corporation. • Prohibition from acting as a trustee.
s 47(8)	Failure to take all reasonable steps to appoint, or appoint correctly: • an auditor; • an actuary; • a fund manager where such person is required to be appointed by *PA 1995 s 47*.	• Fine of up to £5,000 for an individual, or £50,000 for a corporation • Prohibition from acting as a trustee

Duty to disclose information

Reg. 11, Occupational Pension Schemes (Disclosure of Information) Regulations 1996	• Failure to provide automatically: • basic information about the scheme to members and	• Fine of up to £1,000 for an individual, or £10,000 for a corporation. • Prohibition from acting as a trustee.

- prospective members;
- information on benefits when they become payable, or are altered, to members receiving those benefits;
- information to a retiring member about his options on retirement;
- notification to members if a scheme ceases to be contracted-out;
- on death of a member, information on his rights to any person who may have rights in consequence;
- a transfer value to a member or prospective member;
- information on any winding up process to members and anyone else who may benefit under the scheme;
- notification to members if a scheme ceases to be a registered

[4.36] *Basic Guide to Pensions*

	stakeholder scheme.	
	• Failure to provide on request:	
	• information on benefits and contributions to members;	
	• information on their rights to any person who may have rights in consequence of the death of a member.	

Reg. 11, Occupational Pension Schemes (Disclosure of Information) Regulations 1996	• Failure to provide on request to members, prospective members, their spouses, anyone else who might benefit under the scheme, and relevant trade unions:
	  • trust deed and rules;
	  • basic information on the scheme;
	  • changes to information provided on joining (to be provided to members only);
	  • annual report;
		• Fine of up to £200 for an individual, or £1,000 for a corporation.
		 • Prohibition from acting as a trustee.

Trustee Duties and Liabilities [4.36]

	• actuarial valuation; • schedule of contributions or payment schedule; • statement of investment principles; • Failure to include an address for queries with information provided.	
s 47(11)	Failure to take all reasonable steps to disclose information to professional advisers as required by regulations.	• Fine of up to £5,000 for an individual, or £50,000 for a corporation. • Prohibition from acting as a trustee.
★s 101(1)	Without reasonable excuse, to neglect or refuse to produce a document when required to do so by OPRA.	On summary conviction, a fine not exceeding level 5 on the standard scale (currently £5,000).

Duty to register

Reg. 7 Register of Occupational Pension Schemes Regulations 1997	• Failure to provide to the Registrar:
	  • specified information within 3 months of the scheme becoming registrable;
	  • further information reasonably required by
		• Fine of up to £1,000 for an individual, or £10,000 for a corporation.

- the Registrar with 3 months of request;
- notification of changes to registered information within 12 months of the change;
- details of the number of members of the scheme on the last day of any scheme year within 56 days of request;
- where a scheme became registrable before 1 April 1997, specified information within 3 months of request;
- Using information supplied by the Registrar for marketing purposes.

Duty to appoint member-nominated trustees

s 21(1) & (2)	• Failure to make arrangements either for member-nominated trustees (or directors), or for an alternative opt	• Fine of up to £5,000 for an individual, or £50,000 for a corporation. • Prohibition from

	out arrangement which has been duly approved by members.	acting as a trustee.
	• Failure to implement the above arrangements.	

Duty to implement an internal dispute resolution procedure

s 50	Failure to implement an internal dispute resolution procedure.	Fine of up to £5,000 for an individual, or £50,000 for a corporation.

Duty to comply with PA 1995 s 67 in amending scheme rules

Reg. 8 Occupational Pension Schemes (Modification of Schemes) Regulations 1996	Failure to comply with the certification requirements or the consent requirements under *PA 1995 s 67* when amending scheme rules.	Fine of up to £5,000 for an individual, or £50,000 for a corporation.

In addition, a trustee who is prohibited from acting as trustee for a particular pension scheme can also be disqualified from acting as a trustee for any other scheme. A person who acts as a trustee while prohibited or disqualified commits a criminal offence under *PA 1995 s 6 or s 30* respectively, and is liable on summary conviction to a fine not exceeding the statutory maximum (currently £5,000) and on conviction on indictment to imprisonment and/or an unlimited fine.

Liability under trust law [4.37]

A trustee commits a breach of trust if he fails to carry out his duties, or does something which he is not empowered to do. Trust law will remedy a breach of trust by compensating anyone who suffers loss as a result, for example a member who has not received his pension. Statute may also provide remedies for a person who has suffered loss because of the trustees' breach of duty. However, statute may also impose penalties on the trustees (see paras [4.34]-[4.36] above). Trust law does not impose penalties in this way.

When is a Trustee liable for Breach of Trust? [4.38]

- A trustee is liable for any breach of trust that he commits by his own act or omission. This liability will continue even after he has ceased to be a trustee.

- As a general principle a trustee is not liable for the acts or omissions of his fellow trustees. However, once a trustee becomes aware of a breach of duty by a fellow trustee, unless he does something to remedy it he will become equally responsible for the breach. This is true even if the breach was made by a former trustee. A trustee may also be found responsible if he fails to check that his fellow trustees are dealing with trust property correctly.

- Where a loss is caused by the joint default of all the trustees, each trustee is individually liable for the whole of the loss. However, they will generally be entitled to recover contributions from each other.

- Where a trustee has delegated duties to an agent such as a fund manager, he will remain liable for breaches of trust committed by that agent unless he took all reasonable steps to ensure that the agent was a suitable person to appoint. Equally, an agent who joins in a breach of trust by trustees will be liable together with the trustees.

What is the extent of a Trustee's Liability? [4.39]

Where a trustee commits a breach of trust, under trust law he will usually be personally liable to compensate the trust fund. In such a situation, the court may order the following remedies:

Compensation for Loss Suffered [4.40]

The trustee who has committed a breach of trust may be required to compensate the trust fund or the members for any loss suffered by them as a result. Indeed, once a breach of duty can be shown to have contributed towards a loss, the trustees will be held responsible for the whole amount of the loss even if the breach was not the main cause of the loss (*Brickenden v London and Loan Savings Co (1934) DLR 465 at 469*).

In calculating the loss suffered by the scheme or the scheme members:

- Any failure to make a gain (such as an increase in value of the assets of the scheme) which would probably have been made but for the breach of trust will be included as part of the loss *(Nestle v National Westminster Bank plc (1994) 1 All ER 118)*.

- Losses that would have been suffered by the fund if the trustees had not breached their duties will not be taken into account, so will not reduce the sums payable by the trustees *(Target Holdings Ltd v Redfern (1994) 2 All ER 337)*.

- The trustees will have to compensate the scheme or the members for all losses that occur before the breach is remedied *(Clough v Bond (1838) 3 My & Cr 490)*. So if, for example, trustees fail to sell some scheme assets because of a breach of trust, the loss includes the highest possible price that could have been obtained for the assets if they had been sold.

If a transaction in breach of trust causes both a loss and a gain, the trustees are only liable for the overall loss. However, if the loss and the gain arise from two distinct transactions, there can be no set-off of one against the other *(Bartlett v Barclays Bank Trust Co. Ltd (No 2) (1980) Ch 515 at 538)*.

Accounting for Profit [4.41]

If a trustee makes a profit out of the trust fund or his position as a trustee, either by breach of trust or in the course of managing the scheme, the court may order him to pay his profits to the scheme.

If the trustee has made a profit by using scheme funds for his own private purposes, he may be required to both replace the money and to pay any profits he has made to the scheme.

Choice of Remedy [4.42]

Where a trustee could be required either to pay his profits to the scheme, or to compensate the scheme for loss, the court will grant one or other of the two remedies. However, although the scheme members cannot have both remedies, the court will enforce the remedy most favourable to them.

Invalidity of Acts [4.43]

If a trustee purchases property that belongs to the scheme, for example buys shares from the scheme, the transaction can be declared invalid by any member of the scheme, or any person who might benefit under it. This is because a trustee who buys property from the scheme is breaching his duty to avoid any conflicts of interest with the scheme. However, this does not prevent a trustee from being a member of the scheme.

If trustees act outside the provisions of the trust deed and rules, even unintentionally, their acts may again be held to be invalid.

Costs [4.44]

A trustee who is found responsible for a breach of trust in court will be ordered to pay the legal costs of the person who brought the court action against him. (*Bartlett v Barclays Bank Trust Co. Ltd (No 2) (1980) Ch 515.*) This does not happen if a compliant is made to the Pensions Ombudsman. Instead, the trustee and the person bringing the complaint each have to pay their own legal costs.

Statutory Liability [4.45]

Although consideration of statutory liabilities other than those under *PA 1995* is beyond the scope of this chapter, it is necessary to mention that trustees may also find themselves subject to statutory liabilities for some kinds of breach of trust. One example is the *DPA 1998* (discussed in para [4.18] above), which imposes criminal penalties on trustees for breach of its provisions, and also provides for them to pay compensation to members in certain circumstances. Another is the offence of criminal theft under the *Theft Act 1968*, which could apply if a trustee makes personal use of scheme funds.

Protection of trustees [4.46]

Given the extent of trustee liabilities, it is hardly surprising that many trustees seek to protect themselves against the consequences of breach of trust. However, there are limits on the steps a trustee can take. For example:

- *PA 1995 s 31* provides that trustees may not be reimbursed out of the trust assets for fines or penalties imposed under *PA 1995 s 10* or *PSA 1993 s 168(4)*.

- *PA 1995 s 33* prevents the exclusion or restriction of liability for breach of any legal obligation to take care or exercise skill in the performance of investment functions, where exercisable by trustees or by a fund manager appointed by them.

However, trustees may be able to persuade an employer to allow them to limit their liability under the scheme rules when the employer is setting up the scheme. The main methods are briefly considered in this section. These are:

- trust deed exclusion clauses;
- indemnity clauses;
- insurance;
- consents; and
- reliance on the *Trustee Act 1925 s 61*.

Trust deed exclusion clauses [4.47]

Trust deeds may contain exclusion clauses protecting trustees. These vary widely, but are all aimed at excluding the personal responsibility of the trustees for breaches of trust. A clause might provide, for example, that 'no trustee shall incur any personal liability whatsoever in the execution or purported execution of any duties, rights or powers under this trust deed and rules except in respect of fraud'. If a trustee protected under this clause committed a breach of trust through an honest mistake, the clause would give him a defence to any claim for breach of trust.

Any trustee who wishes to rely on an exclusion clause must carefully check to see whether he is protected under its exact terms. Exclusion clauses are construed restrictively by the courts, so if there is any ambiguity, the trustee is unlikely to be protected. However, as long as the clause is clear, it appears that the courts will give effect even to very wide-ranging exclusions. The case of *Armitage v Nurse (1997) All ER 705* established that a trust deed can exclude trustees' liability for negligent breaches of trust, though not for breaches that are reckless, deliberate or dishonest. However, Lord Justice Millett commented that it is difficult to justify the exclusion of liability for negligence, especially in the case of professional trustees, as this undermines the rights of the scheme's beneficiaries. A more sensible approach is to exclude liability for only innocent breaches of trust.

An exclusion clause may also provide that trustees will not be liable for the acts of their managers or agents. Such a clause reinforces the statutory protection in *PA 1995 s 34(4)*, which provides that trustees will not be responsible for the acts or defaults of a fund manager provided that they have taken all reasonable steps to satisfy themselves that the fund manager has the appropriate knowledge and experience, and is carrying out his work competently and in accordance with *PA 1995 s 36* (see para [4.12] above).

However, statute may also prevent a trustee from obtaining protection from an exclusion clause. *PA 1995 s 33* prevents the exclusion or restriction of liability for breach of any legal obligation to take care or exercise skill in the performance of investment functions by trustees or fund managers. However, trustee liability for the actions of a properly appointed fund manager, can be excluded under *PA 1995 s 34(6)*.

It has been suggested that the *Unfair Contract Terms Act 1977* may also apply to trustee exclusion clauses applying to trustees appointed after 1 February 1978. If so, such clauses must be 'reasonable' under the terms of the *Unfair Contract Terms Act 1977 s 2(2)* if they are to be effective.

Indemnity clauses [4.48]

Indemnity from Employer [4.49]

Pension scheme trustees may seek an indemnity from the scheme employer before taking a proposed course of action, in case it could be considered to be in breach of trust. For example, trustees might ask for an indemnity if the employer asks them to merge the scheme with another pension scheme. It is also common for trust documents to contain a general provision that the trustees will be indemnified for their actions by the employer provided they are acting honestly and in good faith.

There is little case law in this area, so there is some question as to whether such indemnities are valid. However, a court would be likely to uphold an indemnity for an innocent breach of trust, such as those covered by a general indemnity for actions taken in good faith.

A final point to note is that an indemnity from an employer is only of use if the company that has given the indemnity has the resources to indemnify the trustees when the need arises.

Indemnity from the Scheme [4.50]

As mentioned above, *PA 1995 s 31* provides that trustees may not be reimbursed out of the trust assets for fines or penalties imposed under *PA 1995 s 10* or *PSA 1993 s 168(4)*. Equally, trustees may not use those scheme funds to purchase insurance against such fines or penalties. There are civil penalties for breach of these provisions, and a trustee commits a criminal offence if he is reimbursed in contravention of the provisions and knows or has reasonable grounds to believe that this is the case.

The question remains whether trustees can seek indemnities from the trust fund in respect of other breaches of duty. To be valid, any such indemnity would need to be contained in the trust deed and rules at the outset, as it is very unlikely that trustees could justify amending scheme rules to include an indemnity for their own benefit. In practice, it is common to find indemnities where the trustees have acted in good faith. The comments at para [4.45] on the validity of indemnities apply equally here: in particular the indemnity will be of no value if the scheme is winding up and in deficit.

Insurance [4.51]

Trustees may also seek to protect themselves by obtaining insurance against their liabilities for breach of trust. However, in practice insurance companies will only offer cover for negligent breaches of trust, not for deliberate breaches.

If trustees decide to obtain insurance, they will want the cost to be covered by the pension scheme. The premiums can be paid out of the scheme funds, but only if there is a specific power in the trust deed allowing this. As with indemnities, it will be almost impossible for trustees to justify amending scheme rules to allow this, so it is important that suitable provisions are included from the outset.

[4.52] *Basic Guide to Pensions*

Under the *Trustee Act 1925 s 19*, as amended by *TA 2000 s 34*, a trustee may insure scheme property against risks of loss or damage due to any event, and can pay the premiums out of the scheme funds. The trustee is, however, subject to a statutory duty to exercise reasonable care and skill when insuring the fund (taking into account any special knowledge or experience he may have) unless this duty is specifically excluded in the trust deed and rules. Where a trustee has an indemnity from the scheme, he should therefore be able to insure the scheme against any loss resulting from payments made under that indemnity.

Trustee Act 1925 s 61 [4.52]

Trustee Act 1925 s 61 gives the court the power to relieve a trustee from personal liability for breach of trust. The power applies where the trustee has acted 'honestly and reasonably, and ought fairly to be excused from the breach of trust and for omitting to obtain the directions of the court in the matter in which he committed such breach'.

It should not be difficult to ascertain whether a trustee has acted honestly. Whether a trustee has acted reasonably is a question of fact, and the test applied is objective. The third limb of the test, whether the trustee should fairly be excused, is a question for the court to consider in the light of all the circumstances. The conduct of a paid or professional trustee is much less likely to be excused than that of a gratuitous trustee.

The final part of the test refers to a trustee's ability to apply to the court for determination of any question arising in the execution of a trust (see para [4.3] above). A trustee seeking to rely on the *Trustee Act 1925 s 61* will normally have to provide a full explanation of why the trustees did not apply to the court for guidance on the matter concerned. As a general rule, *s 61* should be considered as a last resort, and in cases of doubt trustees are well advised to seek directions from the court.

Exercise of trustee powers [4.53]

Decision making [4.54]

As a general principle, trustee decisions must be unanimous unless the trust deed and rules provide otherwise. However, *PA 1995 s 32* allows trustees of an occupational pension scheme to take decisions by majority unless the trust deed provides otherwise. Subject to the scheme rules, the trustees may require a minimum number of trustees to be present before a decision can be made.

Trust deed and rules [4.55]

The trust deed and rules may contain provisions dealing with trustee meetings and decision making. If so, the trustees must comply with the rules, or their decisions may be invalid and in breach of trust (see para [4.43] above).

Notice of meetings [4.56]

In practice, trustee decisions will be made either at trustee meetings, or in a written statement signed by all the trustees. Where a meeting is held, *PA 1995 s 32* provides that notice of meetings must be given to 'each trustee to whom it is reasonably practicable to give such notice'. The notice must:

- be given not less than 10 working days before the meeting;
- be sent to the last known address of each trustee; and
- specify the date, time and place of the meeting.

There is an exception from the notice requirement for 'an occasion on which it is necessary as a matter of urgency to make a decision' (*Occupational Pension Schemes (Scheme Administration) Regulations 1996, reg 9*).

Minutes of meetings [4.57]

The trustees of occupational pension schemes are obliged by statute to keep written records of trustee meetings. The *Occupational Pension Schemes (Scheme Administration) Regulations 1996*, require the record to state:

- the date, time and place of meeting;
- the names of all trustees invited;
- the names of trustees attending/failing to attend;
- the names of other persons attending;

- any decisions made;
- whether any decisions have been made since the last meeting; and
- if so, the date, time and place of decisions made since the last meeting, and who participated in making those decisions.

There are limited exceptions from the regulations, for example for an occupational pension scheme with only 1 member.

Useful addresses [4.58]

OPRA, Invicta House, Trafalgar Place, Trafalgar Street, Brighton, East Sussex, BN1 4DW (**www.opra.gov.uk**)

The Pensions Ombudsman, 11 Belgrave Road, London SW1V 1RB

Association of Pension Lawyers, Cheviot House, 70 Baxter Avenue, Southend on Sea, Essex, SS2 6JA (**www.apl.org.uk**)

National Association of Pension Funds, NIOC House, 4 Victoria Street, London SW1H 0NX (**www.napf.co.uk**)

Pensions Management Institute, PMI House, 4-10 Artillery Lane, London E1 7LS (**www.pensions-pmi.org.uk**)

Pensions Benefits Law Reports (**www.pensionslaw.com**)

Pensions Law Reports (**www.incomesdata.co.uk**)

Useful texts [4.59]

OPRA Guides for Pension Scheme Trustees

Pensions Law and Practice – Robin Ellison (Sweet & Maxwell)

Sweet & Maxwell's Law of Pension Schemes – Nigel Inglis-Jones (Sweet & Maxwell)

Underhill and Hayton Law of Trusts and Trustees – David J Hayton (Butterworths)

The Pensions Practice 1997 – Robin Ellison (Pendragon)

5 – People in Pensions

> This chapter covers the following:
>
> - People involved in pensions.
>
> - The role of people in pensions.

Introduction [5.1]

An employer will decide to give pension benefits to its employees as an aid to recruitment or retention of staff. The type of scheme it offers will largely depend on the demands of the marketplace in which the employer operates and the benefits offered by its competitors. Another determining factor will be the likely costs involved. Once this decision is made a scheme will be established and various people will need to be involved to ensure its smooth operation.

If the scheme is a group personal pension managers will be appointed, but if an occupational money purchase or final salary scheme is chosen, trustees will be appointed to hold the assets of the scheme and pay the benefits it promises. There are various types of trustees which will be described in this chapter, while Chapter 4 contains a detailed analysis of their powers and duties.

Under the *Pensions Act 1995* (*PA 1995*), s 47 the trustees of a scheme are obliged to appoint certain professionals to assist them in their task. An auditor, fund manager and an actuary will generally be necessary, and their roles are discussed here. Other advisers will be needed from time to time, and their appointment and function are also examined.

The scheme will be subject to the requirements of the Inland Revenue if it is to take the benefit of the tax advantages available to an exempt-approved scheme under the *Income and Corporation Taxes Act 1988* (*ICTA 1988*). If it is contracted out of SERPS, it will also

[5.2] *Basic Guide to Pensions*

need to comply with the requirements of the Department of Social Security (now the Department for Work and Pensions). Contracting out is dealt with in more detail in Chapter 3.

The Occupational Pensions Regulatory Authority (OPRA) will require the scheme to be registered with it, and will ensure its compliance with pensions legislation including, in particular, *PA 1995* and the numerous regulations passed under it.

Lastly the Pensions Advisory Service (OPAS) and the Pensions Ombudsman may be called upon to resolve disputes concerning the administration of the scheme, and ultimately there may be issues which can only be decided by the courts.

Fig 1.1 People involved in pension schemes

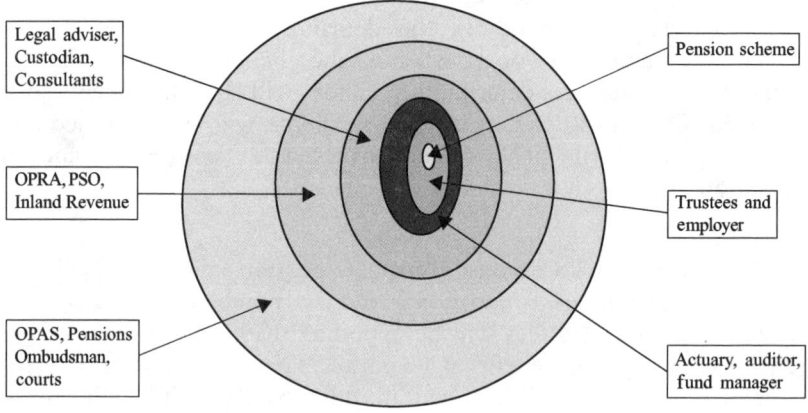

The employer [5.2]

The employer will be a party to any trust deed establishing a money purchase or final salary scheme. At the point of establishing the scheme, the employer has the opportunity to decide the balance of powers between it and the trustees in certain crucial areas. Careful consideration will be given to the drafting of powers relating to the future amendment of the scheme, the augmentation of benefits, the granting of early retirement, and the decisions on contribution rates and commutation factors. The trust deed will also set out whether administration costs are to be borne by the employer, in addition to its normal contributions, or from the fund.

An employer may participate in a centralised or multi-employer occupational pension scheme which will result in lower administration costs, and many of the powers under the pension scheme will be exercised by the principal employer on its behalf. In the case of an approved occupational pension scheme the Inland Revenue will need to be assured that the employers are sufficiently closely associated, i.e. one directly or indirectly controls the other, or both are controlled by a third party. It also will accept that employers are associated if they have a permanent community of interests, such as common management or shareholders, or interchangeable, or jointly employed staff. Alternatively, there are some industry-wide schemes specifically established for non-associated employers, such as those established by trade unions.

It is a condition of Inland Revenue approval that the employer makes more than token contributions to a pension scheme. They must amount to at least 10% of the total contributions to the scheme (Inland Revenue PN 5.1 IR 12 (2001)). Contributions may be suspended however, but an actuarial certificate is necessary in the case of a final salary scheme. A temporary suspension of an employer's contributions of under two years does not require reporting to the Inland Revenue.

The employer will need to put in place payroll systems to ensure that its contributions (and those of the members) which are deducted from their salaries are promptly passed over to the trustees. Members' contributions must be paid over within 19 days of the end of the month in which they are deducted, or 14 days where minimum payments are made because the member is contracted-out of SERPS on a protected rights basis *(PA 1995, s 49(8)* and the *Occupational Pension Schemes (Scheme Administration) Regulations 1996 SI 1996 No 1715, reg 16).* Failure to do so is no longer a criminal offence but may attract a fine from OPRA. An employer has eight weeks after a minimum funding requirement (MFR) valuation to agree a schedule of contributions with the trustees of a final salary scheme *(PA 1995, s 58).* A payment schedule will need to be established and maintained in accordance with *PA 1995, s 87* in the case of a money purchase scheme.

The employer will also need to supply the trustees with membership information to enable them to administer the scheme, such as details of members' ages and pensionable salaries. The requirements of the *Data Protection Act 1998 (DPA 1998)* should be borne in mind. Not only is the employer a data controller in its own right but it will also be a data processor for the trustees. The employer may be required

[5.2] *Basic Guide to Pensions*

by the trustees to enter into an agreement confirming that it will abide by the principles in *DPA 1998* relating to such matters as security and disclosure of information.

As the pension scheme is a benefit forming part of the employment package, it will need to be referred to in the employees' contract of employment. It is important that it is made clear that the scheme is governed by the trust deed and rules and that information about the scheme is contained in the scheme booklet. It is also wise to draw attention to the fact that the employer may change or terminate the scheme. Otherwise it is arguable that a change in the scheme, or its discontinuance, may constitute a change in the employee's contractual terms of engagement and a claim for constructive dismissal could result.

In exercising its powers and duties under the trust deed the employer should also have regard to its duties of good faith to its employees. Long recognised as a principle applicable in the field of employment law, the case of *Imperial Group Pension Trust v Imperial Tobacco (1991) 2 AER 597*, made it clear that this duty is also implied in the exercise of an employer's duties and powers under a pension scheme. It must not act in a way which seriously undermines the relationship of trust and confidence between it and its employees. In the case of *Hillsdown Holdings plc v Pensions Ombudsman (1996) PLR 427*, it was decided that the employer was in breach of this duty when it threatened the trustees that if they did not agree to its scheme merger proposals, it would suspend contributions and swamp an over-funded scheme with new members. The duty of good faith does not prevent an employer taking into account its own interests. On the other hand a fiduciary duty of an employer must be exercised solely in the best interests of the trust's beneficiaries. The power to appoint trustees is such a power, but often there is a fine line to be drawn between a fiduciary duty and one of good faith.

Subject to its contractual obligations to its employees and to the terms of the trust deed and rules, the employer retains the right to terminate the scheme by ceasing to make contributions. Many employers, fearful of the escalating costs particularly of final salary schemes, have in recent times used this power. Other useful powers in this context are powers to close the scheme to new entrants or to amend the scheme to reduce benefits in respect of future pensionable service.

Trustees [5.3]

Where a money purchase or final salary scheme is established under trust, the employer will appoint trustees to hold the scheme's assets on behalf of the members and to be responsible for its administration and operation. The trustees are subject to statutory requirements, the terms of the trust deed and rules, and also trust law. Trustees' duties are discussed in detail in Chapter 4. Where a scheme is set up under contract, the employer will appoint managers. Here there will be individual investments made by the managers through a fund manager or custodian on behalf of each member separately and such arrangements are not subject to trust law.

Eligibility to be a trustee [5.4]

Any person capable of holding land may be a trustee. In effect this means any individual over the age of 18. There is no central register or list of qualification requirements for trustees. Under *PA 1995, s 29*, however, OPRA may disqualify from acting as a trustee any of the following:

- a person convicted of an offence involving dishonesty;
- an undischarged bankrupt;
- a person who has made an arrangement with his creditors and has not been discharged in respect of it;
- a person disqualified as a company director; or
- a trustee company, if any director of that company has been disqualified for any of the reasons set out above.

OPRA may also disqualify a person from acting as a trustee if it considers he is incapable due to a mental disorder or, if the trustee is a company, it is insolvent.

If permitted by its memorandum and articles of association, a company may also act as a trustee, and there may be a combination of individual and corporate trustees on the board of trustees of large pension schemes. It is sometimes seen as an advantage that a company remains the trustee while its directors may change from time to time without the need for formal deeds of appointment or removal. Also any liability will fall on the corporate entity, but increasingly the courts are looking behind the corporate veil to hold individual directors personally responsible.

A trust corporation is a corporate trustee which is formed under United Kingdom law, has a place of business in the United Kingdom and whose constitution empowers it to act as a trustee. It must either be incorporated by a special Act of Parliament or a Royal Charter or be a registered company with an issued share capital of at least £250,000 of which £100,000 is paid up. Unlike other corporate trustees it can act alone to give a valid receipt for the proceeds of sale on land. Otherwise two individual trustees are necessary for this purpose (*TA 1925, s 14*).

Neither the scheme actuary nor the scheme auditor can be a trustee of the scheme.

However desirable it may be, there is no requirement for trustees to have any training before or during their appointment. Under the *Employment Rights Act 1996, ss 58–60* trustees of occupational pension schemes who are also employees or officers of the employer company are to be allowed time off from their duties to carry out their trustee functions and undertake training. They are also entitled to payment for that time off and may complain to an employment tribunal if the employer fails to comply.

Appointment and removal of trustees [5.5]

Under the provisions of the trust deed the power of appointment and removal of trustees usually lies with the employer, and, as a fiduciary power, must be exercised in the best interests of the members. Often the trust deed will specify a minimum and maximum number of trustees who must be in place at any time.

In addition to the provisions of the trust deed, *TA 1925, s 36* grants a statutory power to appoint trustees to the person named in the trust deed, that is generally the employer. A new trustee or trustees may be appointed in place of a trustee who:

- is dead;
- remains outside the United Kingdom for a continuous period exceeding 12 months;
- desires to be discharged from the trust;

- refuses to act;
- is unfit to act, for example because of bankruptcy;
- is incapable of acting, for example, because of lunacy, age or infirmity or, in the case of a company, dissolution;
- is an infant; or
- is removed under a power in the trust deed.

Under *TA 1925, s 39* any trustee may by deed retire from the trust if afterwards there will either be a trust corporation or two individuals to act as a trustee, and the appointor consents. This may be negated by the trust deed specifically stating a minimum number of trustees. If a trustee resigns and his resignation takes the number of trustees to below the permitted minimum, his resignation will not be effective and he will remain a trustee of the scheme, and therefore still be personally liable for the exercise of the trusts of the scheme.

OPRA may prohibit an individual from acting as a trustee of a particular scheme, if he has committed serious and persistent breaches of trust or legislation. The person may be disqualified from acting as a trustee in connection with any scheme (*PA 1995, ss 3, 10*). OPRA has powers under *PA 1995, s 7* to appoint replacement or additional trustees if it considers it necessary for the proper administration of the scheme.

On the appointment of a new or additional trustee it must be ensured that all the scheme investments are legally owned by all the trustees. Under *TA 1925, s 40* all land and chattels automatically vest in a new appointee. However, stocks and shares do not, and it is therefore wise for the deed appointing the new trustee to ensure that all trust property and investments are held in the names of the new appointee and the continuing trustees.

Remuneration of trustees [5.6]

Unless specified in the trust deed establishing the pension scheme, trustees are prohibited from being remunerated for their role as trustees or indeed from being compensated for their personal trouble or loss of time. Senior officers and directors of the employer may act as individual trustees but are rarely entitled under the trust deed to be remunerated. However their benefit packages may reflect their extra responsibility and work undertaken as a trustee.

Professional trustees will of course require remunerating for their role and so it should be ensured that the trust deed contains an appropriate charging clause.

Member-nominated trustees [5.7]

In order to ensure member representation on the board of trustees, PA 1995, s 16 requires an occupational pension scheme to give its members the opportunity to nominate up to one third of the trustees. These are member-nominated trustees (MNTs).

The trustees are obliged to ensure compliance with the terms of PA 1995 relating to the appointment of member-nominated trustees. To do this, they may either use the ready-made rules set out in the *Occupational Pensions Schemes (Member Nominated Trustee) Regulations 1996 SI No 1216*, or adopt their own rules so long as these have been approved under the statutory consultation procedure (see below).

The main requirements for member-nominated trustees are as follows:

- one third of the trustees must be member-nominated subject to a minimum of two member-nominated trustees where the scheme has more than 100 members, or one where the scheme has fewer than 100 members. A greater number of member-nominated trustees requires the consent of the employer;
- those who have been chosen under the rules must become member-nominated trustees automatically;
- they must be appointed for a term of between three and six years;
- they must have the same functions as other trustees; and
- they must not be removed unless the other trustees agree, and if they are scheme members they must cease to be trustees if they cease to be members.

It is possible under PA 1995, s 17 for the employer to suggest its own arrangements as an alternative to the use of the PA 1995 rules or rules formulated by the trustees. It could propose entirely new arrangements, or it might suggest continuing the scheme's arrangements which were in place before the implementation of PA 1995. This is called an employer opt-out.

The member-nominated trustee requirements of *PA 1995* have been avoided in many instances by the use of the employer opt-out. As a result the Government has introduced a change in the *Child Support, Pensions and Social Security Act 2000*. Under *s 43* of this Act employer opt-outs are no longer possible and, at the end of any current employer opt-out or current arrangements, it will be necessary for the trustees to ensure full compliance with the member-nominated trustee requirements of the *PA 1995*.

If there is a trustee company rather than individual trustees, *PA 1995, s 18* requires member-nominated directors to be appointed in the same way as member-nominated trustees.

There are some schemes which do not have to have member-nominated trustees as they are exempt from *PA 1995, s 16*. These include certain executive schemes, certain industry-wide schemes and insured schemes, unapproved schemes, death benefit only schemes, and schemes with a statutory independent trustee.

If there is a bulk transfer without consent, or an employer begins or ceases participation in the scheme or becomes a wholly-owned subsidiary of an employer which does not participate in the scheme, the trustees may decide that any member-nominated trustee arrangements currently in place should come to an end. The trustees will then be obliged to put in place fresh arrangements implementing the member-nominated trustee requirements of the *PA 1995*.

Independent trustees [5.8]

If an insolvency practitioner is appointed in relation to a participating employer, or if the official receiver becomes the liquidator of an employer or the receiver of a bankrupt individual employer, the insolvency practitioner or official receiver must ensure that one of the trustees of a pension scheme is independent. In this context independence is defined in *PA 1995, s 23(3)* and in the *Occupational Pension Schemes (Independent Trustee) Regulations 1997 SI No 252, reg 2* as being a person who:

- has no interest in the assets of the employer or of the scheme (otherwise than as a trustee);
- has not provided services to the trustee or the employer in relation to the scheme during the last three years;
- is neither connected with, nor an associate of:

- the employer;
- the insolvency practitioner acting in relation to the employer;
- the official receiver acting in relation to the employer;
- the person who has an interest in the assets of the employer or of the scheme (otherwise than as a trustee); or
- a person who has provided services to the trustees or the employer in relation to the scheme during the last three years.

The insolvency practitioner must appoint an independent trustee if there is not already a sufficiently independent person appointed as a trustee. An independent trustee may lose his independent status whilst acting as a trustee and will then automatically cease to be a trustee (unless he is the sole trustee of the scheme).

An independent trustee will exercise all the discretionary powers of the trustees and those discretionary powers of the employers which must be exercised in the best interests of the members. He will be instrumental in winding up the pension scheme or in arranging for the scheme to be taken over by a new employer if the insolvent employer is sold.

Professional trustees [5.9]

Many schemes have a professional trustee on their board. He or she may have considerable knowledge and experience in the pensions field and be a trustee of several different pension schemes at any one time. Often professional trustees are corporate trustees. A professional trustee will require to be remunerated and the trust deed must provide for this.

Pensioneer trustees [5.10]

A pensioneer trustee is required for every small self-administered scheme, that is a scheme which generally has fewer than 12 members. Small self-administered schemes are highly regulated occupational pension schemes, in view of the Inland Revenue's perception that the small number of members may act together to bend their rules for their own ends. The pensioneer trustee will liaise with the Inland Revenue, and so must be approved by it as a person widely concerned with occupational pension schemes who has had dealings with the Inland Revenue over a period of time.

The pensioneer trustee must not be connected with any member trustee or participating employer of the small self-administered scheme and must not be a member of the scheme himself.

Once appointed the pensioneer trustee cannot be dismissed unless an immediate successor is appointed.

The pensioneer trustee's role is to:

- ensure compliance with regulations governing small self-administered schemes;
- refuse to consent to winding up of the scheme other than in accordance with the scheme's rules;
- be a co-signatory for the purposes of the scheme's bank accounts;
- hold the scheme assets jointly with the other trustees; and
- report to the Inland Revenue on specified matters such as loans, investments etc.

If the Inland Revenue considers a pensioneer trustee to be failing in his duties to act prudently, it may remove his pensioneer trustee status at any time.

Custodian trustees [5.11]

A custodian trustee may be appointed to ensure the safe-keeping of a pension scheme's investments. The Public Trustee (established under the *Public Trustee Act 1906*) and certain banks and insurance companies may act as custodians. They will generally not be involved in the day-to-day management of the trust, and will act on the instructions of the other trustees.

The scheme actuary [5.12]

An actuary is a professional pensions' adviser whose expertise is in calculating probabilities with reference to the members' mortality rates.

He will recommend the assumptions and methods used to value the scheme's assets and liabilities, and will carry out periodic valuations. He will recommend the employer's contribution rates for final salary schemes and be involved in benefit issues such as how cash equivalents are calculated. He may also give strategic investment advice.

PA 1995, s 47 requires that the trustees of all final salary schemes must appoint a scheme actuary. This must be an individual (rather than a firm) who is a member of either the Institute or the Faculty of Actuaries. He may also be a person approved by the Secretary of State to act in that capacity.

A scheme actuary is not required for:

- unfunded schemes;
- unapproved schemes;
- public service schemes or schemes backed by government guarantee; or
- money purchase schemes.

As actuarial valuations are required under the *Pension Schemes Surpluses (Valuation) Regulations 1987* for money purchase schemes every three and a half years, trustees of money purchase schemes will generally appoint an actuary or firm of actuaries to act on their behalf.

The scheme actuary appointed under *PA 1995, s 47* has specific obligations under *PA 1995* particularly in relation to producing MFR valuations. The scheme actuary has a duty under *PA 1995, s 48* to "blow the whistle" to OPRA if he has reasonable cause to believe that any administrative duty imposed on the trustees, professional advisers or employers is not being carried out, and if that failure is likely to be of material significance to OPRA.

Any trustee of a pension scheme (or person connected with a trustee) is prohibited from acting as an actuary to that scheme. However a trustee and a scheme actuary may work for the same actuarial consultancy.

An appointment of the scheme actuary must be in writing and must specify:

- the date the appointment is due to take effect;

- to whom the adviser is to report; and
- from whom the actuary is to take instructions.

The actuary must acknowledge notice of his appointment within one month of receipt. If the actuary resigns, a statement must be made specifying any matters connected with the resignation that might significantly affect the interests of the members or prospective members under the scheme. Otherwise a declaration must be made that no such circumstances apply. If an actuary is removed or resigns, a replacement must be appointed within three months. The actuary must inform the trustees immediately should any conflicts of interest arise. There is a reciprocal duty of disclosure between the actuary and the trustees requiring each to disclose information to the other which may be required for the proper exercise of their respective functions.

Auditor [5.13]

An auditor is a person authorised by the Institute of Chartered Accountants of England and Wales or other similarly recognised supervisory body to audit accounts. Under *PA 1995, s 47* every occupational pension scheme in the United Kingdom must appoint a scheme auditor except:

- unapproved schemes;
- unfunded schemes;
- death benefit only schemes;
- schemes with under two members;
- public service pension schemes;
- schemes backed by government guarantee and certain schemes established by statute; and
- money purchase small self-administered schemes in which all members are trustees and all trustee decisions are made unanimously.

An auditor must not be:

- a member of the scheme;
- a trustee;

- any person connected with or an associate of a trustee;
- a person employed by the trustees;
- a participating employer or an employer in the same group of companies as the participating employer; or
- a director, officer or employee of any participating employer or any company within the same group.

An accountancy firm cannot provide both a trustee of the scheme and its auditor even if they are different people.

Again it is the duty of the trustees rather than the employer to appoint the scheme auditor and the same provisions relating to his appointment apply as to the appointment of the scheme actuary.

The auditor must prepare and audit the scheme accounts within seven months of the end of the scheme year and provide an auditor's statement regarding payment of contributions. The accounts must contain a statement that they have been prepared and audited in accordance with the *Occupational Pension Schemes (Requirement to Obtain Audited Accounts and a Statement from the Auditor) Regulations 1996 SI No 1975*.

The auditor is under a similar duty as the scheme actuary to whistle-blow under *PA 1995, s 48*.

Administrator [5.14]

An administrator is a person charged with liaising with and supplying information to the Inland Revenue. *ICTA 1988, s 611AA* indicates that the scheme trustees should generally be the administrator for this purpose provided that they are resident in the United Kingdom. If the trustees are not resident in the United Kingdom they must appoint someone who is so resident to act as an administrator. The trustees may decide to appoint someone else to fulfil the role of administrator provided that he or she is resident in the United Kingdom.

Legal and other advisers [5.15]

There is no statutory requirement for trustees to appoint a legal adviser. They are however under a duty to obtain advice from appropriate people on areas in which they are not qualified or do not have a full understanding. There may therefore be an implicit responsibility on trustees to obtain legal advice on issues such as compliance with relevant legislation.

As a result of *PA 1995, s 47* trustees may not rely upon the advice of a lawyer who has not been appointed by them in writing in accordance with that section. It is not therefore open to the trustees to rely upon advice given to them by lawyers appointed by the employer.

Other professional advice may be needed from time to time and in all cases appointments must be made in writing and in accordance with *PA 1995, s 47*.

Fund managers [5.16]

If a scheme holds investments which are regulated by the *Financial Services Act 1986* a fund manager must be appointed in accordance with *PA 1995, s 47*. If the trustees rely on the advice of someone not properly appointed by them, they may be held liable by OPRA and subjected to fines or prohibition orders.

Trustees must be careful to appoint suitable fund managers and should look to their track record as a measure of their expertise. It is however important for trustees to be very clear about their strategy for investments and to ensure that potential fund managers are aware of their requirements and have proven that they can perform in the chosen field of investments.

The National Association of Pension Fund Managers (NAPF) has issued a set of questions it would be prudent for trustees to ask potential fund managers to ensure that they understand the trustees' objectives and investment philosophy and have the relevant expertise. These questions include :

- Does the manager appear to understand the trustees' philosophy and does it appear he will be able to implement this?

- How well will the trustees be likely to build an appropriate relationship with the manager?

- Will the manager be able to give sufficient dedication to the fund? Is the fund of the right size and correct profile for the manager concerned?
- Will a sufficient range of specialist skills or knowledge be available (a) within that organisation and (b) to manage the fund?
- Will the fund always receive appropriate attention – what happens for example during the absence of individuals?
- Are trustees clear as to the fees that will be charged? Are there likely to be any hidden charges?
- Would there be any obstacles to taking appropriate remedial action in the event of unacceptable performance?

Pension consultants and administrators [5.17]

Pension administrators are often employed by trustees to run the day-to-day administration of the scheme. For schemes which are fully insured often the insurance company will provide a comprehensive administrative service. Many administrators also offer a consultancy service to help with such matters as changes in scheme design and member communications.

Inland Revenue [5.18]

Schemes which are exempt approved, by the Inland Revenue under *Chapter I Part XIV* of *ICTA 1988*, enjoy certain tax advantages. The employer and employee obtain tax relief on their contributions and the employee is not charged to tax on his employer's contributions as a benefit in kind. Tax relief is granted on the investment income of the fund and when pensions are paid, part may be taken in the form of a tax-free lump sum.

To be exempt approved by the Inland Revenue the scheme must be established under irrevocable trusts and be approved as such by the Inland Revenue. Mandatory approval is given to schemes complying with *ICTA 1988, s 590(3)*, but most schemes seek discretionary approval under *ICTA 1988, s 591*.

The discretionary practice of the Inland Revenue in granting and continuing its approval is set out in its practice notes. Schemes must ensure that both contributions and benefits do not exceed the limits set out in the practice notes and they must adopt rules reflecting the Inland Revenue's requirements.

Certain information must be provided to the Inland Revenue from time to time so that the Revenue can check that the scheme continues to operate within the prescribed parameters. The Inland Revenue plays a greater role in monitoring small self-administered schemes and there are specific regulations for these schemes limiting its discretion to approve.

OPRA [5.19]

The Occupational Pensions Regulatory Authority (OPRA) was established by *PA 1995, s 1*, and has wide powers to regulate the operation of occupational pension schemes. It is funded by a levy collected from all occupational pension schemes. Not only can it prohibit a person from being a trustee for a particular scheme but it can also disqualify a trustee from acting in relation to any pension scheme. Trustees can also be suspended and in certain circumstances OPRA can appoint additional trustees and replace disqualified trustees.

OPRA has the power to exact civil penalties (currently up to £5,000 for an individual or £50,000 for a company) for breaches of the *PA 1995*. It can also penalise an actuary or auditor for failure to whistleblow in accordance with *PA 1995, s 48*. If a scheme is no longer required or it is necessary to protect the interests of most of the scheme members, OPRA may authorise a scheme to be wound up. *PA 1995, s 69* gives OPRA powers to make modification orders if it is necessary to amend a scheme's provisions to enable a surplus to be returned on winding up of a scheme. It can also apply to the court for an injunction preventing assets of the scheme from being misappropriated and it has powers also to apply for an order requiring repayment of money to a pension scheme where a refund or loan to an employer has been wrongly made. It can direct trustees to pay benefits which should have been paid by the employer, and it can direct trustees to circulate a statement it has prepared to members of a scheme.

OPRA has wide powers to enable it to obtain the documentation and information it requires to carry out its functions. This includes entering premises to search for and take possession of documents or to find out whether regulatory provisions are being complied with.

It is an offence attracting a fine and/or imprisonment not to co-operate with OPRA.

OPAS [5.20]

The Pensions Advisory Service is a non-profit making voluntary organisation funded by the DWP via OPRA which offers a useful free service to individuals seeking help or advice about their occupational or personal pensions. It can consider disputes at any stage. It has no statutory powers and so any agreement it brokers must be accepted by the parties.

Pensions Compensation Board [5.21]

Established by *PA 1995, ss 78–80*, the Pensions Compensation Board enables compensation to be made to the trustees of occupational pension schemes established by a trust. Compensation is not available to:

- small self-administered schemes with under 12 members, all of whom are trustees, and where trustee decisions must be taken unanimously;
- public service pension schemes and schemes backed by government guarantee;
- unapproved schemes;
- schemes with under two members; and
- death benefit only schemes.

Compensation is only made in very limited circumstances. The employer must be insolvent and the value of the scheme's assets must have fallen below 90% of the MFR as a result of an offence of dishonesty. The Board must then consider it reasonable in all the circumstances that it should assist the members.

Pensions Ombudsman [5.22]

Since October 1990, the Pensions Ombudsman has been dealing with complaints of maladministration concerning occupational pension schemes. Maladministration includes bias, neglect, inattention delay, incompetence and arbitrariness. Complainants may be the member himself, the member's widow or widower or any surviving dependants, and a complaint must be brought within three years of the occurrence of the event complained of or within three years after the complainant knew or ought to have known of that event. Generally the Pensions Ombudsman will only investigate complaints which the scheme's own internal dispute resolution procedure and OPAS have failed to resolve.

Complaints may be brought against trustees, administrators or employers and may also be made in connection with a dispute between trustees of two pension schemes, for example following the scheme merger. He may also examine a dispute between different trustees of the same occupational scheme.

The investigation procedure is based upon written statements and responses from the parties, although the Pensions Ombudsman has power to demand that oral evidence be given. He will then issue his written determination which is binding on the parties and enforceable in the county court. The determination may be appealed on a point of law to the High Court. Each party is responsible for his own costs in the Pensions Ombudsman's investigation.

Useful addresses [5.23]

OPRA, Invicta House, Trafalgar Place, Trafalgar Street, Brighton, East Sussex, BN1 4DW.

The Pensions Ombudsman, 11 Belgrave Road, London, SW1V 1RB.

OPAS, 11 Belgrave Road, London, SW1V 1RB.

6 – Scheme Documents

> This chapter covers the following:
>
> - Scheme documents.
>
> - Information contained in scheme documents.

Introduction [6.1]

The documents of any occupational pension scheme are central to an understanding of its nature. Employers and trustees look to them to establish their powers and duties. The benefits to which members are entitled are set out, and indeed members are entitled to see the main scheme documents. The Inland Revenue will grant its approval on the basis of the documents presented to it. The Contracted-Out Employment Group (COEG) of the Inland Revenue National Insurance Contributions Office will need to see its requirements relating to guaranteed minimum pensions (GMPs) or protected rights set out in the scheme deeds. Also, throughout the scheme's life accounts and valuations will be key to understanding its funding and membership.

The aim of this chapter is to examine these documents, and look at the information they contain.

Documents establishing a scheme [6.2]

In order to satisfy the Inland Revenue's requirement that an occupational pension scheme must be held under irrevocable trusts so that it might obtain tax exempt status, many pension schemes are set up under a formal trust deed. However this is not essential; all that is necessary is for the scheme's assets to be separate from those of the employer and this can be achieved by a declaration of trust or by an appropriately drafted insurance policy. A trust deed is also used for funded unapproved schemes, as again it is important for the members that its funds are not mingled with those of the employer.

A definitive trust deed is of necessity a long and detailed document, and often it is not possible to agree all its terms by the time it is intended that a new scheme should be operational. In this case a temporary, interim deed is used to outline the scheme's trust structure and obtain the conditional approval of the Inland Revenue. It will not give a full description of the benefits to be provided by the scheme, but it will contain an undertaking that definitive documentation will be completed within a reasonable time. In addition, the essential features of the scheme need to be communicated to all prospective members, and a copy of this announcement will need to be produced to the Inland Revenue, and may be relied upon by any member seeking to enforce payment of his benefits.

If the interim documentation is satisfactory, the Inland Revenue will permit the scheme to operate on the interim documentation, but full approval will not be granted until the definitive deed is executed. It will then be backdated to the inception of the scheme.

The definitive deed is usually divided into two parts. The first sets out the powers and duties of the employer and the trustees, establishing the trust framework within which the scheme will operate. The second part sets out the scheme's benefit structure, details of the contributions to be paid, and a procedure for winding up the scheme should it be necessary. Modern pension scheme documentation usually includes Inland Revenue and contracting-out requirements by way of separate sections in or after the second part. The Inland Revenue produces model rules setting out the limits it imposes on benefits and contributions, and updated versions of the model rules produced by the now defunct Occupational Pensions Board are often used to govern the requirements governing GMPs and protected rights.

Both under general principles of trust law and under the *Occupational Pension Schemes (Disclosure of Information) Regulations 1996 SI No 1655 (the Disclosure Regulations), reg 3*, members are entitled to see these documents as well as any deeds subsequently amending them. A copy must be supplied, for which the cost of copying, postage, and packing may be recovered. A prospective member, a spouse of a member or prospective member, a beneficiary and recognised trades unions have the same right of disclosure and in each case, disclosure must be effected within two months of request.

During the life of a pension scheme it will need to adapt to many changes, and this will result in further documentation.

Deeds of removal, retirement and appointment of trustees [6.3]

Over time trustees will retire or be removed and be replaced, and this will need to be recorded. Often the definitive documentation will require this to be done by deed, but sometimes it may be effected by resolution of the principal employer. In all cases, care should be taken to ensure continued compliance not only with the definitive deed's provisions concerning the appointment and removal of trustees, but also with the member-nominated trustee requirements of the *Pensions Act 1995* (*PA 1995*) including any employer opt-out of its provisions.

Deeds of amendment [6.4]

There are also changes to the scheme either prompted by new legislation, or by a change in benefit structure. For these, deeds of amendment will have to be produced. Significant changes will bring *PA 1995, s 67* into play. Under this, any power of amendment cannot be exercised if it might affect the accrued rights or entitlements of any member unless the consent of the members concerned has been obtained, or an actuary has certified that those accrued rights and entitlements are not adversely affected. Accrued rights are rights to future benefits which have accrued under the scheme. The term 'entitlements' is less clear as it is not defined by *PA 1995*, but it is generally accepted as meaning pensions in payment. It is the responsibility of the trustees to ensure compliance with this section even if the power of amendment is exercisable by the principal employer alone, and failure to comply will invalidate the changes made. It is good practice to keep the original certificate with the amending deed for future reference.

Deeds of adherence or participation [6.5]

Also, deeds of adherence or participation may be required when a new employer begins to participate in a scheme. Such a company may be:

- a wholly-owned subsidiary of the principal employer or controlled by it (control here is as defined in the *Income and Corporation Taxes Act 1988* (*ICTA 1988*), *s 416* for close companies and *ICTA 1988, s 840* for other corporate bodies);

- controlled by a third party which also controls the principal employer; or
- associated with the principal employer through a permanent community of interest (for example, common shareholding or management).

There are also industry-wide schemes, usually sponsored by a professional or trade association, in which the Inland Revenue permits the participation of employers which are not associated with each other.

Sales of companies may mean that a company which participates in a scheme severs its links with the principal employer. However, it may take time for the purchaser to set up its own pension arrangements and in this case the Inland Revenue will normally agree to the company continuing to participate in the vendor's scheme for a limited period, but not beyond twelve months without good reason. Similarly if a part of a participating employer's business is being sold, it may be required that the transferred employees remain in the scheme, and again the Inland Revenue has no objection to this for a limited period, but will not of course permit new employees of the purchaser to join the scheme.

Scheme booklet [6.6]

Membership of an employer's pension scheme is voluntary, and so a clearly written booklet is essential if employees are to be persuaded of the advantages of joining. Today it often forms part of a larger communications exercise, which may include newsletters, videos and presentations. Also, members cannot realistically be expected to understand fully the benefits of the scheme by reading its rules, and so the booklet serves to explain the scheme's basic benefit structure.

There are a number of items which should be included in a booklet so that it provides the basic scheme information required by the *Disclosure Regulations, reg 4* to be given to every prospective member, and to every member within two months of joining the scheme. Briefly this information is as follows:

- the categories of employees who are eligible to join, and whether they have to complete an application form, are automatically admitted unless the employee indicates otherwise, or require the consent of the employer;

- eligibility criteria – such matters as age limits, and length of service required;
- any period of notice a member must give to leave the scheme, and end his pensionable service;
- whether, and on what conditions, a member may rejoin the scheme having left;
- how the employer's contributions are calculated;
- how the employee's contributions are calculated;
- arrangements for the payment of additional voluntary contributions;
- whether the scheme is approved by the Inland Revenue;
- details of employments contracted out by reference to the scheme;
- details of the benefit structure, and in particular:
  - the normal pension age;
  - how pensionable earnings are calculated;
  - what benefits are payable and how they are calculated;
  - details of survivors' benefits;
  - whether any benefits are discretionary;
  - details of increases which are made to pensions in payment, and whether these are discretionary;
- the arrangements made for giving estimates or statements of guaranteed cash equivalents, refunds of member's contributions for those leaving with under two years' qualifying service, and for preserving or transferring the rights of early leavers;
- whether and in what circumstances the trustees will accept a transfer into the scheme;
- if the trustees have decided that cash equivalents shall not take into account discretionary benefits, a statement to this effect;
- a summary of the way transfer values are calculated;
- a statement that an annual report is available on request;

- whether information has been given to the Registrar of Occupational and Personal Pension Schemes;
- details of the scheme's internal dispute resolution procedure, including the job title and address of the person to be contacted;
- a statement that the Pensions Advisory Service (OPAS) is available to assist with disputes;
- a statement that the Pensions Ombudsman may investigate and determine disputes, and his address;
- a statement that the Occupational Pensions Regulatory Authority (OPRA) may intervene in the running of schemes where trustees, employers or advisers have failed in their duties, and its address; and
- the address to which enquiries should be sent.

Other information which, although not mandatory, may usefully be contained in a booklet includes:

- details of the trustees, and compliance with the member-nominated trustee requirements of *PA 1995*;
- information concerning the *Data Protection Act 1998*, including a statement that members' consents to the processing of their personal data will be inferred;
- information about the trustees' policies with regard to pension sharing on divorce, and in particular any intention to make a charge to cover the production of information and administration;
- a statement that if the booklet and the scheme's deed and rules differ in any material respect, then the deed and rules will prevail;
- a statement that the scheme can be amended, and may also be terminated by the employer;
- a statement that a member may not assign his scheme benefits;
- worked examples of the calculation of benefits; and
- a statement that the scheme assets are kept separate from those of the company.

Statement of investment principles [6.7]

A statement of investment principles is required by *PA 1995, s 35* to be prepared, maintained and revised as appropriate for all occupational pension schemes except:

- schemes approved under *ICTA 1988, s 615(6)*;
- small self-administered schemes;
- wholly insured schemes;
- unapproved schemes; and
- schemes whose solvency is guaranteed by a Minister of the Crown.

Trustees must take appropriate written financial advice, and consult the sponsoring employer (one of a number of employers may be nominated for consultation) before preparing or revising the statement. The statement sets out the investment strategy for the scheme and must cover:

- how the minimum funding requirement (MFR) is to be complied with;
- kinds of investment to be held, and the balance between them;
- the risk acceptable to the trustees;
- the expected rate of return on investments;
- the realisation of investments; and
- whether there is a policy on social, environmental and ethical matters (that is, socially responsible investment) and if so, what it is.

The statement must be disclosed to a member or beneficiary or authorised trade union within two months of request in accordance with the *Disclosure Regulations 1996, reg 6*.

Audited accounts [6.8]

Audited accounts and an auditor's statement regarding the payment of contributions must be obtained within seven months of the end of the scheme year. This is required by the *Occupational Pension Schemes (Requirement to Obtain Audited Accounts and a Statement from the Auditor) Regulations 1996 SI No 1975)* (the *Audited Accounts Regulations*) for all schemes which are obliged to appoint a scheme auditor, except those insured schemes which earmark policies for each member. Failure to comply must be reported by the scheme auditor to OPRA.

Pension fund accounts should be produced in line with the Statement of Recommended Practice ('SORP') which is produced by the Pensions Research Accountants Group. The SORP is not mandatory but should be used in all but exceptional cases and the *Audited Accounts Regulations* require the accounts to include a statement as to whether they have been prepared in accordance with it, and if not, to indicate any material departures from it. The auditor is also required to state whether in his view the financial statements show a true and fair view of the scheme's transactions during the year, and further whether contributions have been paid in accordance with the schedule of contributions or payment schedule.

The audited accounts and auditor's statement must be included in the trustees' annual report, a free copy of which must be provided to members, beneficiaries and recognised trades unions within two months of request. The accounts relating to the last five years must also be made available for inspection, and, if copies of these are provided, the cost of copying and postage may be recovered under the *Audited Accounts Regulations, reg 6*.

Company accounts [6.9]

The sponsoring company must also show any pension scheme surplus or deficit as an asset or liability of the company in its statutory accounts. Financial Reporting Standard FRS 17 requires that assets are taken at market value, while liabilities are calculated using corporate bond yields. FRS 17 is being phased in over a transitional period and must be fully adopted for accounting periods ending on or after 22 June 2003. The fear is that it will produce volatile results as assets will generally reflect equity markets, while liabilities will move in line with bond yields.

Actuarial valuation report [6.10]

Trustees of all final salary and money purchase schemes (except small self-administered schemes, certain insured schemes and simplified defined contribution schemes) must obtain a valuation as required by *ICTA 1988, Sch 22* once every three years and six months. This is required to establish that the fund is not too large in relation to the scheme's liabilities for the purposes of continued Inland Revenue approval. If a scheme is found to be more than 105% funded on prescribed, conservative assumptions then the scheme's administrator must within six months submit proposals to the Inland Revenue to eliminate the excess, generally over a period of five years. These proposals may include benefit improvements, the suspension of employer or employee contributions, or a refund to the employer if the scheme rules allow. If the excess is not reduced it will cease to enjoy the advantages of tax-exempt status and be taxed, generally at 25%.

In addition, once every three years trustees of final salary schemes are required by *PA 1995, s 41* to obtain an ongoing valuation to determine the contributions to be made to the scheme. They also need a valuation to ensure the scheme is complying with the MFR as required by *PA 1995, s 57*. Such valuations are unnecessary not only for money purchase schemes, but also for:

- public service pension schemes and government guaranteed schemes;
- unapproved schemes;
- UK schemes established for non-UK businesses providing benefits for those working abroad;
- schemes for one member, and
- death benefit only schemes.

The actuary, when signing his valuation, should also give a statement in the form prescribed in the *Occupational Pension Schemes (Minimum Funding Requirement and Actuarial Valuations) Regulations 1996 SI No 1536, Sch 6*. This indicates whether the resources of the scheme are likely in the normal course of events to meet the scheme's liabilities as they fall due, bearing in mind the contributions which are to be made to it. He must also summarise the methods and assumptions he has used. This statement is then included in the trustees' annual report.

The latest actuarial valuation must be available for inspection by a member, beneficiary or recognised trade union within two months of request. Alternatively a copy may be provided at a charge to cover copying and postage.

Trustees' annual report [6.11]

Under the *Disclosure Regulations, reg 6* the trustees of an occupational pension scheme must produce an annual report within seven months of the end of the scheme year. A free copy must be supplied to a member, beneficiary or recognised trade union within two months of request. It is designed to provide relevant information not only to members but also to professional advisers and regulatory bodies such as OPRA. As such it is usually a long document and often a shorter 'popular' version is produced for distribution to the scheme's members.

The report should include the following:

- trustees' report;
- investment report;
- financial statement including:
  - the scheme auditor's report on financial statements for scheme year and payment of contributions; and
  - the scheme actuary's valuation statement and MFR certificate on contributions;
- compliance statement.

The trustees' report details how and by whom the scheme is managed, and sets out developments during the year. Although not essential, it may usefully include details such as the composition of the trustee board, the number of trustee meetings held during the year, details of the sponsoring employer, and a contact name and address in the case of complaint. Important events which have shaped the financial development of the scheme, even if they occurred outside the period covered by the accounts, may also be included. The following list sets out the information which *must* be given:

- the names of those who served as trustees during the year;
- the scheme's provisions for the appointment, removal and retirement of trustees. If there is a corporate trustee and no

[6.11] *Basic Guide to Pensions*

individual trustees, the provisions in that company's articles of association about the appointment and removal of directors;

- the names of professional advisers and others who have acted for the trustees during the year, noting any changes;

- a contact address for further information;

- the number of members and beneficiaries at any one date in the year. Although not essential, it may also be useful to note changes from the previous year;

- unless the scheme is a wholly insured money purchase scheme, if any cash equivalents were not calculated and verified in accordance with the *Occupational Pension Schemes (Transfer Values) Regulations 1996 SI No 1847*, an explanation should be given;

- unless the scheme is a wholly insured money purchase scheme, details of any reduced cash equivalents or guaranteed cash equivalents paid during the year, together with an explanation of the reason for the reduction;

- a formal statement that the accounts of the scheme have been prepared and audited in accordance with regulations made under *PA 1995, s 41(1)* and *(6)*. If they have not, an explanation is required;

- if the auditor's statement is negative or qualified, an explanation, and details of any remedial action should be given;

- details of who has managed the scheme's investments, and the extent of any delegation by trustees;

- confirmation of whether a statement of investment principles has been produced if required, and that a copy is available on request; and

- the trustees' policy on the custody of scheme assets, unless the scheme is wholly insured. It might also indicate the controls in place to ensure safe custody.

A trustees' investment report is required for all schemes except those which are wholly insured. It may include details of any change of investment manager, or alterations to the statement of investment principles, and may provide an explanation of the trustees' performance objectives, and a brief discussion of the extent to which these have been met. The following information however *must* be included:

- details of any investments not made in accordance with the scheme's statement of investment principles (if it is required to have one), together with an explanation and details of any proposed remedial action;
- a review of the scheme's investment performance during the year and over the previous three to five years, including an assessment of the nature, disposition, marketability, security and valuation of the assets;
- a copy of any statement made on the resignation or removal of the actuary or auditor; and
- details of any employer-related investments, together with details of any remedial action if these do not comply with PA 1995, s 40.

The trustees' compliance statement may include a review of changes to the scheme's benefits or rules which are not sufficiently significant to be included in the trustees' review of the financial development of the scheme. It may also include an explanation of the tax status of the scheme, and a brief summary of the benefits provided by the scheme. It *must*, however, provide the following information:

- except in the case of a money purchase scheme, the increases to pensions in payment and to deferred pensions, together with an indication of the extent to which they were discretionary. If different increases have been given for individuals or groups of individuals, the minimum, maximum and average increases should be given; and
- unless the scheme is a wholly insured money purchase scheme, a statement of whether discretionary benefits are included in the calculation of transfer values and if so, the method of assessing their value.

Schedule of contributions and payment schedule [6.12]

PA 1995, s 58 requires trustees of all final salary schemes which are subject to the MFR to prepare and from time to time revise a schedule of contributions. This must show the employer's and employees' contributions (except AVCs), and contributions required to cover the scheme's expenses if these are paid separately. The dates when these are due must be stated, and the scheme actuary must certify that the schedule provides for contributions which will maintain the 100% MFR funding of the scheme, or enable this to be reached by the end of the schedule period. This period is generally five years from the signing of the MFR valuation, and so the schedule may require amendment following a subsequent MFR valuation of the scheme.

The schedule is to be agreed by the trustees and the employer within eight weeks after the signing of the MFR valuation. If no such agreement is reached, the trustees may decide upon the schedule, imposing an employer contribution rate sufficient to meet the MFR. They must ensure the schedule is in place within twelve weeks of the valuation being signed.

For most money purchase schemes, *PA 1995, s 87* requires that a schedule of payments is prepared and maintained. Schemes for which a schedule is *not* required are:

- unapproved schemes;
- relevant earmarked schemes;
- certain public service pension schemes;
- occupational pension schemes with only one member;
- death benefit only schemes; and
- small self-administered schemes where all the members are trustees and every member has to agree on each decision.

For each scheme year the payment schedule must show the rates and due dates of payment of employer and member contributions, and the amounts to be paid by the employer in respect of expenses. If the scheme is contracted out of SERPS on a money purchase basis, the minimum payments are included in the contributions indicated in the payment schedule.

Within two months of request the schedule of contributions or payment schedule must be made available for inspection or a copy must be supplied to a member, beneficiary or recognised trade union.

All member contributions must be paid to the scheme within 19 days from the end of the month when they were deducted from their pay. Late payment of all contributions is viewed very seriously by OPRA, although it is no longer a criminal offence. The scheme actuary and auditor are bound to report this to OPRA, and the trustees also have

30 days to inform OPRA. The only time when the trustees are not required to report to OPRA is if the member contributions are received within ten days of the due date, and payment has never been late before, or has only once been late in the preceding twelve months. If contributions remain outstanding the trustees must inform the members within 90 days of the date they were due.

Contracting-out certificate [6.13]

If the employment of any members of a scheme is to be contracted out of SERPS, the scheme will require a contracting-out certificate from COEG in order that reduced National Insurance contributions may be paid. The certificate will indicate an employer's contracting-out number (ECON) and a scheme contracting-out number (SCON) to be quoted in all future correspondence.

Before obtaining a contracting-out certificate, a notice of intention or explanation must be given to the employees in the employments concerned, and to any independent trade union of the employees. Manuals available from COEG (CA14C for final salary schemes, CA14D for money purchase schemes and CA14E for mixed benefit schemes) contain specimen forms of such notices which must contain information which is specified in the *Occupational Pension Schemes (Contracting-out) Regulations 1996 SI No 1172* (the *Contracting-out Regulations*), *reg 3*. The notice period should be three months. However if there is no trade union involved, or if any trade union which is involved agrees, the period may be reduced to one month. Any notice must be sent not only to any independent trade union, but also to the scheme trustees and administrator, and, if the scheme is insured, to the insurer. Objections may be addressed to the Commissioners of the Inland Revenue or to the employer within the notice period.

A notice of explanation is given where changes occur which will not result in any change of contracted-out status for the employees concerned. It is given in a similar way to a notice of intention, and again COEG's manuals contain specimen forms, but there is no notice period.

An election to contract out must be made within three months of the expiry of the notice. Again specimen forms of election are available from COEG and contain specified information which must be included under the *Contracting-out Regulations, reg 6*. In addition, in the case of a final salary scheme, the scheme actuary must give a Certificate 'T' confirming that the scheme satisfies the requirements of *PA 1995* relating to the MFR, employer-related investments and winding up. He is also required to give a certificate confirming the reference scheme test is met.

Once issued, a contracting-out certificate may be varied. COEG simply requires to be informed of minor changes, but major alterations will require the full process of issuing a notice of intention or explanation, and the submission of an appropriate completed form to COEG within three months.

A contracting-out certificate may be surrendered. Consultation with any trade union must be undertaken, and again notices of intention or explanation must be duly given and COEG informed by the completion of the appropriate form.

Internal dispute resolution procedure [6.14]

Under *PA 1995, s 50* trustees of occupational pension schemes must put in place a two-stage procedure for the resolution of disputes. Only schemes which have only one member, or in which all the members are trustees are exempt from this requirement. The *Occupational Pension Schemes (Internal Dispute Resolution Procedures) Regulations 1996 SI No 1270* set out the details to be incorporated in the procedure, which is often incorporated in the scheme booklet. See Chapter 7 for further information.

Useful addresses [6.15]

COEG
Chillingham House
Benton Park View
Benton Park Road
Longbenton
Newcastle upon Tyne
NE98 1ZZ

7 – Information for Scheme Members

> This chapter covers the following:
>
> - The ways in which trustees and employers communicate with their pension scheme members.
>
> - The legal requirements and the practical ways in which communication happens.

Information or communication? [7.1]

The legal requirements are primarily found in the *Pensions Act 1995* and the *Occupational Pension Schemes (Disclosure of Information) Regulations 1996 SI No 1655*. Collectively we will refer to these as the *Disclosure Regulations*. These are an extension of Regulations originally put in place in 1986.

The *Disclosure Regulations* have undoubtedly meant that all pension scheme members are provided with or have access to a great deal more information about their scheme than was the case before 1986. However, many people might question whether they are any better informed, so in this chapter we look not only at the legal requirements for disclosure of information but also at how to communicate effectively with members.

Disclosure Regulations [7.2]

The *Disclosure Regulations* set out in great detail the information which must be provided to scheme members. They define precisely:

- what information must be provided;
- what type of member or beneficiary it must be provided to;
- whether it must be provided automatically or only on request;

- within what timescales the information must be provided;
- whether a request can be refused if a similar request has been made in the recent past; and
- possible fines or penalties for not complying with the *Regulations*.

By information, we mean:

- the documents setting up the scheme (i.e. the trust deed and rules);
- basic information about the scheme – the *Regulations* effectively provide a checklist of contents for a pension scheme booklet;
- the annual trustees' report and accounts – again the *Regulations* provide a checklist of contents;
- the latest actuarial valuation report – the *Regulations* prescribe the form of a statement on scheme funding which must be provided by the actuary for inclusion in the scheme accounts; and
- information to individuals about their own personal benefits, that is, an annual benefit statement (again the regulations provide a checklist of contents), a statement of benefits on leaving, retirement or death, or a transfer value calculation.

In Appendix B of this book, we set out a summary of the main provisions of the *Disclosure Regulations* as they impact on the day-to-day running of pension schemes. The relevant checklists for items to be included in booklets, trustees reports, accounts and benefit statements are set out in the *Regulations* and would be available from any good pension consultant.

Failure to comply with the *Disclosure Regulations* can lead to the Occupational Pensions Regulatory Authority (OPRA) imposing a fine on the individual or the body responsible, or prohibiting trustees from acting as trustees.

Fines could be:

Up to £200 for individuals or £1,000 for corporate trustees	Generally for failure to provide information which is available on request and has been requested.

Up to £1,000 for individuals or £10,000 for corporate trustees	Generally for failure to provide information which should be provided automatically.

Communication material [7.3]

Armed with a knowledge of the *Disclosure Regulations*, employers and trustees must then set about communicating with members about the scheme and each member's benefits. In this section we look at the different ways in which this is done in practice.

Scheme booklet [7.4]

This is the main reference point for most scheme members, and so a well-written booklet can add a great deal to members' understanding and appreciation of the scheme. Whilst the *Disclosure Regulations* do not specifically say there must be a scheme booklet, they set out a lengthy checklist of basic information about the scheme which must be provided to prospective members immediately where practicable, and in any event no later than two months after a member joins the scheme.

Virtually all schemes decide to combine this information in a scheme booklet. The box below shows a summary of the contents of a typical booklet, although the full *Disclosure Regulations* specify precisely what must be included. Unfortunately the amount of information which must be provided under the *Regulations* means that most pension scheme booklets run to at least 20 pages.

Many schemes have sought to counter this by also producing a shorter, glossier, 'sales' brochure which sets out just the key features of the scheme to encourage employees to join.

A typical pension scheme booklet will cover:

- eligibility conditions;

- how to join or opt out;

- the level of member contributions;

- arrangements for AVCs;

- when benefits are payable;
- how benefits are calculated in different circumstances;
- how benefits increase once in payment;
- the calculation of spouse's or dependant's benefits;
- details of how transfers in and out are dealt with;
- details of Inland Revenue approval;
- contracting-out arrangements, if any;
- procedures for resolving disputes and outside bodies who can help;
- the address for further enquiries.

Note: This is not intended to be a full description of the *Disclosure Regulations* relating to basic scheme details.

Trustees report and accounts [7.5]

Each year the trustees of a scheme are responsible for producing a trustees report to accompany the audited scheme accounts. In essence it is a report on the scheme year, and the box below shows the type of information included. As for the scheme booklet, the *Disclosure Regulations* specify a lengthy checklist of information to be included.

A typical trustees' report will cover:

- details of the trustees and their advisers;
- information from the actuary about the funding position of the scheme;
- numbers of members in each category;
- any increases in benefits awarded during the year;

> - details of investment management arrangements;
>
> - a report on investment and investment performance during the year.
>
> Note: This is not intended to be a full description of the *Disclosure Regulations* relating to the trustees' report.

It is not uncommon for trustees also to produce a shorter, or 'popular' trustees report. This is not intended to comply with the *Disclosure Regulations* but aims to be more eye-catching and answer the main questions a member might have, such as:

- where is the money?
- how much is in the fund?
- is this going to be enough?
- who looks after the scheme?
- what has happened during the year?
- how can I pay more?
- where can I find out more?

Benefit statements [7.6]

A benefit statement is often the most powerful form of communication as it shows what the scheme will provide for the individual member.

Money purchase schemes [7.7]

Under the *Disclosure Regulations*, a benefit statement must be provided to all members (actives, deferred pensioners and pensioners) at least once a year. The *Regulations* stipulate a list of items which should be included. A typical example is shown in the box below. With effect from April 2003 such statements must include a projection of expected benefits at normal retirement age. Clearly this requires assumptions to be made about future investment returns and annuity rates and so there should be suitable warnings that the figures are only estimates.

Sample benefit statement for a money purchase scheme

ABC Pension Scheme: Statement of benefits as at 31 March 2002

Name:	Mrs A Smith
Date of birth:	9 October 1965
Date pensionable service commenced:	14 September 1987
Normal retirement date:	9 October 2025
Current pensionable salary:	£22,500 a year

Your personal details set out above have been taken from our membership database. If any are not correct, please contact Mr A Pensions-Manager at ABC Head Office quoting the correct details.

In the year to 31 March 2002, the following contributions were paid to the scheme on your behalf:

Your contributions

Compulsory contributions	£840
Voluntary contributions	£240
Company contributions	£1,680
Total invested for you	£2,760

At 31 March 2002, the value of your fund is shown below, together with an estimate of the pension this might provide on retirement.

Current fund value	£40,000
Estimated pension from normal retirement date	£4,300 a year

If you remain in the scheme until your normal retirement date, we estimate that your total pension including the value of future contributions (compulsory and voluntary) will be £9,500 a year.

The pension figures shown in this statement are in current salary terms and assume that the investment return on your fund will exceed your salary growth by 2% a year. The figures are only estimates and cannot be guaranteed as the benefits you receive will depend on the actual investment return achieved and annuity rates at the time you retire. We have assumed that you will buy a pension which increases each year in line with the increase in the Retail Price Index and which continues at the rate of 50% to your widower on your death.

Final salary schemes [7.8]

The *Disclosure Regulations* do not require an annual statement to be provided to members automatically, although a prescribed list of benefit statement information must be provided on request. However, the vast majority of schemes understandably take the view that it is important that members know what benefits to expect from the scheme and send an annual benefit statement to each active member automatically. A typical example is shown in the box below. A few schemes also provide an annual statement to deferred pensioners.

Sample benefit statement for a final salary scheme

XYZ Pension Scheme: Statement of benefits as at 31 March 2002

Name:	Mrs A Smith
Date of birth:	9 October 1965
Date pensionable service commenced:	14 September 1987
Normal retirement date:	9 October 2025
Current pensionable salary:	£22,500 a year

Your personal details set out above have been taken from our membership database. If any are not correct, please contact Mr A Pensions-Manager at ABC Head Office quoting the correct details.

Your benefits build up at the rate of 1/60th of your final pensionable salary for each year of pensionable service.

This means that if you were to stay in pensionable service to your normal retirement date with no change in your pensionable salary, your pension would be: £14,250 a year

[7.9] *Basic Guide to Pensions*

> Part of this pension may be exchanged
> for a tax-free cash sum under current
> legislation. The maximum cash sum you
> could take would be: £32,000
>
> which would leave you with a pension of: £11,340 a year
>
> Should you die in service before retirement
> or after retirement your widower would
> receive a pension of: £7,125 a year
>
> In addition if you were to die before
> retirement your beneficiaries would receive
> a lump sum of: £67,500
>
> Had you left service on 31 March 2002, your pension payable from normal retirement date would have been £5,437 a year, which would be increased between leaving and normal retirement as set out in the scheme booklet.

Benefit statement strategies [7.9]

There have been a number of developments in the way schemes provide benefit statement information. These include:

- non-member benefit statements. These are provided to employees who have not chosen to join the pension scheme and show the benefits they would receive if they did. This can prove an excellent tool in improving the take-up rate of a scheme.

- combined pay and benefit statements. A single statement would show pension benefits alongside pay and other remuneration or benefits such as share options, bonus, company car, holiday entitlement, health insurance, sickness cover and so on. This helps to reinforce pensions as a major employee benefit. Such statements often shown the total cost of all benefits provided, so employees appreciate the value of the non-cash benefits they receive.

- internet/intranet based benefit statements. This is covered in more detail in para [7.17]. Companies are increasingly arranging access to pension information via an internet or intranet site, often avoiding the issue of many thousands of benefit statements in paper form.

Combined pension forecasts [7.10]

At the time of writing, proposals are being considered which would require schemes to provide an integrated benefit statement which would include details of State pension benefits as well as benefits from the current scheme, and possibly those of former employers. This has many practical difficulties but if it could be achieved would be an enormous help for individuals looking to plan their retirement.

Statements of entitlement [7.11]

When benefits come into payment, a statement of entitlement must be provided as follows.

Benefits on retirement [7.12]

Ideally before retirement, but certainly no later than one month after retirement (two months if retirement is before normal retirement date) the member must be told:

- the amount of their benefit;
- how the benefit will be paid;
- how the benefit may change in future (e.g. pension increases);
- any benefits and options available on death.

A member with money purchase benefits must be provided with a statement of the options available under the scheme at least six months before normal retirement date (or the member's selected retirement age).

If a benefit in payment changes in any way the member has not been informed of, the member must be told, ideally before the change but certainly no later than one month after the change.

Benefits on death [7.13]

Information on benefits payable, pension increases and any options available must be provided as soon as possible, and in any event no later than two months after the trustees are informed of the death.

Benefits on withdrawal [7.14]

Information on benefits and options on withdrawal must be provided within two months of the trustees becoming aware that the member has left.

Transfer values [7.15]

If a member requests a transfer value statement, this must be provided within three months of the request. This will be one of the following:

- For active members in all schemes and deferred pensioners in a money purchase scheme, an estimate of the current transfer value, as the final amount cannot be known until the member leaves service (in a final salary scheme) or the transfer payment is made (in a money purchase scheme).

- For deferred pensioners in a final salary scheme, a guaranteed statement of transfer value. If the member asks for the transfer payment to be made at any point in the three months following the date of calculation, the amount paid can be no less than (but need not be any more than) this guaranteed amount.

Certain information set out in the *Disclosure Regulations* must accompany a transfer value quotation or estimate.

Pensioners may occasionally request a transfer value calculation. This would be because a court needs a value placed on a pensioner's benefits for the purpose of a divorce settlement.

Presentations [7.16]

It is common (and generally very good practice) for presentations to staff to accompany significant changes to any pension scheme. Sometimes an annual meeting of scheme members is held to provide members with information in addition to the annual trustees' report. Presentations have the major advantage that any questions members raise can be answered immediately.

Other forms of communication to members [7.17]

A wide variety of other forms of communication are used by trustees and employers in providing information and guidance to members. These include:

- a regular pensions newsletter;
- articles in a staff magazine or bulletin;
- video or DVD;
- explaining the pension scheme at interviews or during the course of induction meetings;
- information by e-mail;
- information on an internet or intranet site.

Pension schemes are just beginning to make use of internet technology. This can start with the provision of static information, such as the pension scheme booklet, the trustees' report, or details of the trustees. However the more advanced sites will have a link to the pensions administration system meaning that members can, with appropriate security and password protection, access details of their own expected benefits (i.e. a benefit statement) and also explore the impact that different options would have (such as paying additional contributions). These developments look set to continue, with an increasing amount of pensions administration being carried out on-line.

Effective communication strategies [7.18]

The most effective communication strategy will vary between different organisations. However, the following principles are usually worth following:

- Use the methods of communication which best fit the organisation. Some companies have particular ways of communicating important messages – a regular newsletter, video or webcast – make good use of the way the organisation normally spreads news.

- Get information to members on time. Nothing detracts from a member's appreciation of a scheme more than an out of date statement or one that has to be requested again and again.
- Keep printed documents up to date, if necessary by use of an addendum.
- Make forms as simple and easy to complete as possible.
- Know your limits in dealing with members – ensure you know what you can and cannot advise on (for instance the restrictions caused by the *Financial Services Act 1986*) and ideally keep a note of other individuals or agencies to whom members can be referred for further advice.

8 – Benefit Calculations

> This chapter covers the following:
>
> - Benefit calculations.
>
> - The records that need to be kept to perform these calculations.

Introduction [8.1]

We consider benefit calculations from the perspective of two pension plans, one defined benefit and one defined contribution. The examples are intended to illustrate how the plans operate in practice.

The model plans are fairly typical of the kind of plan designs that are often adopted. However, one significant difference from common practice is that plans are rarely only defined benefit or defined contribution. For instance, virtually all defined benefit plans offer an additional voluntary contribution facility (see Chapter 11) which provides benefits on a defined contribution basis. Equally some defined contribution plans have defined benefit elements – as an example, some defined contribution plans were contracted out on a GMP basis (see Chapter 2) and so will have a defined benefit underpin. For simplicity of illustration we will not consider these hybrids.

Structure of model plans [8.2]

The benefit structures of the defined benefit plan and defined contribution plan are set out below. The example calculations throughout this chapter will be based on these plans.

Defined benefit plan [8.3]

Definitions

Final pensionable salary	Average of last three years' pensionable salary (immediately preceding date of leaving, death or retirement).
Normal retirement age	65 (normal retirement date = 65th birthday).
Pensionable salary	Basic salary less the Basic State pension – both at the coincident or preceding 1 January.
Pensionable service	Service as a member of the plan.

Benefits on normal retirement

Annual pension	1/60th of final pensionable salary for each complete year (and pro rata complete months) of pensionable service.
Lump sum	By commutation: 3/80ths of final pensionable salary for each complete year (and pro rata complete months) of pensionable service.

Benefits on early retirement

Early retirement pension	Calculated as normal retirement pension, but reduced by early retirement factor.
Early retirement factor	$1/4$% for each month (3% for each year) that retirement precedes normal retirement date.
Lump sum	By commutation: 3/80ths of final pensionable salary for each complete year (and pro rata complete months) of pensionable service.

Benefits on late retirement

Benefit accrual	Ceases at normal retirement date.
Late retirement pension	Calculated as normal retirement pension, but increased by late retirement factor.
Late retirement factor	$3/4$% for each month (9% for each year).
Lump sum	By commutation: calculated as normal retirement pension, and increased by late retirement factor.

Benefits on death in service

Lump sum	Four times pensionable salary at date of death.
Spouse's pension	50% of member's pension based on final pensionable salary at date of death and total completed and potential (complete years and pro rata complete months) pensionable service to normal retirement age.

Benefits on death after leaving service

Spouse's pension	50% of member's deferred pension at date of death (i.e. including any increases applied in deferment).

Benefits on death after retirement

Lump sum	If death occurs in first five years after retirement – lump sum payable equal to the balance of outstanding instalments for the remainder of the five-year period, based on the rate of pension payable at death.
Spouse's pension	50% of pension which would have been payable had the member not commuted any pension for a lump sum at retirement.

Ill health benefits

Pension	1/60th × final pensionable salary (at date of early retirement) × total completed and potential (complete years and pro rata complete months) pensionable service to normal retirement age.
Lump sum	3/80ths of final pensionable salary for each year (and pro rata complete months) of employment.
Contracted-out basis	• On guaranteed minimum pension basis before April 1997.

[8.4] *Basic Guide to Pensions*

	• On reference scheme test after April 1997.
Increases to benefits in deferment	• Guaranteed minimum pension element receives fixed rate revaluation.
	• Excess is increased by statutory revaluation provisions i.e. price inflation (capped at 5% per year for the entire period of deferment).
Pension increases	• Guaranteed minimum pension element receives statutory increases.
	• Excess (over GMP) earned before April 1997 receives no increases.
	• Pension earned after April 1997 is increased by limited price indexation (LPI) i.e. price inflation capped at 5%.

Commutation factors	Age	Factor
	60	10.2
	61	9.96
	62	9.72
	63	9.48
	64	9.24
	65	9
	66	8.76

Defined contribution plan [8.4]

Definitions

Normal retirement age	65 (normal retirement date = 65th birthday).
Pensionable salary	Basic salary received during current calendar month.
Contributions to the member's account	
Employee	None required.
Employer	6% of pensionable salary + any employee contribution up to 3% of pensionable salary is matched.

Death in service   Lump sum of 6 × salary at date of
                         death is added to the member's account
                         which is then applied to provide
                         benefits.

Retirement from the defined benefit plan   [8.5]

Let us suppose a member reaches normal retirement date on 1 March 2001. This is how we would calculate benefits for a member of the defined benefit plan.

Member's details   [8.6]

Date of birth – 1 March 1936

Date of joining plan – 16 May 1975

Salary history

Year	Basic salary at 1 January	Basic State pension at 1 January
1994	£17,750	£2,917.20
1995	£18,500	£2,995.20
1996	£19,500	£3,060.20
1997	£20,500	£3,179.80
1998	£21,500	£3,247.40
1999	£22,650	£3,364.40
2000	£23,800	£3,471.00
2001	£25,000	£3,510.00

Calculation of normal retirement pension   [8.7]

In order to calculate the member's benefits we need to know the pensionable service and the final pensionable salary.

The period of pensionable service is the number of complete years and complete months of membership. The member joined the plan on 16 May 1975 and reached normal retirement date on 1 March 2001. Therefore, pensionable service = 25 years and 9 months.

Final pensionable salary is the average of the member's pensionable salary on 1 January for the three years preceding retirement. From

[8.7] *Basic Guide to Pensions*

the data we have, to calculate the member's final pensionable salary, we first need to calculate pensionable salary – this figure is arrived at by subtracting the basic State pension from the member's basic salary.

Final pensionable salary = £20,368.20, which is calculated:

$$\frac{[(25,000 - 3,510) + (23,800 - 3,471) + (22,650 - 3,364.40)]}{3}$$

So pension that the member receives at 65 will be:

$$1/60 \times 25^{9/12} \times £20,368.20 = £8,741.35$$

However, see para [8.9] for the effect that the lump sum has on the member's pension. You should also be aware that the maximum amount of pension (and lump sum) is governed by Inland Revenue limits: these are summarised in para [8.48].

Graph 8.1 illustrates how pensionable salary and final pensionable salary vary over time.

Graph 8.1 The relationship between salary, basic State pension, pensionable salary and final pensionable salary

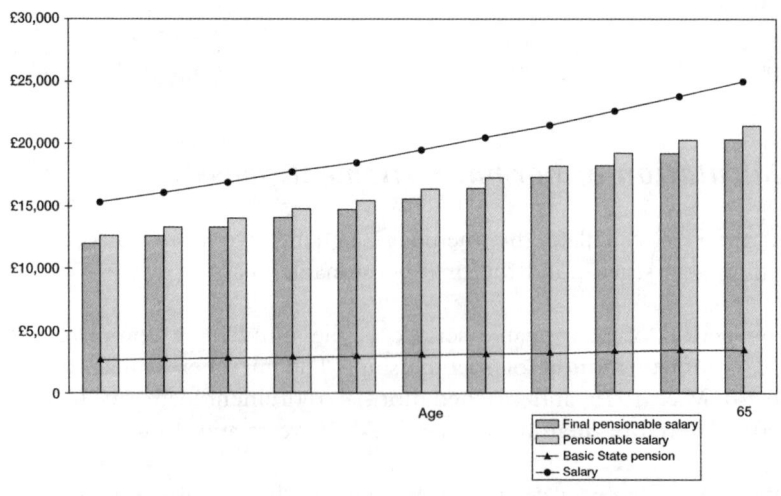

Calculation of normal retirement lump sum [8.8]

We have all of the data to calculate the member's lump sum at normal retirement date – the data we use is the same as that for the calculation of pension: we just apply a different fraction (3/80 rather than 1/60) to reach the lump sum. The lump sum the member will receive is £19,668.04 which is reached by the following calculation:

$$3/80 \times 25^{9/12} \times £20,368.20$$

Effect of lump sum on normal retirement pension [8.9]

The member does not simply receive the lump sum and the pension set out above. The lump sum is paid by 'commuting' part of the pension – effectively part of the pension is paid early as a lump sum. The rate at which this early payment is accounted for is determined by the commutation factors which are adopted by the plan.

As a side issue, in recent years improving mortality (i.e. people are expected to live longer) and lower interest rates have caused commutation to be less valuable for members, as commutation factors have not generally changed to reflect the developing conditions. However, the fact that lump sums are tax-free still makes them attractive to members.

At normal retirement age (i.e. when our member is 65) the commutation factor in the defined benefit plan is 9. The member's pension before commutation is £8,741.35 and the lump sum is £19,668.04. The amount of pension the member receives is reduced by the lump sum divided by the commutation factor. So the member's pension is:

$$£8,741.35 - (£19,668.04 \div 9) = £6,556.01$$

Calculation of early retirement pension [8.10]

Let us suppose the member had wanted to take early retirement on their 60th birthday (on 1 March 1996). Several key factors will be different and these will affect the pension:

[8.10] *Basic Guide to Pensions*

- the member will be younger than would have been the case at normal retirement age and therefore the pension will be expected to be payable for a longer period of time – to account for this, the plan applies an 'early retirement factor' for each month by which retirement precedes normal retirement date; and

- the member will have completed a shorter period of pensionable service which will affect the benefit – in this case the period of pensionable service will be the period from 16 May 1975 until early retirement date on 1 March 1996. Therefore, pensionable service will be 20 years and 9 months.

As you would expect, final pensionable salary will also be different from the previous example because we will be averaging salaries from different years. On early retirement final pensionable salary is the average of pensionable salary on 1 January for the three years preceding early retirement and is calculated as follows:

$$\frac{[(19,500 - 3,060.20) + (18,500 - 2,995.20) + (17,750 - 2,917.20)]}{3}$$

$$= £15,592.47$$

We mentioned the early retirement factor that will be applied. This factor is $1/4\%$ for each month that retirement precedes normal retirement date. In this case, early retirement is five years (60 months) early so the factor is 15% – put another way, the member receives a pension of 85% (100% - 15%) of the full amount to account for retiring early.

The pension that the member receives on early retirement at 60 (before commutation) will be:

$$1/60 \times 20^{9/12} \times £15,592.47 \times 85\% = £4,583.54$$

Graph 8.2 illustrates the pre-commutation pension on retirement under para [8.7] against the pension on early retirement. For illustration, the graph also shows increases which are applied to the pensions when they come into payment which we will discuss at para [8.21].

Graph 8.2 How a member's pension can differ on early and normal retirement

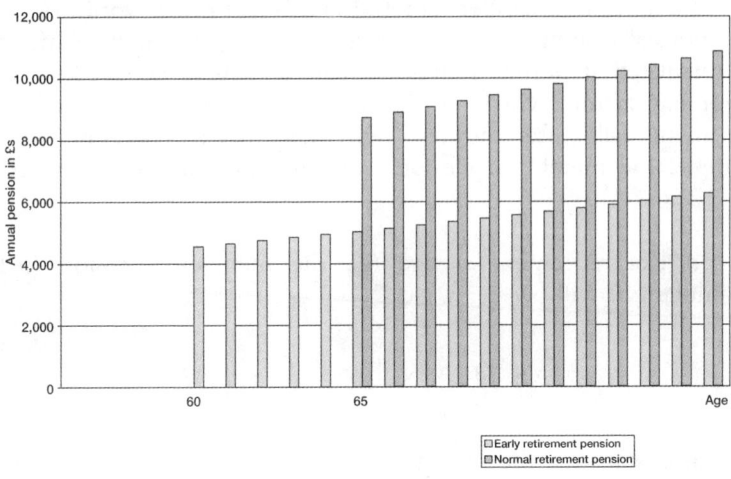

Calculation of early retirement lump sum and effect on pension [8.11]

In common with most defined benefit plans, our model defined benefit plan does not apply an early retirement factor to the lump sum. Therefore in this example, the lump sum payable on early retirement is calculated:

$$3/80 \times 20^{9/12} \times £15,592.47 = £12,132.90$$

However, although an early retirement factor is not applied, the plan does apply a different commutation factor on early retirement. At age 60 the factor applied is 10.2. It is important to remember that commutation factors increase for younger ages: £1 paid for life from age 60 is more valuable than £1 paid for life from age 65 because a pension from age 60 is expected to remain in payment for longer.

The member's early retirement pension before commutation is £4,583.54 but this is now reduced by the lump sum divided by the commutation factor. So the member's early retirement pension is:

$$£4,583.54 - (£12,132.90 \div 10.2) = £3,394.04$$

Calculation of late retirement pension and lump sum [8.12]

Now suppose the member retires at age 66, in other words, one year after normal retirement date. In this case, the pension and lump sum are calculated at normal retirement date and then increased by a late retirement factor, which in this case is $3/4$% for each month that retirement falls after normal retirement date. Therefore in this example, the member's pension and lump sum will be increased by 9% (12 × $3/4$%).

So, on late retirement at age 66, the member's pension (before commutation) will be:

$$£8,741.35 \times 1.09 = £9,528.07$$

The lump sum (i.e. the normal retirement lump sum increased by the late retirement factor) will be:

$$£19,668.04 \times 1.09 = £21,438.16$$

The late retirement pension is then reduced by the commuted amount of the lump sum, and so the member's late retirement pension will be:

$$£9,528.07 - (£21,438.16 \div 8.76) = £7,080.79$$

Retirement from the defined contribution plan [8.13]

Benefits arising from a defined contribution pension plan are calculated in a different manner to those provided under a defined benefit plan.

When retiring from a defined contribution plan a member will use their 'pot' of money (probably more properly called their 'account' but we will call it their pot, because that is the terminology that is commonly used) to buy a pension, usually from an insurance company.

No early retirement factors are applied since these are effectively included in annuity prices – the younger a member when a pension is purchased, the higher the price of the annuity and the lower pension that can be bought with the same amount of money. In addition, a member who retires earlier is likely to have a smaller defined contribution pot because the money will have been invested for a shorter period.

Key factors affecting the amount of pension under the defined contribution plan [8.14]

There are three main factors which will affect the amount of pension a member receives from a defined contribution plan:

- the amount of money paid in;
- the investment return (which to a certain extent is a function of how long the money is invested – £1 invested in 1970 is likely to be worth more than £1 invested in 2000); and
- annuity rates at the date the pension is purchased.

Graph 8.3 The value of £1,000 invested in UK equities in 1981

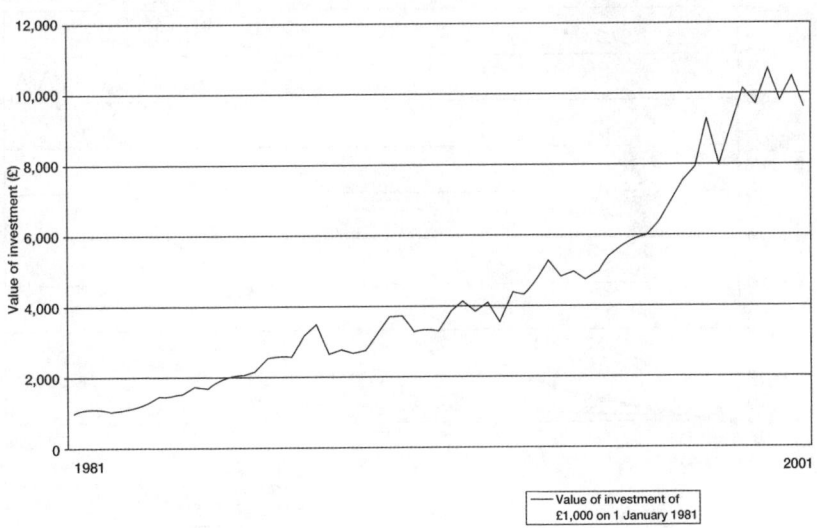

[8.14] *Basic Guide to Pensions*

By way of illustration, Graph 8.3 shows the return that would have been achieved if £1,000 had been invested in UK equities for the period from January 1981 to January 2001.

Again for illustration, Graph 8.4 shows the growth of a defined contribution member's pot based on the investment growth shown in Graph 8.3, but in this case:

- at the start of the graph, the member is earning £10,000;

- the total contribution rate is 10% per year (i.e. in the first year £1,000 is contributed); and

- salary is assumed to increase by 2.5% each year.

The lower line shows the investment return shown in Graph 8.3 (it looks like a lower return because a different scale has been used). You should note that these graphs are only to illustrate possible investment returns and, for instance, do not show the effect of charges.

Graph 8.4 The growth over time of a member's pot with regular contributions when invested in UK equities against £1,000 invested in UK equities in 1981

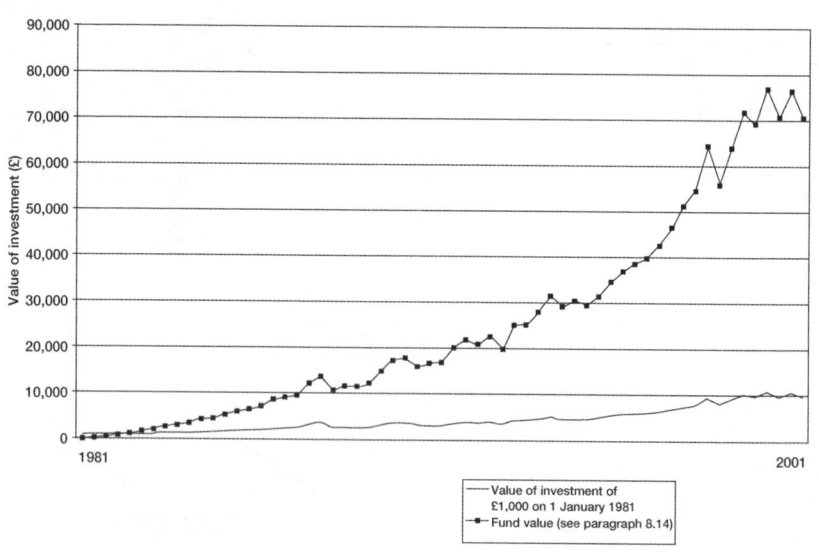

Graph 8.5 shows the capital cost of purchasing a pension equal to 50% of the member's salary. Over time the member's salary increases – thereby increasing the cost of an annuity, but the member's life expectancy falls – so the cost of purchasing an annuity falls. As the graph illustrates, the net effect over time is that the amount of money needed to buy a pension for the rest of the member's life will fall.

Graph 8.4 is superimposed and as you can see, the member suffers a 'double whammy' on early retirement – less money has been invested and annuity rates (i.e. the cost of buying a pension) are higher. Comparing the situation to the defined benefit plan, this explains why early retirement factors are applied.

This book does not deal with financial planning issues, however, this graph does start to show the 'moving target' nature of planning for retirement under a defined contribution arrangement.

Graph 8.5 Investment returns against annuity prices as a member ages

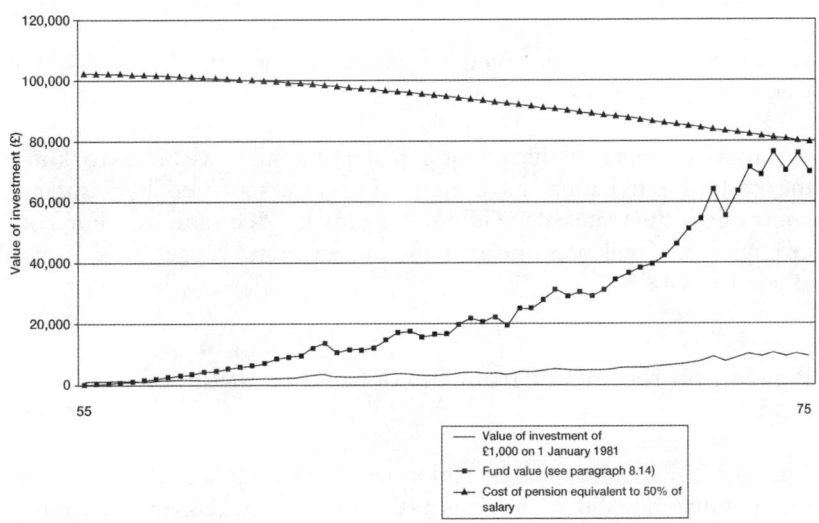

Calculation of retirement benefits under a defined contribution plan [8.15]

Enough of the theory about how a member's pot might grow. We will now consider the calculation of benefits under the defined contribution plan with some practical examples.

[8.16]   *Basic Guide to Pensions*

The first factor we established as affecting benefits under a defined contribution plan is the amount paid in. The following table shows how the total contribution paid by the employer and employee will increase under the model defined contribution plan as the employee contributions increase:

Employee contributes	Employer contributes	Total contribution
0%	6%	6%
1%	7%	8%
2%	8%	10%
3%	9%	12%
4%	9%	13%
5%	9%	14%

For this example, let us consider a member who has paid a contribution of 2% each year. In this case, the employer would pay its regular contribution of 6% and would pay another 2% to match the employee's contribution. This would mean that a total contribution of 10% is paid in each year.

Let us presume that the member retires at age 60 when the pot is valued at £190,000.

In order to calculate the pension that is payable, we need to know the cost of purchasing an annuity. The prices offered by insurance companies fluctuate depending on market conditions. For our examples, we will presume that the annuity rate at age 60 is 19 and at age 61 is 18.5.

Pension on retirement from the defined contribution plan [8.16]

The pension is calculated by taking the fund value and dividing it by the annuity rate. So if the member retires at age 60, the pension is calculated as:

$$£190,000 \div 19 = £10,000 \text{ a year}$$

If, instead of retiring at age 60, the member continues to work for another year, then:

- additional contributions will be paid into the member's pot;

- the pot will accrue further investment returns (including returns on the contributions paid during the additional year); and
- the cost of purchasing an annuity will (assuming unchanged market conditions) reduce (because the member will have a shorter life expectancy when the pension is purchased).

Taking the example above:

- if the member was earning £30,000, and if the same 10% contribution level is maintained, then £3,000 will be contributed during the year;
- the member's pot will accrue investment returns and we will assume a return of 6% for the purpose of this example;
- the contributions that are paid in will also receive investment returns, however, not all of the contributions will be invested for the whole year, so we will assume a return of 3% on contributions; and
- as we have noted already, the annuity rate will change from 19 to 18.5.

If the member's pot is valued at £190,000 at age 60, over the next year it will increase by:

£3,000 to take account of contributions paid in

£11,400 (190,000 × 0.06) to account for investment returns

£90 (3,000 × 0.03) to account for investment returns on contributions paid

So at age 61, the member's pot will be valued at £204,490 (i.e. £190,000 + £3,000 + £11,400 + £90).

Again, the member's pension is calculated by taking the fund value and dividing it by the annuity rate. So if the member retires at age 61, the pension is calculated as:

$$£204,490 \div 18.5 = £11,053.51$$

So by taking retirement one year later, the member's pension has increased from £10,000 to £11,053, in other words by 10.5%.

Lump sum on retirement from a defined contribution plan [8.17]

The calculation of lump sum payments under the defined contribution plan and the interaction with the pension are much more straightforward than under a defined benefit plan.

The only restriction on the amount of lump sum that a member can take is the Inland Revenue limit (see para [8.48]). The amount that the member chooses to take is paid out of the member's pot. Then instead of commuting a pension as would be the case under a defined benefit plan, there is simply less money available for the member to purchase an annuity and hence a lower pension will be purchased by the member.

Taking the retirement at age 60 example set out in para [8.16], if the member takes a lump sum of £40,000, then the pot available to purchase the pension will be reduced from £190,000 to £150,000. Remembering that the annuity rate is 19, this means that the member's pension will be:

$$£150,000 \div 19 = £7,894.74$$

Leaving the plan [8.18]

When a member leaves service before a retirement pension is available, they become a deferred member. Between the date of leaving the pension plan and retirement, the pension must be increased. As an alternative to a deferred pension, the member can ask the plan to transfer the value of the benefits accrued to another pension plan (usually of their new employer), or a personal pension/stakeholder plan.

Increases under the defined benefit plan between leaving and retirement [8.19]

A deferred pension is calculated in the same way as a normal retirement pension, but is based on final pensionable salary and pensionable service at the date of leaving the plan. A member's pension is made up of different elements – under the model defined benefit plan, these elements receive different increases in deferment as detailed below:

- the element relating to guaranteed minimum pension (GMP) is revalued at the 'fixed' rate (however, see Chapter 2 for a fuller explanation about GMP revaluation); and

- everything else is revalued in accordance with statutory provisions (this means broadly that it is increased in line with the lower of price inflation and 5% for each year during the period of deferment).

The fixed rate of revaluation for GMPs varies depending on the date the member left the plan as detailed in this table:

Date of leaving	GMP fixed revaluation rate
before 5 April 1988	8.5%
6 April 1988–5 April 1993	7.5%
6 April 1993–5 April 1997	7%
6 April 1997–5 April 2002	6.25%
After 6 April 2002	4.5%

For illustration, let us take a member who leaves service on 1 January 1996 at age 60 and becomes a deferred member rather than retiring. For this example we will assume the member is male (and therefore his GMP is revalued to 65, his GMP pension age). Taking the figures that we used in para [8.10], we know the member's pensionable service and final pensionable salary.

So this member's deferred pension at 1 March 1996 is:

$$1/60 \times 20^{9/12} \times £15,592.47 = £5,392.39$$

As the member is not retiring early, no early retirement factor is applied. We will assume that the pension is made up of two components:

Guaranteed minimum pension (GMP)	£1,031.67
Excess over GMP	£4,360.72
	£5,392.39

So when the member retires at age 65 on 1 March 2001, the two elements of pension would have to be increased as set out in Graph 8.6.

Graph 8.6 A member's income before and after retirement

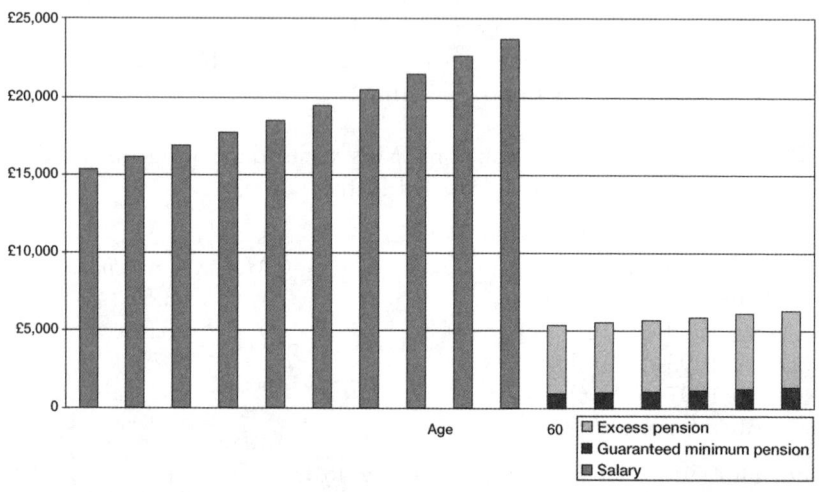

The GMP would be increased for the period 1 March 1996 to 1 March 2001 at the fixed revaluation rate of 7%. There were four complete tax years during this period, so the GMP at 1 March 2001 is calculated as follows:

$$£1,031.67 \times (1.07)^4 = £1,352.31$$

For the excess pension we need to make a comparison, between the statutory revaluation percentage and 5% compound. To make the comparison we take the revaluation percentage at 1 March 2001 which is appropriate for a member who left service five years ago. In this case the figure is 14%, so the comparison is:

the revaluation percentage i.e. 14%, and

increases at 5% would give a cumulative increase of
27.6% (i.e. $(1.05)^5 - 1$)

Benefit Calculations [8.20]

The excess is increased by the lesser of these two amounts (i.e. the revaluation percentage) and so the revalued excess is calculated at:

$$£4,360.72 \times 1.14 = £4,971.22$$

Therefore the revalued pension at age 65 is:

$$£1,352.31 + £4,971.22 = £6,323.53$$

Increases under the defined contribution plan between leaving and retirement [8.20]

On leaving a defined contribution plan, a member's pot will continue to receive investment returns. Graph 8.7 shows how a defined contribution member's pot could grow on leaving service. Notice that when contributions cease to be paid, the fund value increases at a slower rate. You should also be aware that the fund value does not start from zero – if it did, in the second year the fund value would effectively double.

Graph 8.7 How the growth of a member's account declines when contributions cease

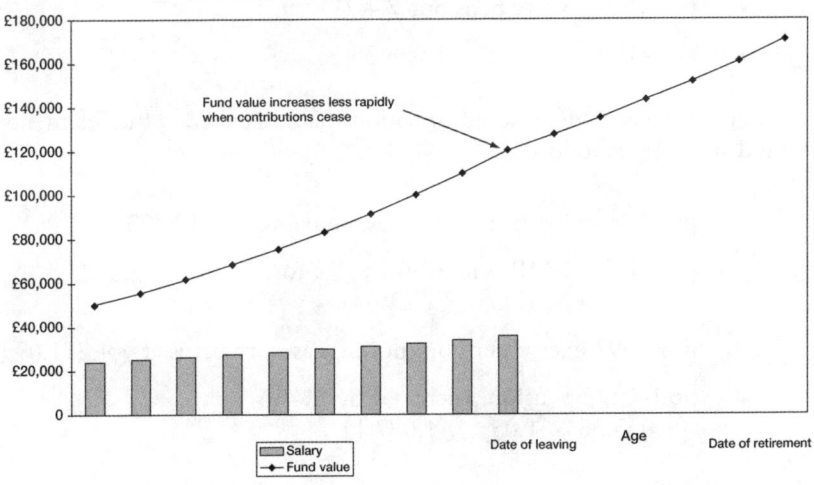

Increases to pensions in payment [8.21]

When looking at pension increases, there is little difference in the treatment of a defined benefit and a defined contribution plan. The key differences arise because differing elements of a pension in payment must be increased at different rates.

The key elements are:

- the pre-April 1988 GMP element which does not get increased in payment;
- the post-April 1988 GMP which is increased by price inflation, but capped at 3%;
- the pre-April 1997 excess above the GMP which does not receive any increase in payment; and
- the post April 1997 pension which receives increases in line with the Retail Prices Index capped at 5%.

As an example, let us consider our member who retired at normal retirement date (see paras [8.7] and [8.9]) with a pension of £6,556.01. The elements of this pension might be broken down as follows:

- pre-1988 GMP: £106.23;
- post-1988 GMP: £1,203.34;
- pre-1997 excess pension: £4,211.09;
- post-1997 pension: £1,035.35.

If after one year the rate of inflation had been 6%, the elements would increase as follows:

- pre-1988 GMP: no increases, remains at £106.23;
- post-1988 GMP: increases by 3% to £1,203.34 × 1.03 = £1,239.44;
- pre-1997 excess pension: no increases, remains at £4,211.09;
- post-1997 pension, increases by 5% to £1,035.35 × 1.05 = £1,087.11.

Therefore after one year, the pension will have increased from £6,556.01 to £6,643.87.

Benefit Calculations **[8.24]**

For a defined benefit member, the plan will provide increases on the appropriate elements of the benefit. For our model defined contribution plan, there are fewer elements (since the plan is not contracted out).

Under a defined contribution plan, differing increases are provided by purchasing annuities which take account of the differing increases that must be provided. In para [8.16], we illustrated the initial pension the member would have received if increases in line with inflation were to be provided. However, if instead the member had chosen to have no pension increases (which could be the case if the account related to pre-April 1997 service), then the annuity rate at 60 may have been 14 and so the pension would have been £13,571 a year (£190,000 ÷ 14). In this case the member would have got a higher initial pension, but it would not have increased in payment.

It should be noted that the increases illustrated here are the statutory minima that must be provided. Plans may, and in practice do, offer increases in excess of these minimum levels and do so quite often in order to simplify their administration.

Benefits on death in service [8.22]

Under the model plans, the benefits payable on death in service differ considerably in their method of calculation. However, both plans do provide the same nature of benefits i.e. a lump sum plus some form of dependants' pension.

Benefits on death in service under a defined benefit plan [8.23]

As would be expected, the defined benefit plan provides benefits which are linked to a member's salary at the date of death.

Calculation of lump sum from the defined benefit plan on death in service [8.24]

The lump sum payable on death in service from the defined benefit plan is equal to four times the member's pensionable salary at the date of death.

[8.25] *Basic Guide to Pensions*

Taking the figures used earlier, assume the member died on 4 June 1996. On 1 January 1996, basic salary was £19,500 and the basic State pension was £3,060.20. Therefore pensionable salary at the date of death was £16,439.80. Accordingly, the lump sum payable on death in service would be:

$$4 \times £16,439.80 = £65,759.20$$

Calculation of pension under the defined benefit plan on death in service [8.25]

The pension payable on death in service under the defined benefit plan is 50% of the pension the member would have received having worked until normal retirement age, but based on final pensionable salary at the date of death. Before we can calculate the benefit, we need to calculate final pensionable salary at the date of death and total potential pensionable service.

The calculation of final pensionable salary uses the same methodology as we applied for the calculation at normal retirement age (see para [8.7]), i.e. we take the average of the last three pensionable salary figures preceding death. Taking the data from para [8.6], final pensionable salary is:

$$\frac{[(19,500 - 3060.20) + (18,500 - 2,995.20) + (17,750 - 2917.20)]}{3}$$
$$= £15,592.47$$

Pensionable service is the period of complete years (and pro rata months) from the date of joining (16 May 1975) until the member's normal retirement date (1 March 2001). Pensionable service is therefore 25 years and 9 months.

We can now calculate the spouse's pension:

$$50\% \times 1/60 \times 25^{9/12} \times £15,592.47 = £3,345.88$$

The lump sum provided on death is not arrived at by commuting the spouse's pension – the figure of £3,345.88 is therefore the full amount of the spouse's pension. It will receive increases in payment as a member's pension would – details of the calculation of pension increases are set out in para [8.21].

Benefits on death in service under a defined contribution plan [8.26]

The benefits under the defined contribution section are calculated in quite a different manner on death in service.

The amount of benefit that can be paid out is affected by the value of the member's pot. The value of the member's pot is:

- the accrued value of the member's pot; plus
- a lump sum equal to six times the member's basic salary at the date of death.

If we take the example of a member who on the date of death, has a pot valued at £150,000 and a basic salary of £30,000. A sum of £180,000 (£6 × £30,000) will then be added to the pot, making a total of £330,000 which will then be applied to provide benefits.

Calculation of lump sum from the defined contribution plan on death in service [8.27]

The lump sum paid from our defined contribution plan on death in service is the maximum allowed by the Inland Revenue – four times the member's final remuneration at the date of death (see para [8.48] for a fuller explanation of Inland Revenue limits).

Let us assume that the member's final remuneration is £32,000 (final remuneration is often greater than basic salary). This would mean that the maximum lump sum that could be paid would be:

$$4 \times £32,000 = £128,000$$

This leaves a balance in the pot of:

$$£330,000 - £128,000 = £202,000$$

Calculation of pension from the defined contribution plan on death in service [8.28]

The calculation of all pensions from a defined contribution plan is quite simple – it is the amount that the pot can buy. However, on death in service a pension is purchased for the widow or widower rather than for the member (with an attaching option to pay the widow or widower on the subsequent death of the member). The cost of the pension for the widow or widower alone is therefore less.

If the remaining pot is worth £202,000 and the annuity rate for the spouse is 15, then the amount of the spouse's pension on death in service will be:

$$£202,000 \div 15 = £13,466.67$$

Benefits on death after leaving service under a defined benefit plan [8.29]

On death in deferment, no lump sum is paid under our model plan and so there is only a pension payable.

If the member of our defined benefit plan leaves service at age 60 (see para [8.10]) on 1 March 1996. From paragraph 8.19, we know that:

Guaranteed minimum pension (GMP)	£1,031.67
Excess over GMP	£4,360.72
	£5,392.39

If the member then dies on 1 March 1998, the GMP will be increased by 7% for the one complete tax year of deferment – see para [8.19]). The increase in the revaluation percentage (i.e. 5.8%) is less than the maximum amount of 5% a year for two years.

So the deferred pension at the date of death is £5,717.53, which is calculated as:

- GMP: £1,031.67 × 1.07 = £1,103.89; plus
- Excess pension £4,360.72 × 1.058 = £4,613.64

So the spouse will receive a pension on death in deferment of £2,858.77 (50% × £5,717.53). This pension will be increased in payment in the same way that the member's pension would have been (see para [8.21]).

Benefits on death after leaving service under a defined contribution plan [8.30]

On death in deferment the same benefit is payable under the defined contribution plan as would be payable on death in service, except there is no additional lump sum of 6 × basic salary added to the member's pot.

Taking the example in para [8.26], if the member had left service immediately before death (therefore assuming the same figures), the value of the pot would have been £150,000. This amount would be available to provide benefits.

Calculation of lump sum from the defined contribution plan on death in deferment [8.31]

It is possible to pay a lump sum on death in deferment and it is common practice on death in deferment for a defined contribution plan to pay the maximum allowed by the Inland Revenue – this is four times the member's final remuneration at the date of leaving service increased by price inflation until the date of death (see para [8.48] for a fuller explanation of Inland Revenue limits).

Using the member's same final remuneration as before (£32,000) would mean that the maximum lump sum that could be paid would be:

$$4 \times £32,000 = £128,000$$

This leaves a balance in the pot of:

$$£150,000 - £128,000 = £22,000$$

Calculation of pension from the defined contribution plan on death in service [8.32]

If the remaining pot is worth £22,000 and the annuity rate for the spouse is 15, then the amount of the spouse's pension on death in service will be:

$$£22,000 \div 15 = £1,466.67$$

Benefits on death in retirement under a defined benefit plan [8.33]

It is typical practice for defined benefit plans to provide a dependant's pension on death in retirement together with a 'guarantee'. This is the case for our model defined benefit plan.

Calculation of lump sum from the defined benefit plan on death in retirement [8.34]

Our model defined benefit plan 'guarantees' the pension for its first five years. What this means is that if the member dies within the first five years, a lump sum will be paid equal to the balance of the remaining payments due over the remainder of the five-year period (at the rate the pension is paid).

Let us consider the member who retired at normal retirement date (see paras [8.7] and [8.9]). On retirement the pension payable was £6,556.01. For an example, we will assume that this member died after two years and received two pension increases – each of 4% (in total taking the increases on all of the elements as described in para [8.21]).

Therefore, at the date of death, the member's pension would have been:

$$£6556.01 \times 1.04 \times 1.04 = £7,090.98$$

There would have been 36 months (i.e. three years) of pension instalments still to pay, so the 'guarantee' lump sum that would be paid would be:

$$3 \times £7,090.98 = £21,272.94$$

Calculation of pension from the defined benefit plan on death in retirement [8.35]

Continuing the same example, on death in retirement, a spouse's pension is payable equal to 50% of the pension which would have been payable if the member had not commuted any pension for a lump sum at retirement.

We know (see para [8.9]) that the full pension at retirement (before commutation) would have been £8,741.35. We know the pension increases that were paid were 4% each year. Therefore the pension that would have been paid at the date of death, ignoring any commutation would have been:

$$£8{,}741.35 \times 1.04 \times 1.04 = £9{,}454.64$$

From this, we calculate the spouse's pension as:

$$50\% \text{ of } £9{,}454.64 = £4{,}727.32$$

Benefits on death in retirement under a defined contribution plan [8.36]

On retirement from the defined contribution plan, members are given the option of what benefits they purchase. In the same way that members can purchase pension increases (see para [8.21]), some may purchase dependants' pensions and/or guarantees.

Whatever choices the member has made are not relevant to the plan – the benefits will be provided by the insurance company with which the pension was purchased and there are no calculations for the plan to be involved with.

Benefits on disability [8.37]

Our two plans differ considerably in the provision of benefit they make for disability – the defined benefit plan provides a quite generous benefit while the defined contribution plan provides nothing. This reflects common practice – very often employers who provide defined contribution arrangements do not offer disability pensions because they provide some form of salary continuance insurance so the member remains in pensionable service until normal retirement age.

Pension benefits on retirement on disability grounds from the defined benefit plan [8.38]

The pension on disability retirement is 1/60 × final pensionable salary (at date of early retirement) × total potential (complete years and pro rata complete months) pensionable service to normal retirement age. No early retirement factor is applied.

For illustration, we will take the early retirement example we considered in para [8.10], but will look at what the benefit would have been if the member had retired on health grounds rather than just taking early retirement.

We know that the member's final pensionable salary is £15,592.47, but the period of pensionable service will be different from that used in the early retirement calculation as we will need to include potential service to normal retirement date.

Much the same as for our calculation of death in service benefits under the defined benefit plan, pensionable service is the period of complete years (and pro rata months) from the date of joining (16 May 1975) until the member's normal retirement date (1 March 2001). Pensionable service (completed plus potential) is therefore 25 years and 9 months.

Thus, the pension on disability is:

$$1/60 \times 25^{9/12} \times £15,592.47 = £6,691.77$$

Compare this with the pension of £4,583.54 which would have been paid if the member had simply chosen to retire early.

As with early retirement, the member can then commute some of this pension for a cash lump sum.

Benefits on divorce: pension splitting [8.39]

The last calculations that we are going to illustrate in this chapter occur when a member divorces. It may be many years between the date of divorce and the date on which the member's benefits come into payment. At the date of divorce, a court may (but does not have to) order that a member's pension will be 'split'. If this happens the plan's trustees must implement the court's order and may have to retain the spouse in the plan (as a deferred member) until retirement.

You may also encounter 'ear-marking' orders – these are very much like deferred maintenance orders. The effect of these is not illustrated here as they do not affect the nature of the benefit calculation, but have more effect on who the benefit is paid to.

Calculating benefits on divorce under the defined benefit plan [8.40]

If a pension splitting order is made, then:

- the member will continue to accrue pension in the normal manner until pensionable service ends, however, the pension will be subject to a 'pension debit' which is the amount ordered by the court to be 'split' in favour of the former spouse; and

- the former spouse will be awarded a 'pension credit' – this will usually be a defined contribution amount equal to the value of the pension debit, but this may be converted into a deferred pension which will be revalued in accordance with the statutory provisions set out in para [8.19] and will come into payment at the spouse's retirement age.

The key point is that the pension debit is based on final pensionable salary at the date of divorce and the member's pension is based on final pensionable salary at the date of leaving service or retirement.

At retirement, the member will receive the full pension less the amount of the pension debit.

Calculating benefits on divorce under the defined contribution plan [8.41]

Under the defined contribution plan, at the date of divorce, the member's pot is split into two equal pots. The former spouse's pot will only receive investment income. However, the member's pot will receive investment returns and regular contributions by the member and the member's employer. Accordingly, the member's pot will grow at a faster rate than the former spouse's pot (provided they are both invested in the same manner). This is illustrated in Graph 8.8. Once the member has left service, both pots can achieve the same investment rates (again, provided they are both invested in the same manner). Note that the spouse and member do not have to retire and take their benefit from their respective pots at the same time.

Graph 8.8 How a member's account is affected on and after divorce

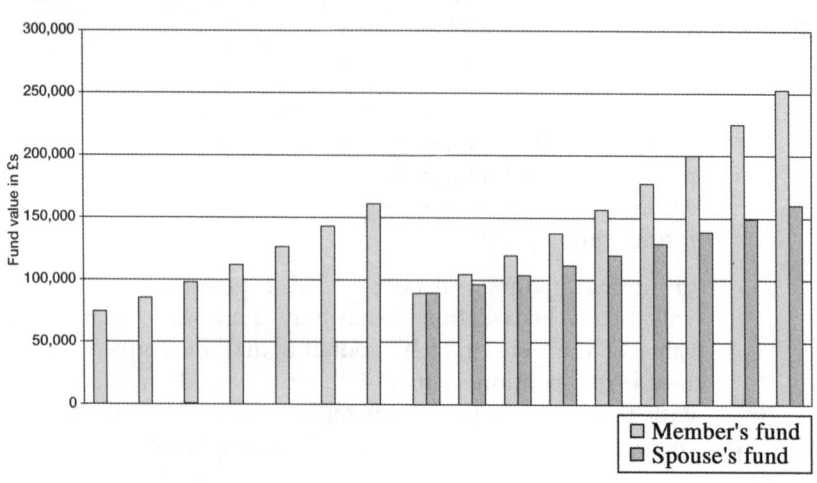

Record keeping [8.42]

As can be seen from the calculations above, pension plans need to keep a lot of information. The lists below summarise the data that needs to be kept in order to calculate benefits. The information is grouped by member event. The information listed here is not necessarily a comprehensive list of the data that every plan should keep, but rather is intended to illustrate the breadth of data that must be held and would be needed to pay the benefits calculated above.

Member joins the plan [8.43]

- Full name (member and spouse).
- Address (member and spouse).
- Date of birth (member and spouse).
- Evidence of marriage.
- Dependants.
- Date of hire by employer.
- Date of joining plan.

Benefit Calculations **[8.45]**

- Benefit category/any special terms or conditions applying.
- Salary (split into basic pay and fluctuating emoluments – see para [8.48]).
- Investment choices (for defined contribution assets).

Ongoing/annual [8.44]

- Salary/fluctuating emoluments.
- Contributions made (including AVCs).
- Marital/dependants' changes.
- (Terms of any) court order made on divorce.
- Investment choices/changes.
- Value of funds contributions are invested in.
- Periods of maternity.
- Periods of sickness.

Although we did not deal with the calculation of benefits following a period of absence due to maternity or sickness, you should be aware that practice in these areas varies. There is a statutory requirement to pension the whole period of paid maternity leave – some employers then choose to pension the whole period of maternity leave (sometimes this is conditional on the employee returning to work after the period of maternity leave ends).

As a minimum, the information that plans may need to hold in connection with maternity includes the date maternity absence begins, the date paid maternity absence ends, the date on which unpaid maternity leave ends and the date on which service terminates (if different).

Leaving service [8.45]

- Date of leaving.
- Rate of revaluation to be applied to each element of pension.
- Salary/fluctuating emoluments on leaving service.
- Fund values (on an ongoing basis).

Retirement [8.46]

- Date of retirement.
- Amount of pension.
- Amount of pre-commutation pension.
- Amount of lump sum.
- Pension increases.
- Where pension payments have been made.
- Spouse/dependants.

Death [8.47]

- Dependants' pensions paid.
- Lump sum/guarantee payment made.

Inland Revenue limits [8.48]

In return for the tax relief given to pension plans, the Inland Revenue limits the amount of benefit that can be taken from a pension plan.

On the following pages we summarise the three main Inland Revenue limits regimes in brief. It should be noted that the information provided is an indication of the important points, for instance, no detail is included about the inclusion of retained benefits i.e. benefits provided in respect of previous employments. For a comprehensive exposition, you should refer to the latest publication of the Inland Revenue Savings Pensions Share Schemes Practice Notes (IR12).

Benefit Calculations [8.48]

	Pre-1987 members	1987–1989 members	Post-1989 members
	Plan set up before 14 March 1989 *and* Employee joined plan before 17 March 1987	Plan set up before 14 March 1989 *and* Employee joined plan between 17 March 1987 and 31 May 1989	Plan set up after 13 March 1989 *or* Plan not approved before 27 July 1989 and employee joined plan after 31 May 1989
Final remuneration	The greater of: (a) the highest: (i) basic pay in the last 5 years, plus (ii) the 3 consecutive-year average of fluctuating emoluments (increased in line with the retail prices index) ending with the same year chosen in (i); and (b) the average of total taxable emoluments for any three or more consecutive years ending not earlier than ten years before the relevant date		
		†Restricted to £100,000 for cash sum commutation only	★Restricted to the earnings cap – £95,400 (April 2001), indexed broadly in line with retail prices index
Maximum employee contribution (including AVCs)	15% of taxable remuneration	15% of taxable remuneration	15% of taxable remuneration★
Maximum employer contribution	No limit	No limit	No limit

	Pre-1987 members	1987–1989 members	Post-1989 members
Normal retirement age (NRA)	60–75	60–75	60–75
Minimum age for payment	50	50	50
Maximum benefit at NRA			
Maximum pension at NRA	2/3 × final remuneration after 10 years' service	2/3 × final remuneration after 20 years' service	2/3 × final remuneration*after 20 years' service
Maximum cash sum at NRA	1½ × final remuneration after 20 years' service	3/80 × final remuneration† × service (maximum 120/80) *or* Higher cash formula if pension greater than 1/60 × service	Greater of: 2¼ × initial rate of pension *and* 3/80 × final remuneration* × service (maximum 120/80)
Maximum benefits on early retirement			
Final salary plans	(actual service ÷ potential service to NRA) × 2/3 × final remuneration if 10 or more years' potential service	(actual service ÷ potential service to NRA) × 2/3 × final remuneration if 20 or more years' potential service	2/3 × final remuneration* after 20 years' service *or* if leaving plan but not service

	Pre-1987 members	1987–1989 members	Post-1989 members
Money purchase plans	2/3 × final remuneration if 10 or more years' potential service to NRA (or actuarial equivalent if paid before NRA)	2/3 × final remuneration if 20 or more years' potential service to NRA (or actuarial equivalent if paid before NRA)	(actual service ÷ potential service to NRA) × 2/3 × final remuneration★ if 20 or more years' potential service
			2/3 × final remuneration★ if 20 or more years' potential service to NRA (or actuarial equivalent if paid before NRA)
Maximum cash sum	(actual service ÷ potential service to NRA) × 1½ × final remuneration if 20 or more years' potential service	3/80 × final remuneration† × service (maximum 120/80) *or* Higher cash formula if pension greater than 1/60 × service	Greater of: 2¼ × initial rate of pension *and* 3/80 × final remuneration★ × service (maximum 120/80)
Maximum benefits on late retirement			
Maximum pension:	1/60 × final remuneration × service (maximum 45/60) *or* 2/3 × final remuneration at NRA after 10 years' service + late retirement increase	1/60 × final remuneration × service (maximum 45/60) *or* 2/3 × final remuneration at NRA after 20 years' service + late retirement increase	2/3 × final remuneration★ after 20 years' service

[8.48] Basic Guide to Pensions

Maximum cash sum	3/80 × final remuneration × service (maximum 135/80) *or* 1½ × final remuneration at NRA after 20 years' service + interest	3/80 × final remuneration† × service (maximum 135/80) *or* Higher cash formula if pension greater than 1/60 × service	Greater of: 2¼ × initial rate of pension *and* 3/80 × final remuneration⋆ × service (maximum 120/80)
Maximum benefits on death in service			
Maximum cash sum	4 × final remuneration at death (or £5,000 if greater) + refund of member's contributions	4 × final remuneration at death (or £5,000 if greater) + refund of member's contributions	4 × final remuneration⋆ at death (or £5,000 if greater) + refund of member's contributions
Maximum spouse's pension	4/9 × final remuneration if 10 or more years' potential service to NRA	4/9 × final remuneration if 20 or more years' potential service to NRA	4/9 × final remuneration⋆ if 20 or more years' potential service to NRA
Maximum benefits on death in retirement			
Maximum cash sum	Total remaining pension instalments for balance of 5 years from commencement	Total remaining pension instalments for balance of 5 years from commencement	Total remaining pension instalments for balance of 5 years from commencement
Maximum spouse's pension	4/9 × final remuneration after 10 years' service	4/9 × final remuneration after 20 years' service	4/9 × final remuneration⋆ after 20 years' service

Maximum increases during deferment				
Pension (final salary)	Greater of 5% p.a. compound and RPI	Greater of 5% p.a. compound and RPI	Greater of 5% p.a. compound and RPI	Greater of 5% p.a. compound and RPI
Pension (money purchase)	Lesser of 5% p.a. compound and RPI	Lesser of 5% p.a. compound and RPI	Lesser of 5% p.a. compound and RPI	Lesser of 5% p.a. compound and RPI
Cash sum	RPI	RPI	RPI (where cash is calculated on 3/80 formula)	
Maximum increases to pensions in payment	Year-on-year greater of 3% and RPI	Year-on-year greater of 3% and RPI	Year-on-year greater of 3% and RPI	Year-on-year greater of 3% and RPI

9 – Funding and Valuations

> This chapter covers the following:
>
> • How a pension scheme is funded.
>
> • The role of the actuarial valuation in the funding process for a final salary scheme.

What is funding? [9.1]

Funding is the name given to the process of setting aside a fund of money, separate from the employer, to provide pension benefits.

Why fund a pension scheme? [9.2]

A pension does not have to be funded in advance. The earliest pensions were simply paid by the person who succeeded to the pensioner's position. Pensions provided by an employer can be paid from the continuing business after the pensioner's retirement. This is indeed the position for the largest group of pensioners, i.e. those of the State. The National Insurance Fund is not a true fund, but merely a means whereby current contributions are turned instantly into current pension payments. Similarly, the State does not maintain a funded pension scheme for many of its own employees. Civil servants, teachers and others rely solely on a promise to pay their pensions, with no funds other than those provided by current contributions and taxation. Furthermore, many employers have set up unfunded pension arrangements to provide benefits on earnings in excess of the earnings cap (see para [3.9]).

However, the vast majority of private sector pension schemes, and many public sector ones, are funded, with a fund of assets held separate from the assets of the employer.

The main reason for funding a pension scheme is to provide security for the members. The existence of a fund should mean that a pensioner is not reliant on the employer staying in business and

Funding and Valuations **[9.3]**

having sufficient profits to pay their pension. An adequate fund means that even if the employer goes out of business, pension benefits will continue to be paid in full.

There are other reasons why employers choose to fund pension schemes, for example:

- it allows them to pay for a member's benefits over the period the member is employed by them. This is particularly important when companies shrink in size – benefits are paid for while the workforce is large and generating income for the employer;
- it allows the employer to provide benefits in a tax efficient way due to the tax relief available if the scheme is approved (see para [3.7]).

Money purchase schemes [9.3]

The rules of a money purchase scheme will usually specify the contributions a member is required to pay to the scheme and also the contributions the employer is required to make to the scheme in respect of him. Usually the rules will provide for the member to have a notional 'individual account' which is credited with his contributions, the contributions his employer makes in respect of him and the investment growth attributable to those contributions. When the member retires, assets equal to the value of his account will be realised and the proceeds will be used to purchase an annuity to provide him with an income.

The amount of pension the member receives from a money purchase scheme will be wholly dependent on the contributions made and the investment growth achieved; it will not in any way be related to the member's earnings before retirement. For many employers a money purchase scheme represents an attractive proposition as the cost of financing the scheme can be predicted with certainty.

The employee, on the other hand, bears all of the risk of investments under-performing but also benefits from any out-performance of investments.

The remainder of this chapter relates primarily to the position of final salary schemes, where deciding what fund should be held and therefore what contributions should be paid to meet the benefits is a more complex process.

Actuarial valuations [9.4]

Funding a final salary pension scheme is rather like saving for your next holiday when you don't know:

- where you are going;
- when you are going;
- when you are coming back; and
- what you are going to do while you are there.

Faced with such a situation, most people would look to make some assumption as to what the holiday will be, and then aim to set aside enough money to meet it. They may then regularly review the position, modifying their assumptions as necessary, to check they are still on course.

The position of a final salary pension scheme is fairly similar, and the regular review of the position is known as the actuarial valuation.

Timing of valuations [9.5]

For most pension schemes an actuarial valuation must be carried out at least once every three years. The effective date of the valuation will usually be the end of the scheme year, as this is when audited scheme accounts are available.

What the actuary does [9.6]

When the actuary carries out a valuation, it is usual to perform no fewer than four separate investigations. These are:

- *the ongoing valuation* – this is the valuation which is used to set the employer's contribution rate to the scheme and is what is most commonly meant when anyone mentions valuation, surplus or deficit;
- *the discontinuance valuation* – this looks at the situation if the scheme were to have been discontinued (i.e. the employer went out of business or ceased to support the scheme) at the valuation date;

- *the minimum funding requirement (MFR)* – this compares the scheme against the minimum level of funding set by the *Pensions Act 1995*;
- *the surplus test* (also sometimes known as the *Government Actuary's Department (GAD)* valuation or, for the technical, the valuation for the purposes of *Income and Corporation Taxes Act 1988, Sch 22*) – this compares the scheme against the maximum funding level set by the Inland Revenue.

Each of these investigations is described in more detail in the following sections.

What the actuary does not do [9.7]

The actuary does not tell you what your pension scheme costs. The exact cost will not be known until the last pensioner dies. At that point you will know what the pension scheme has cost. This is largely unaffected by the funding strategy or the actuarial assumptions. Less paid in now will mean more will have to be paid in later. The actuary, by means of the ongoing valuation, advises on the speed at which the fund is built up to provide the benefits. The trust deed and rules will specify precisely who sets the employer contribution rate, although in most cases nowadays it is effectively an agreement between the employer and the trustees based on the advice of the actuary.

The water tank

A pension scheme is often compared to a water tank and many people find this is a helpful analogy. In the picture below, the tank represents the pension fund, and the water represents the money in the fund.

The drain out of the bottom of the tank is the outflow of money to pay pensions, cash sums, transfer payments, expenses and all other amounts due. This is a function of the benefit structure and the experience of the scheme (for instance, how long pensioners survive).

There are three pipes leading into the tank. These are:

- *Member contributions* – usually a fixed percentage of salary (sometimes zero) and therefore based on the number of active members at any point in time and their salaries.

- *Income from investments* – this depends on what the assets are invested in and how those assets perform.

- *Employer contributions* – as can be seen in the picture, this is the control mechanism (the tap) for the whole process. The employer contributions can be varied, as a result of successive actuarial valuations, in order to influence the level of water in the tank (money in the fund).

In this context, the past service valuation is the process by which you measure the level of water in the tank and the future service valuation tells the employer how much the 'tap' of employer contributions should be opened or closed.

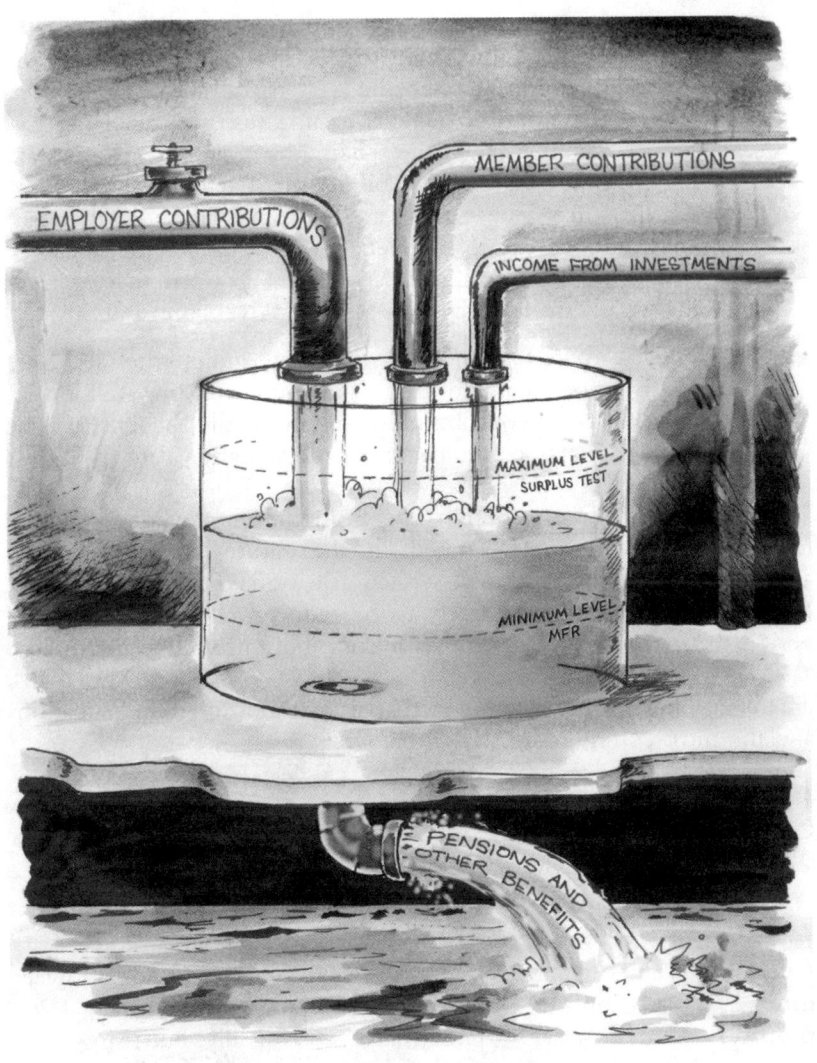

The ongoing valuation [9.8]

The ongoing valuation is usually what determines the recommended rate of employer contributions. There are two parts to it:

- *Past service valuation* – this compares the value of benefits earned by all members up to the valuation date against the value placed on the scheme's assets at that date. If assets exceed the value of benefits earned (usually called the past service liabilities) then the scheme has a surplus. If assets are less than the past service liabilities the scheme has a deficit. A surplus may be used to reduce future employer's contributions, improve benefits or, in extreme circumstances, may be refunded to the employer (less tax). A deficit is almost universally made up by increased employer contributions.

- *Future service valuation* – this determines the level of contribution required from the employer (in addition to any member contributions) to meet the benefits to be earned by active members after the valuation date.

The recommended contribution rate from the employer is then the level of contribution determined in the future service valuation adjusted on account of the past service valuation. If there is a surplus, employer contributions are likely to be reduced to run it off over a period. If there is a deficit, employer contributions will be increased.

There are numerous different actuarial methods used in valuations and the most common are shown below.

Common valuation methods

	Past service	Future service	Comments
Current unit method	Values benefits based on current salary (usually allowing for increases to benefits in line with legislation).	Values the next year's benefits, plus what is needed to pay for a year's salary growth on the past service benefits to the extent that this	Tends to lead to lower contribution rates initially, but rising steeply over time as members build up more pensionable service

Funding and Valuations **[9.9]**

		exceeds what has been allowed for in the past service valuation.	
Projected unit method	Values benefits based on projected final salary.	Values the next year's benefits, based on projected final salary.	Produces a stable contribution rate where the profile of the workforce does not change over time (that is, new entrants replace leavers and average ages etc. remain stable).
Attained age method	Values benefits based on projected final salary.	Values all benefits to be earned by members up to retirement.	Produces a stable contribution rate for schemes closed to new entrants where the average age increases over time. Often used for closed schemes or small pension schemes. Tends to lead to higher contribution rates initially and, if the scheme remains open, surplus appearing at successive valuations

Actuarial assumptions [9.9]

In carrying out any valuation, the actuary must make a large number of assumptions about future events. These can be split into two groups:

Economic assumptions. These include:

- the rate of investment return expected on current and future assets of the scheme;
- the rate of salary growth;
- the rate of price inflation;
- the rate of pension increases on deferred pensions and pensions in payment.

Demographic assumptions. These include:

- rates of mortality of current and future pensioners;
- rates of withdrawal of members from active membership;
- rates of early retirement at each age (separately for voluntary and ill-health retirement);
- the proportion of members who are married or who have dependants who may receive benefits.

It is usually the economic assumptions, and in particular the differences between them, which have the biggest impact on the results of the valuation.

Valuation of benefits [9.10]

In order to place a value on a benefit, the actuary must do three things:

1. Project the amount of benefit which could be paid in some future year (using the economic assumptions).
2. Estimate how likely that amount is to be paid in that year (using the demographic assumptions).
3. Calculate how much money should be set aside now (assuming it will earn the assumed rate of investment return in the future) to provide for this benefit.

The three stages above are repeated for all the possible benefits which could be paid to members, and the results totalled to give a value of the benefits.

Valuation of assets [9.11]

Historically many actuaries have not used the declared market value of the assets of the scheme in their past service valuation. Instead it has been common practice to use a value based on the future income those assets are expected to produce. This tended to produce a stable asset value (as opposed to market value which tends to be highly volatile) but one which rarely coincided with market value.

Increasingly this method is being replaced by the use of market value in valuations, or in some cases, to reduce volatility, a smoothed market value.

Sample valuation result

The following shows a sample valuation result for a scheme valued on the projected unit method of valuation.

Past service valuation	£m
Past service liabilities	
Pensions in payment	12.5
Deferred pensions not yet in payment	5.7
Active members' benefits, based on service to the valuation date only and projected final salary	17.6
Total	35.8
Value placed on the scheme's assets at the valuation date	38.2
Surplus	2.4
Level of funding (assets as a percentage of liabilities)	107%
Future service valuation	
Value of benefits to be earned by active members in the year following the valuation date expressed as a percentage of active members' salaries	16.2%
plus Contributions to meet expenses and life assurance	2.2%
less Members' contributions	(5.0%)
Future service employer contribution rate	13.4%
less Adjustment to employer's contribution rate to run off the surplus of £2.4 m over 15 years	(2.5%)
Recommended employer contribution rate	10.9%

The discontinuance valuation [9.12]

At any point in time, the benefits each member of the scheme has accrued can be calculated, based on service up to that date and final pensionable salary at that date. If the scheme were discontinued each member would be entitled to a pension, immediate or deferred as appropriate, equal to this benefit and subject to whatever increases are guaranteed under the scheme, as overridden by statutory requirements.

On discontinuance, the trust deed and rules of the scheme would specify how the trustees can provide these benefits. Normally there is a choice of three courses of action:

1. Buy an insurance policy for each member which guarantees to pay the benefit (an annuity policy or deferred annuity policy).

2. Transfer benefits to another scheme or an individual pension scheme such as a personal pension scheme or a stakeholder pension. This will often require the member's consent so it cannot be assumed it will always be possible.

3. Continue to run the scheme and pay the benefits as they fall due.

The discontinuance valuation will place a value on these benefits assuming one of these courses of action, and will compare the answer with the assets held to determine whether the scheme has enough money or not to provide these discontinuance benefits. This gives the trustees of the scheme a measure of the security of members' benefits – is the fund adequate to provide what would have been promised to members if the employer were to go out of business?

The minimum funding requirement (MFR) [9.13]

Historically there has been little formal guidance as to the minimum acceptable funding level in a pension scheme, except that a final salary scheme which was contracted out of the State Earnings Related Pension Scheme (SERPS) had to hold enough money to cover its contracted-out liabilities.

Many employers and pension scheme trustees have taken the view that they wish to maintain assets sufficient to cover their liabilities on a discontinuance basis (i.e. to have a discontinuance surplus, rather than a discontinuance deficit). However should a discontinuance deficit arise for whatever reason, it has been a matter for discussion between employers and trustees as to how to restore the funding position.

This has now changed, with effect from April 1997, when the minimum funding requirement or MFR was introduced. This specifies, from the first actuarial valuation after 6 April 1997, a minimum level of funding and the precise form of remedial action should assets fall below this level. As part of this process, the actuary must certify, after each actuarial valuation, a *schedule of contributions* to the scheme which is at least sufficient to meet the MFR. This schedule must be reviewed annually, and if the actuary does not think the schedule remains adequate a new contribution rate must be agreed and a new schedule signed.

If a scheme is less than 100% funded on the MFR (i.e. it has a deficit, rather than a surplus on the MFR basis), then employer contributions must be paid to target being over 100% funded within five years (or 6 April 2007 if later). If a scheme falls below 90% funded (that is, assets cover less than 90% of the liabilities), then employer contributions must target getting back to 90% within twelve months (or 6 April 2003 if later). This could potentially require large contributions from employers over a short timescale.

The actuarial assumptions underlying the MFR are specified precisely in legislation and actuarial guidance.

The MFR has recently been subject to a lengthy review. It had been widely criticised as unduly influencing investment decisions, with some schemes having to invest, to protect their MFR funding level, in a way which might not be in the best long-term interests of the pension fund or the wider economy. At the time of writing the Government has recently proposed that the MFR be scrapped, although as yet we do not have a definite timescale for this. In its place will be an ongoing funding statement for each scheme setting out its own funding objectives and assumptions and the method of dealing with any underfunding.

There are also proposals for interim changes to some aspects of the current MFR (for instance extending the periods to reach 90% and 100% cover).

The surplus test [9.14]

At the time a formal actuarial valuation is carried out, the actuary will also calculate the surplus (if any) in accordance with Regulations made for the purposes of *Income and Corporation Taxes Act 1988, Sch 22* (originally *Finance Act 1986, Sch 12*). This valuation is carried out for the Inland Revenue to enable them to be satisfied that the amount of money invested (and therefore attracting the tax reliefs set out in para [3.7]) is not excessive.

Most of the actuarial assumptions to be used in the surplus test are specified in regulations, although there is scope for the actuary to use some scheme-specific assumptions. The assumptions specified are generally more conservative (i.e. more cautious, so less likely to show a surplus) than those which would be adopted for the ongoing valuation of the scheme.

Thus, a scheme may well disclose a surplus in its ongoing valuation but have no surplus on this surplus test basis. Similarly, a large surplus disclosed by the valuation may well prove to be a small surplus on the statutory basis.

Under the surplus test, a surplus of 5% of the liabilities (i.e. a funding level of 105%) is permitted. If the funding level is higher than this, then a plan of action must be put in place which is designed to reduce the funding level to below the 105% level within five years by one or more of the following means:

- reduction in employer contributions;
- reduction in employee contributions;
- benefit improvements;
- refund of surplus to the employer, less tax.

Schemes which are closed to new entrants may put in place a plan to reduce the excessive funding over the period until the last active member leaves service, if this is longer than five years.

The valuation report [9.15]

At the conclusion of the process the actuary will produce a formal report on the valuation, which includes the results of these four investigations, certificates for the authorities and a statement for inclusion in the trustees' report and accounts. It will also show details of the data used, the benefits valued, the assumptions used and the experience of the scheme since the previous valuation.

10 – Investment

> This chapter covers the following:
>
> - The duties of the trustees of a pension scheme with regard to the investment of its assets.
>
> - The major types of asset held by UK pension schemes.
>
> - The different ways in which schemes structure their investments.
>
> - Investment manager selection and monitoring

Trustees' investment duties [10.1]

The trustees of a pension scheme have the power to invest the assets of the scheme as they see fit, but subject to constraints set out in the law and in their own trust deed and rules. The trust deed and rules of a scheme will usually set out certain investment powers and may apply certain restrictions on investment. For instance, the trust deed may stipulate a ban on investment in the sponsoring employer, above the statutory limit of 5% (see para [10.7]).

The prudent man [10.2]

If the trustees can, under the rules, make a proposed investment, should they? The law says that the trustees must look after trustee investments as if they were looking after them for someone else. One may take risks on one's own behalf, but must be more careful with other people's money. The trustees have to act with due prudence.

The best interests of the scheme members [10.3]

Trustees must put aside their own personal interests and views. They must put the best interests of their beneficiaries first, and normally the best interests of the beneficiaries are their financial interests. The points are illustrated by the case of *Cowan v Scargill* in 1984 – the National Union of Mineworkers case (see below). The judge did not uphold the union trustees' views. The mineworkers' scheme had a good proportion of members who had retired and were pensioners, plus many members who had left the industry but kept an entitlement to a preserved pension in the scheme – deferred pensioners. It was not in their best financial interests to invest money in areas relating to UK coal mining if a better return could be obtained elsewhere, and so the judge decided in favour of the management trustees, who agreed with the investment managers' proposal.

Sir Robert Megarry's judgment in Cowan v NUM (1984)

Although this court case was dealing with a final salary scheme, the statements from the judge on the duties and responsibilities of trustees are also relevant to trustees of money purchase schemes.

The pension scheme for mineworkers had a five-year investment plan which was up for review. The investment managers were suggesting that more money should be invested overseas and in oil and gas stocks. The scheme had five union trustees and five management trustees and no provisions for breaking a deadlock. The union trustees opposed the investment managers' proposals because they thought the money should be invested in this country, not overseas, and in the coal industry, not in competing industries. The judge, Sir Robert Megarry, ruled in favour of the management trustees, who were supporting the investment manager's proposals. Some notable statements by the judge include:

> 'The duty of the trustees is to exercise their powers in the best interests of the present and future beneficiaries of the trust; holding the scales impartially between different classes of beneficiaries is paramount. They must of course obey the law but subject to that they must put the interests of their beneficiaries first.'

> 'When the purpose of the trust is to provide financial benefits for the beneficiaries, the best interests of the beneficiaries are normally their best financial interests. In the case of a power of investment, the power must be exercised so as to yield the best return for the beneficiaries, judged in relation to the risks of the investment in question.'

> 'The standard required of a trustee in exercising his powers of investment is that he must take such care as an ordinary prudent man would take if he were minded to make an investment for the benefit of other people for whom he felt morally bound to provide.'
>
> 'That duty includes the duty to seek advice on matters which the trustee does not understand, such as the making of investments, and on receiving that advice to act with the same degree of prudence. This requirement is not discharged merely by showing that the trustee has acted in good faith and with sincerity. Honesty and sincerity are not the same as prudence and reasonableness. Accordingly, although a trustee who takes advice on investments is not bound to accept and act upon that advice, he is not entitled to reject it merely because he sincerely disagrees with it, unless in addition to being sincere he is acting as an ordinary prudent man would act.'
>
> 'In considering what investment to make, the trustees must put on one side their own personal interests and views. Trustees may have strongly held social or political views. They may be firmly opposed to any investment in South Africa or other countries, or they may object to any form of investment in companies concerned with alcohol, tobacco, armaments or many other things. In the conduct of their own affairs, of course, they are free to abstain from making any such investments. Yet if under a trust investments of this type would be more beneficial to the beneficiaries than other investments, the trustees must not refrain from making the investments by reason of the views that they hold.'

Expert advice [10.4]

Trustees should obtain, and take heed of, proper expert investment advice. The obligation is to take heed of it, not necessarily follow it. Trustees must be wary of rubber stamping the advice of their experts.

Diversifying investments [10.5]

Trustees must have regard to the need for diversification of investments. They should not put all their eggs in one basket. If they do this and are successful, they will be acclaimed. If they fail, they will face the risk of being sued for breach of trust.

Investments must be suitable [10.6]

Trustees must hold investments which are suitable. Not only must the investments be suitable in themselves, they must also be suitable having regard to a scheme's liabilities. An example of this would be an investment in property when a number of members' retirements are coming up on the horizon. If, in a small scheme, a number of members are due to retire shortly, there will be a need for cash to pay the tax-free lump sums and perhaps purchase annuities for them. Property is notoriously difficult to realise quickly. Putting the money on deposit would be more suitable having regard to the scheme's liabilities.

In addition, the investments must be suitable in light of the nature of the liabilities of the scheme. The appropriate mix of assets will depend on the mix of liabilities between active, deferred pensioner and pensioner members. This is covered in more detail in para [10.11].

The suitability of a certain investment will also depend on the funding level of the scheme itself. A scheme with a healthy surplus has far greater investment freedom in terms of matching its liabilities than one with a deficit, as it can afford to take more risk in order to seek to achieve better investment returns.

A poorly funded scheme usually cannot afford the risk of investments performing poorly, so will tend to opt for safer, less volatile, assets but with a lower anticipated rate of return.

Self investment [10.7]

Broadly, self investment, or employer-related investment, is investment in the sponsoring employer, and includes loans, property which is occupied by the employer and shares in the company. There is a legal limit on these types of investments of 5% of the value of the fund for most schemes.

Statement of investment principles [10.8]

The trustees of most schemes must maintain a written statement of investment principles. The statement must cover the trustees' policy for complying with the minimum funding requirement (for final salary schemes and hybrid final salary/money purchase schemes), and:

- the kinds of investments to be held;
- the balance between different kinds of investments;
- risk;
- expected return and realisation;
- the trustees' policy, if any, on socially responsible investment (broadly whether they or their investment managers place any restrictions on the investments held on social, moral or ethical grounds) and corporate governance (the way the trustees or investment managers use their influence as shareholders in the running of the companies they invest in).

Before preparing or revising the statement the trustees must consider the advice of a suitable expert and consult the employer.

What do pension schemes invest in? [10.9]

The main type of asset held by pensions schemes are as follows:

UK equities These are shares in UK companies, and most well-known companies will have their shares quoted on the UK stock market. The holders of the shares together own the business and they usually receive dividends paid out of the profits of the business.

The value of the shares is dependent on many factors, not least being the profitability of the company. The value can go up or down, and if the company goes bankrupt they may end up having no value at all.

Overseas equities Similar to UK equities, but these are shares in overseas companies, and are quoted on non-UK stock markets. The main regions in which UK pension funds invest are:
- North America
- Europe
- Japan
- The Pacific Region (including Australia, Singapore, Hong Kong)

[10.9] *Basic Guide to Pensions*

Some pension funds invest a small amount of their assets in emerging markets (developing countries, in many parts of the world, including South America, Africa, Eastern Europe and Asia).

Property Land, buildings etc. It would be unusual to find a pension scheme investing in residential property; they mainly invest in good quality commercial property such as offices, shops and factories. Only the largest pension funds would invest in properties directly (i.e. own individual properties) themselves. Other funds, if they wish to invest in property, would usually do so by some form of pooled fund (rather like a unit trust – see para [10.16]). The reason for this is that units in a pooled fund spread the risk through owning a number of properties, and can be easier to buy and sell.

Gilts The full title is British Government gilt edged stocks, and they represent the borrowing of the British Government. The investor is entitled to fixed interest payments every six months, and a guaranteed return of capital at the redemption date. There is a large variety of gilts, with high and low interest payments, redemption dates in the near future or many years away (or not at all in a few cases), and some gilts have a range of redemption dates to be chosen by the Government.

Additionally, there are index-linked gilts which are the same as gilts except that the interest and return of capital are guaranteed to increase in line with price inflation.

As an example, the Treasury 8pc 2002–06 pays interest of £8 per annum, and will be redeemed at £100 at any time of the Government's choosing between 2002 and 2006.

What return each investor actually receives depends on the price they pay in the market, which varies with general interest rates.

Other Government bonds Similar in concept to gilts but issued by overseas governments.

Investment **[10.10]**

Corporate Bonds	Fixed interest securities (like gilts) but issued by companies. When buying such assets, there is a risk, therefore, that the company will not in future be able to meet the required interest or redemption payments.
Cash	Pension schemes will usually hold a small amount of money in cash (in an interest-paying account) in order to meet the requirements for cash to pay benefits. At times, investment managers may choose to hold larger amounts of money in cash if they think this is more attractive than any other type of asset.
Other asset classes	Some schemes will invest in other asset classes. These include: • *Venture capital* (also known as private equity) – investment in start-up companies, management buy-outs, or other companies too small to be quoted on a stock exchange. • *Derivatives* – these are financial instruments which give the holder the right or the option to buy or sell a given asset at a fixed price on some future date. They may be used in a number of ways, for instance to protect the fund against adverse market movements, adverse currency movements, or to allow the investment manager to take a more extreme position without having to physically buy or sell an asset. The latter use often underlies what are known as hedge funds. The amount invested is only a small part of the ultimate cost of exercising the option. • *Insurance policies* – often a scheme (usually a small scheme) will buy annuity policies in order to pay pensions in payment. If these policies are in the name of the trustees of the scheme, they are effectively an asset of the scheme which happens to pay an income equal to a particular pension in payment.

Investment strategy [10.10]

Investment strategy is the term usually used to describe the allocation of the assets of a scheme to each major asset class. This is the most significant element contributing to investment performance – the difference in returns between different asset classes is normally far greater than the difference in returns between different managers when asked to invest in the same manner.

Setting strategy in a final salary scheme [10.11]

In a final salary scheme, investment strategy will be dictated by:

- the nature of the liabilities of the scheme;
- the level of funding of the scheme;
- the attitudes to risk of the trustees and the sponsoring employer.

The key decision for trustees is the balance between risk and expected return. The most important element of this is the balance, in the fund, between equities and bonds (meaning gilts or other bonds). Equities are generally expected to provide a greater long-term rate of return than bonds. Also equities are expected to provide a 'real' return over price inflation, that is, in periods of high inflation they provide greater returns than in periods of low inflation (again measured over long time periods). This is especially important for a final salary scheme where most, if not all, of the benefits are linked to earnings or price inflation.

However, returns from equities tend to be volatile. In some years world stock markets go up dramatically and in others, they fall in value. Returns from equities therefore cannot be guaranteed.

In contrast, bonds are not expected to provide long-term returns as high as equities, but their values are more stable (although they do still fluctuate up and down as expectations of future interest rates and future inflation change). More importantly, they do provide a guaranteed rate of return. If you buy a gilt at a certain price and you know you will keep it until redemption (i.e. until you have received all the interest payments and the return of capital) then you know in advance precisely what return you will achieve. Because of this feature, pension schemes will often hold gilts or bonds, in particular to cover their liabilities for pensions in payment or deferred pensions, where the amount of the benefit is known. Buying appropriate gilts or bonds gives a degree of certainty that the assets will be adequate to pay the benefit.

The decision for the trustees of a scheme is then to what extent do they invest in equities to seek to achieve a higher rate of return, but knowing this is likely to lead to a more volatile funding position than if they were to invest in gilts or bonds. The sponsoring employer has to be consulted on the setting of investment strategy, as it is the employer who will be required to contribute more to the scheme if the investment performance is not adequate.

Clearly a better funded scheme (i.e. one with a healthy surplus) will have more scope to invest in equities than a poorly funded scheme as the short-term volatility of returns should not lead it into financial difficulties. Also a scheme with most of its liabilities relating to active members will tend to invest more heavily in equities than one with mainly deferred pensioners and pensioners. This is because the scheme with active members will be looking for a real return relative to salary growth. Also it is unlikely to need to sell any assets to pay benefits, so if equity values fall it can normally wait for values to recover – it need not sell assets at depressed prices.

The investment strategy of the average UK pension fund at the end of 2000 is shown below.

UK pension fund investments

The average UK pension fund invested its assets in the following proportions as at 31 December 2000:

	%
UK equities	48
Overseas equities	23
UK gilts/bonds	10
UK index-linked gilts	6
Overseas bonds	4
Property	5
Cash/other	4
Total	**100**

Source: The WM Company

Setting strategy in a money purchase scheme [10.12]

In a money purchase scheme (including a personal pension or stakeholder scheme) the issues of risk and return are similar to those in a final salary scheme. However, the key differences are as follows:

- It is the member, not the employer, who bears the investment risk – the investment return achieved determines the level of benefit a member receives.

- It is usual for the member to have an element of individual choice as to what investment strategy to follow – typically there will be a range of funds invested in different ways from which he or she can choose.

- Apart from any assets taken as a cash sum, the remaining funds will usually be used to buy an annuity policy on retirement to provide the pension.

The third point is important as annuity prices are determined based on the prices of gilts and bonds. The annuity provider will buy these assets to back the annuity policy, so it sets its annuity prices based on gilt and bond prices. Thus, if a member is invested in gilts or bonds leading up to retirement, any change in the value of the member's fund will be matched by a similar change in the price of the annuity the member will buy, and the resulting pension should not change significantly. In contrast, if the member's fund were invested in equities just prior to retirement, and the equity market fell, then unless gilt or bond markets fell as well, the resulting pension would reduce.

As, in a money purchase scheme, members are usually able to choose to switch money between the different funds available; it is possible for members to change their investments appropriately as they approach retirement and thus reduce the volatility of their expected pension. However, it is also becoming increasingly common for money purchase schemes to have, as an investment option, a fund which automatically makes adjustments to the investment strategy in the years leading up to retirement. This is commonly called *lifestyling*. An example is shown below.

Lifestyling in a money purchase scheme

The aim of lifestyling is to achieve the following:

- Heavy investment in equities for most of the member's working lifetime, as this gives the greatest expected return.

- A gradual switch into gilts, in the years leading up to retirement, for the part of the fund which will be used to buy an annuity. This reduces the volatility of the expected pension.

- A final switch into a cash deposit fund for the part of the fund which will be taken as a cash sum on retirement. This guarantees that the cash value will not reduce once in this fund.

A typical lifestyling pattern is shown below. In this example the switch into gilts starts eight years from retirement and into cash three years from retirement.

Typical lifestyling pattern

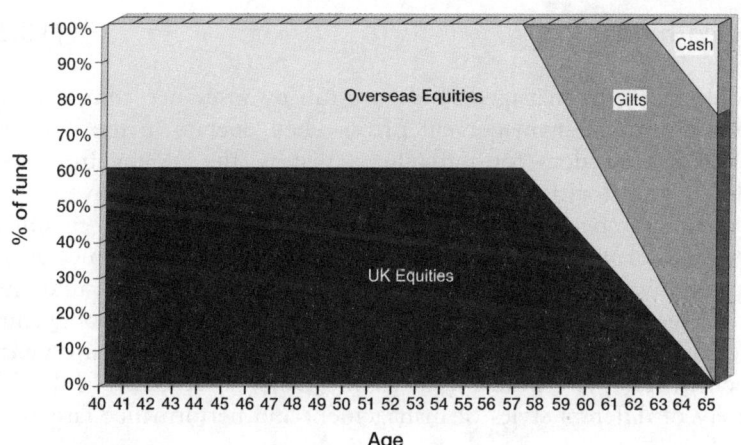

Investment structure [10.13]

While investment strategy is the way in which money is divided between the different asset classes, investment structure is the way in which money is invested, namely the types of investment managers who are chosen and the job that each of them is asked to do.

Insured, pooled or segregated [10.14]

These are the three main methods by which money is held by investment managers for UK pension schemes.

Insured schemes [10.15]

The smallest schemes are often insured, that is, the contributions paid by the employer and employees are paid as a premium to an insurance company. This is more than just an investment approach, as in these cases the insurance company will usually provide administration, actuarial advice, documentation and all other services required in running the scheme. Historically, the money would have been invested in some form of with-profits insurance policy. However, even for insured schemes nowadays, it is quite common for the investments to be in a pooled fund managed by the insurance company (see para [10.16] below)

Pooled funds [10.16]

Pooled funds, or managed funds, are run by insurance companies and other investment management firms. They operate in the same way as a unit trust does for individuals, that is, the money from many different investors is pooled and invested together. Each investor buys a certain number of *units* in the fund, and they buy or sell units as they add or remove money. The price of each unit increases or decreases with the investment return achieved on the underlying assets. See below for an example of the operation of a pooled fund. Pooled funds are now very common and are used by many pension schemes. They are available in all the major asset classes and with a variety of different styles of management and performance targets.

> ### Example of the operation of a pooled fund
>
> At 1 January, the total assets in the pooled fund were worth £100m.
>
> This was allocated to 50 million units, each with a value of £2.00. A number of different investors held units in the fund, and between them they held all 50 million units.
>
> On 1 January, a new investor, Pension Scheme A, invested £10m in the pooled fund. As the unit price on that date stood at £2.00, Pension Scheme A was granted 5 million units.
>
> Thus, immediately after the transaction, the total fund was £110m, representing 55 million units at £2.00 each.
>
> By 31 December, the assets of the fund had grown to £121m due to the investment return earned. No investor had added or removed any money, so there were still 55 million units. This meant that the unit price was now £2.20 (£121m ÷ 55 million).
>
> On 31 December, Pension Scheme A decided to remove its investments. It sold its 5 million units, each worth £2.20, so it received £11 million. Left in the pooled fund was £110 million and 50 million units, each with the same unit price of £2.20.

Segregated management [10.17]

The largest pension funds often operate segregated management. Here an investment manager invests some or all of the assets of a scheme as a separate portfolio, not pooled with any other pension schemes. The advantage of doing this is that the trustees of the scheme can give the investment manager specific instructions in relation to their assets. However, the assets invested in this way will generally be substantial (normally in excess of £100m) in order to make such an approach cost effective.

Within the general categories of pooled or segregated management, there are a number of different approaches which can be taken. These are set out in the next section.

Approaches to investment management

Balanced management [10.18]

A balanced manager is one who has complete freedom to decide which asset classes to invest in (i.e. UK equities, overseas equities, gilts, bonds, property, cash etc.) as well as which particular investments to choose within each asset class (e.g. what UK companies to invest in within the category of UK equities). Balanced management means that investment strategy is effectively being set by the investment manager without the involvement of the trustees.

Having said this, investment managers operating in this way do not tend to deviate very far from the average position of other pension scheme investment managers (the 'peer group') in terms of the allocation of money between asset classes. If they did, and their judgement was wrong, their investment return would be well below their competitors and they would lose business. Thus funds operating balanced management tend to have similar investment strategies which may or may not be appropriate for the liabilities and funding level of the pension scheme in question. This is one of the reasons why balanced management is becoming less common for pension schemes.

Scheme-specific investment strategy [10.19]

Due to the fact that balanced management may not always be appropriate for a particular pension scheme, it is becoming increasingly common for schemes to adopt their own, scheme specific, allocation of money between asset classes, and then give an investment manager little or no scope to deviate from this. This ensures that the trustees' own investment strategy is being followed.

It is common in such an arrangement for the trustees to appoint specialist investment managers, each handling one or more asset classes. These managers would have been picked for their expertise in particular areas and would not be asked to manage investments for the scheme outside those areas. Thus, for instance, a scheme may choose one manager for UK equities, one for overseas equities, one for property and one for bonds.

Index-tracking (passive management) [10.20]

Most investment managers, even if they are only asked to invest in one particular asset class, will retain the freedom to choose the individual investments they buy and sell within that asset class. This is known as active management. However, there is a further possibility known as index-tracking or passive management. Here the investment manager simply aims to match the performance of a particular index. For example, a passive or index-tracking approach to UK equities might involve structuring a profile to match the performance of the FT All Share Index.

Such an approach, if carried out competently, should guarantee a return no better than and no worse than the appropriate index.

In summary, the different approaches to investment management can be described as follows:

	Yes	No
i Do the trustees determine the allocation between asset classes?	Scheme-specific investment strategy	Balanced management
ii Does the investment manager decide which individual investments to buy or sell?	Active management	Passive (index-tracking) management

Other alternatives [10.21]

There are a range of alternatives or combinations of the methods set out above. For instance, trustees may adopt what is known as a core/satellite approach. Here there is an index-tracking 'core' to the scheme's investments, with additional specialist managers appointed to manage a part of the scheme's assets on an active basis (the 'satellites').

Investment manager selection [10.22]

There are three main types of organisations who typically offer investment management services to pension fund trustees.

| **Life assurance companies** | Such companies not only offer insurance-based products but also offer direct exposure to investment markets through separate investment management. |

Merchant banks/ stockbrokers	These organisations will offer a variety of financial services and will have specialised investment departments within their organisations which will deal with pension fund investment.
Independent fund managers	This covers a number of companies whose business is exclusively investment management and, in a few cases, is exclusively investment management for pension funds.

Once the trustees have decided upon an investment strategy and their investment structure, their investment consultant will be able to put forward a shortlist of suitable investment managers.

Past performance [10.23]

Good relative performance over the long term may be indicative of a good investment process. Additionally, many trustees in the process of selecting investment managers feel more comfortable placing their scheme's assets with a manager who has an established performance track record. Therefore, a consistent past performance is one of the criteria to be considered in producing a list of possible investment managers.

Other aspects [10.24]

Past performance is not necessarily a guide to the future. Indeed, the team of people who produced the performance in some years may have been replaced, or the approach to investment may have been changed. To take account of these factors and to ensure they are in a position to advise their clients properly on the choice of investment managers, many consultants undertake a series of visits to a large number of investment managers. These visits are designed to enable them to get a greater understanding of each manager's approach to investment, to assess their success in achieving their stated objectives and to gauge their ability to take on further clients. In helping their clients to select investment managers, they are able to take account of many of the qualitative elements of an organisation which can contribute to its success or failure in investment management.

Performance targets [10.25]

Once appointed, each investment manager should be set a clear performance target, namely:

- what index or survey will their performance be measured against;
- by how much (if anything) are they expected to outperform this measure; and
- over what timescale will their performance be measured.

Thus, for instance, an active UK equity manager might be set the following benchmark:

'To produce a return, measured over rolling three-year periods, of 1% per annum in excess of the return on the FT All Share Index.'

Monitoring the investment manager [10.26]

Trustees will usually monitor the investment manager's actions. This monitoring can be split into two elements:

- monitoring the investment performance (i.e. the returns achieved by the manager); and
- monitoring the behaviour of the manager.

There are a number of performance measurement organisations in the UK who collect and analyse data from a large number of pension schemes, as do many investment consultants. Monitoring the behaviour of the manager (in short, did they do what they said they were going to do and if not, why not?) will usually fall to the investment consultant. A performance measurer will usually be able to identify not just the overall performance but the contributors to that performance (i.e. what did the manager do well and what did they do badly?). It is also good practice for the trustees to meet their investment managers on a regular basis.

11 – Additional Voluntary Contributions

> This chapter covers the following:
>
> - What additional voluntary contributions are.
>
> - Why they must be offered.
>
> - What types are available.
>
> - The benefits which can be produced.
>
> - The various ways in which they can be invested.
>
> - How to compare the investment returns offered.

Introduction [11.1]

Occupational pension schemes can be contributory or non-contributory as far as the member is concerned. There must always be some measure of contribution from the employer (even if this is temporarily suspended due to the high level of funding). In both types of pension scheme there must be provision for the member to contribute more than the rules normally require. This provision is by way of additional voluntary contributions (AVCs).

According to the National Association of Pension Funds (NAPF) Annual Survey 2000, about 19% of private occupational scheme members pay AVCs. Interestingly only about 6% of public sector final salary scheme members take the opportunity and this is generally supposed to reflect higher benefit levels under those schemes.

The normal level of contribution is usually set as a percentage of pensionable earnings, often 5%. However, pensionable earnings is often defined at a level less than total taxable earnings. The maximum permitted contribution by a member is 15% of total taxable earnings from the employment to which the pension scheme relates, but this 15% is limited by the overall earnings cap to 15% of the cap at any given time.

As an example we might think of a salesman earning commission and with a company medical plan in a pension scheme that defines pensionable earnings as 'basic pay'. His actual annual earnings are:

Basic pay	£30,000
Commission	£12,000
Medical plan	£650
Total earnings	£42,650

His maximum permitted contribution is thus:

$$£42,650 \times 15\% = £6,397.50$$

The pension scheme allows a contribution of:

$$£30,000 \times 5\% = £1,500.00$$

He could contribute a total of £4,897.50 more in a year than the scheme normally allows. This is a substantial amount of tax effective saving.

Why AVCs? [11.2]

Why should a member pay more into a pension scheme than they absolutely have to? The answer is initially simple, but becomes more detailed as greater consideration is given to the question.

Paying AVCs is a very good and tax effective method of saving. They fall under the 'EET' (exempt, exempt, taxed) tax system:

- exempt from tax on contribution;
- exempt from tax on build up;
- taxed on payment.

This is normally thought of as the most advantageous system as it allows the greatest capital to be built up over a given period. It is also the system used by most countries in the EU with the notable exception of Germany.

[11.2] *Basic Guide to Pensions*

There is also the point that once the money has been paid into the AVC scheme it cannot be drawn out and spent on anything else. Provided the member is happy to lock away assets for retirement the system is secure and very directed.

Obviously AVCs are not the only tax effective savings vehicle available. It is possible to draw up a small table of options based upon flexibility, moving from least to most flexible:

Savings vehicle	Flexibility	Comments
AVC	Low	Pension only after 50
Personal pension	Low	Pension only after 50★
Stakeholder pension	Medium	Pension or tax-free cash after 50★
ISA	High	Cash at any time

★Since 6 April 2001 a member earning less than £30,000p.a. can choose to pay into a personal pension including a stakeholder pension under the 'concurrency rule'.

Provided the member wants an enhanced pension an AVC is a good deal. But why try to provide more anyway? Each member is different and will have different reasons for saving, but some of the major drivers tend to be:

- *Short-term member* – the member has only joined the scheme at (say) age 40, will not receive full benefits and has no other provision. AVCs can increase the actual pension payable from retirement.

- *Intends to retire early* – the member realises that early retirement penalties can be considerable. A combination of shorter membership and actuarial reduction of the pension built up to take account of the fact that the pension will be paid for longer can seriously reduce the actual pension in payment.

- *Wants additional peripheral benefit* – a pension scheme may provide a 50% spouse's pension and the member may wish to increase this to the maximum 66%. Increases to pensions in payment may be limited to 3%p.a. and the member wishes to increase rate.

Additional Voluntary Contributions **[11.4]**

Types of AVC

Occupational [11.3]

All occupational schemes must make available a vehicle which members can use to make AVCs. Some will take the easy way out and only offer one vehicle, but many make a range of choices available.

If an occupational scheme is insured and run by an insurance company, then the product available from that company will be used. Schemes which are independently run have a choice of products (set out below) from which the trustees will select a range to be offered.

The most common form of AVC is a regular payment deducted from pay monthly and automatically paid into the vehicle chosen by the member from the range on offer. For members who receive bonuses paid on a basis other than monthly (annual, quarterly, etc.) arrangements can be made for them to forgo all or part of each bonus and have this treated as an AVC.

The basic rule is that the member must not exceed the overall 15% limit on total contributions, i.e. ordinary contribution plus AVC combined.

Once an AVC is paid it is locked into the pension scheme and can only be paid as a pension at retirement. It is not possible to take AVCs as additional tax-free cash at retirement unless the member started to pay them before 8 April 1987. However, the very existence of an AVC pension can lead to a better tax-free cash calculation in the main scheme.

The trustees have a general duty to ensure no one receives benefits above normal Inland Revenue limits and this includes a check on the benefits being bought by AVCs.

Free-standing AVCs [11.4]

From 6 October 1987, free-standing AVCs (FSAVCs) were introduced to give members greater flexibility. A member is no longer restricted to the choice of providers permitted by the trustees. Independent providers offer AVCs to which a member can pay directly. The total of normal contributions and all AVCs in any one year must not exceed the 15% limit. Only one FSAVC from one supplier can be used in any one year and the same restrictions apply on taking pension as opposed to cash.

There is an additional requirement in that FSAVC payments of over £2,400p.a. require the provider to make regular 'head room' checks that the benefit being bought overall does not exceed normal Inland Revenue limits.

Controlling directors in small and medium sized companies are not allowed to use FSAVCs.

Stakeholder [11.5]

Employers who are not exempt under the *Stakeholder Pension Schemes Regulations 2000 SI No 1403, regs 22 and 23*, must make available a stakeholder pension to persons earning less than £30,000 p.a. (see para [2.26]). The most a person can pay into a stakeholder is £3,600p.a. and this is in addition to the 15% limit on scheme contributions (ordinary, AVC and FSAVC combined). In fact there are not likely to be many people earning below £30,000p.a. who could afford to pay both sets of contribution.

Stakeholder benefits can be taken at any age between 50 and 75 without reference to the main scheme, adding flexibility.

Personal pension [11.6]

A personal pension is an alternative to a stakeholder. Since 6 April 2001 a member earning less than £30,000p.a. can choose to pay into a personal pension under the 'concurrency' rules.

There is already at least one personal pension being advertised as having lower charges than stakeholders and this could be a viable alternative. Personal pension benefits can be taken at any age between 50 and 75 without reference to the main scheme, adding flexibility.

Types of benefit [11.7]

AVCs can be used to provide different types of benefit. They are all aimed at pension provision (unless started before 8 April 1987 when tax-free cash is permitted). The type of pension provided can vary.

Money purchase [11.8]

The vast majority of AVCs (and all FSAVCs) are of the money purchase type. AVCs are accepted from the members and invested. The pension paid is the value of the annuity which can be bought by the cash fund accumulated in the money purchase account. In some cases, where the investment is in the fund of the pension scheme itself there may be advantageous annuity rates offered by the fund.

Fixed pension [11.9]

This system has become more unusual as money purchase has become more common. Essentially the actuary to the scheme calculates what pension a given contribution from a given age may be expected to purchase and this fixed amount is paid no matter what the investment return has been. Not unexpectedly the actuary tends to be conservative in the assumptions used and the pension frequently does not appear to give very good value for money. It does, however, have the advantage of certainty and the member is protected from adverse investment conditions, particularly a downturn in the stock market or interest rates close to retirement.

Added years [11.10]

This is similar to the fixed pension system, but a number of additional years (or part years) of service are calculated for the agreed AVC level. For instance, if a person has a normal expectation of receiving 30/60ths at normal retirement date, an AVC of 5% might be calculated to provide an additional 1/60 giving a total of 31/60 ths instead of the normal benefit level. In this system all of the investment risk is transferred from the member to the scheme, and a corollary of this is that the actuary, again, tends to use conservative assumptions.

Advantages/disadvantages [11.11]

Most AVC systems place the investment risk with the member. They are of the money purchase type and the member receives whatever investment returns to retirement and annuity rates at retirement will purchase. The fixed pension system takes some of this risk away from the member, but at the cost of conservative assumptions made by the actuary. The added years system does much the same. An extra disadvantage of both fixed pension and added years is that it does not matter (in the long run) to the employer if the actuary uses overly conservative assumptions as, in the end, there will be a contribution holiday because the scheme becomes over funded. There are no contribution holidays for AVC-paying members.

If a member has a choice, as some do, between a money purchase type and a known benefit type they must decide what is more important: certainty or a 'just' return.

Investment [11.12]

All AVCs have to be invested in one way or another. Even holding money in cash is a form of investment. The range of investments available is decided by the trustees, and the NAPF Annual Survey 2000 shows that most large schemes will tend to offer at least two alternatives. The trend is definitely towards greater choice in the same way that the trend in money purchase schemes is to greater choice. The range of investments in FSAVCs is already wide and each provider will have a good range from which to choose.

Trustees (and members for FSAVCs) should take into account not only likely investment returns but also the level of charges which are involved. This is particularly important with FSAVCs because many schemes effectively subsidise in-scheme AVCs by paying the costs directly or arranging size discounts with the provider.

Building society [11.13]

It is well known that returns from building society accounts have not kept pace with stock market returns in the long term. Over the period 1990 to 1999 cash deposits returned 7.9% p.a. and the UK stock market 14.9% p.a. (source: Bacon & Woodrow. Cash deposits

Additional Voluntary Contributions **[11.14]**

used rather than actual building society returns as competition between societies leads to varied rates at different times.) This would tend to suggest that building society investment should not be recommended.

However, there are times when such investment could be useful. This is particularly so in cases where free (or very cheap) switching is permitted between various investment types. If a member has been investing in stock market-based products, has achieved a good return and is approaching retirement, the member could lose some or all of the return on a stock market downturn. It may well be a good idea to lock in some or all of that return by switching to a product which maintains the cash value of the assets.

A possible alternative which might be suggested is to place the asset in a bond-based product as annuity rates are based (at least partly) on bond rates. The problem with this is that an increase in interest rates would lead to a reduction in bond values and thus a capital loss to the member. This would, of course, be partly offset by a consequent increase in annuity rates, but the member is still likely to suffer some loss. By switching to cash the member would retain the full capital value and also gain from the rise in annuity rates, resulting in a higher pension.

With profits **[11.14]**

There are two basic types of with profit contract, unit linked and true with profit. Unit linked will be dealt with in para [11.15]; this section concentrates on true with profit.

Since the problems of Equitable Life most interested people have a better understanding of the operation of a with profit assurance policy. The essentials are quite simple:

- the member pays premiums to an insurance company;
- in return, the insurance company offers a guaranteed payment on death before a given age, plus a minimum guaranteed payment at the given age, plus 'profits';
- 'profits' are decided by the insurance company and added to the policy value each year as bonuses, once added they cannot be taken away;

[11.14] *Basic Guide to Pensions*

- there may well be an additional 'terminal bonus' in the last year.

It is the calculation of profits and bonus levels which causes the problem. The insurance company invests the premiums received and uses the investment return to underpin the guaranteed values, to declare bonuses and to increase reserves. The reserves are intended to see the insurance company (and policyholders) through bad investment periods. The insurance company should be able to maintain bonus levels even when stock markets fall by calling on their reserves.

Unfortunately, competition between insurance companies concentrated on the level of bonus declared and the overall return achieved on with profit policies. This led some companies (Equitable Life amongst them) to retain lower amounts in their reserves in order to pay larger bonuses and be able to 'beat' the competition. When an unexpected event arises there are insufficient reserves and the insurance company cannot pay out the levels it had promised.

The Equitable Life problem is too recent for us to be certain what effect it will have on other companies over time; it will probably be 2010 or later before this is clear. However, some companies have already indicated that they will be even more conservative in their bonus declarations than in the past and that their reserves will be maintained at a relatively high level.

This *may* be good news for long-term savers, those with 20 or more years to go, provided the insurance company actually releases money from those reserves in 20 plus years' time. It is not such good news for shorter-term savers as these people will see the lower bonuses and greater allocation to reserves from which they are less likely to reap the benefit.

AVC payers are likely to be those aged 40 and over, who can afford to pay AVCs because they are starting to enjoy more free spending availability as some of their family and mortgage commitments have reduced. They are exactly the group least likely to benefit from lower bonuses and higher reserves in with profit policies. There is a further complication to take into account on with profit policies and this is 'free assets'. Insurance companies have assets which are not specifically allocated to any given liability – they are 'free'. The greater the level of free asset compared to with profit liability, the greater the security of the with profit bonuses. Free assets for some companies are shown below.

	Free assets	With profit liabilities	
	£ billion	£ billion	%
Axa	3	6.2	48
CGNU	14	39	34
Standard Life	11	29	38
L&G	6	15	43
Scottish Widows	6	15	38
Prudential	21	54	40
Equitable Life	1	20	7

From the figures given it may be thought surprising that questions were not asked about Equitable Life long before problems arose. Their free asset cover was very low. The whole with profit investment field is difficult to assess because:

- charges are hidden in the premium rate and bonus rate;
- investment performance is hidden by the use of reserves;
- surrender terms are either not disclosed at the point of sale or may be penal.

There is no way of managing the risk of low annuity rates at retirement date unless there is a guaranteed annuity, and look what happened to Equitable Life because of these!

Overall the viability of with profits policies for funding AVCs has been called seriously into question.

Unit-linked [11.15]

Unit-linked arrangements are effectively the same as investing in a normal unit trust. The arrangement may be under the umbrella of an insurance policy or a free-standing unit trust; whether or not a policy is used depends on the provider. In either case the vehicle will have been approved for pension scheme purposes and will be treated for tax purposes as if it were itself a pension scheme.

All the usual rules for an individual buying a unit trust privately should be taken into account by members when selecting their investment.

- Does the investment fit their risk profile?
    - Is all equity too risky?
    - Would a balanced trust suit this member?
    - Are they close to retirement and looking to reduce risk?
- Does the investment cover the period they are dealing with?
    - Are we looking long term, say ten plus years?
    - Is the member close to retirement?
    - Does the member want to retire early?

Scheme assets [11.16]

Instead of (or in addition to) other forms of investment the trustees may decide to allow members to invest directly in the pension fund itself. This type of investment can mimic any of the other types. A simple method is to pay to the member's account the rate of return achieved by the fund as a whole. It is also possible to separate out the various components of the fund's assets and to pay the appropriate rate of return. A member could be offered the return on UK equities, or UK fixed interest, etc.

The main problem with this method is that the interests of the member and the trustees may not coincide. For instance, the trustees may have decided that, due to a large number of anticipated retirements in the next few years there is likely to be a major call for cash resources and that equity investment should not only be restricted but also be conservative. The member may be aged 30 and feel that an adventurous equity policy could be sustained for some years in their AVCs. The trustees have a duty to look after the interests of the membership as a whole, not solely of one particular member.

Additionally, members may well feel it would be sensible to be able to spread their investment risk by having alternative managers other than the trustees themselves. A wider range of investment possibilities is probably of greater assistance to the member, although the fund may form part of this wide range.

Matching [11.17]

Matching is not so much a method of investment as an addition to investment. In some schemes the employer will offer to match (within limits) AVCs paid by the member. This is more frequent in money purchase schemes than final salary arrangements.

In a scheme where the normal rate of contribution is:
- employer – 5%;
- employee – 3%,

the employer may offer to match 100% of the employee's next 3% of contribution. At a maximum the contributions would become:
- employer – 8%;
- employee – 6%.

The employee would still have the ability to direct this investment as far as their own 3% AVC is concerned. The employer may reserve the right to continue to direct the investment of the whole of their contribution or may agree to permit the additional matching contribution to be directed by the employee.

The exact level of matching can cover a wide range. Matches of 50% of the employee extra, or double or even triple the employee extra are not unknown.

This system is common in savings plans offered in the United States (401k plans) and is becoming more common in the UK.

The basic intention is that the employer is able automatically to concentrate input on the people most interested and most appreciative of the scheme. Cost is kept under control by not spending money on people who are not willing to help themselves. This begs the question of ability to pay on the part of the member. Higher-paid members tend to take up this type of offer leaving the lower paid (who may well need the extra contribution more but are unable to afford it) to languish on a lower level of benefit.

AVC projections [11.18]

Chapter 10 of this book covers investment and investment performance. This section does not seek to expand on that chapter.

Rough guide [11.19]

Projections are usually made by both insurance providers and investment managers as to the amount that can be expected to have accumulated by normal retirement age as a result of making AVCs. It is sensible for trustees to have a table of projections drawn up by their actuary if investment directly in the pension fund is permitted. The trustees should not forget to have this table updated from time to time.

The difficulty with projections is that they need to combine two elements:

- investment return to normal retirement age;
- annuity rate at normal retirement age.

Members starting AVCs now must take the resultant proceeds as a pension, but the AVCs themselves build up to a lump sum. There is some talk that this rule may be relaxed and tax-free cash payments again might be permitted. Investment returns normally depend upon the return available over time on a range of asset types, e.g. equities, fixed, interest, property, etc. However the rate of conversion from a capital sum to a pension (the annuity rate) depends upon the return available on Government bonds at the date of conversion. The higher the interest rate available, the higher the pension that can be given. Bearing in mind the problems created for Equitable Life by guaranteeing too high an interest rate, the probability is that conversion rates quoted (even if not guaranteed) will not be generous.

Because of the uncertainty over interest rates years into the future it is better to compare only the likely investment returns to normal retirement age and to ignore the annuity rate. It will in any event be almost the same for all people retiring at the same date.

Range of assumptions [11.20]

Different assumptions may be required for different forms of investment because the expenses involved will be different. It is impossible to state what return will actually be achieved in the future. Returns in the past *may* be a guide if they appear to have been consistent over a long period of time. The costs of running a unit trust type can (normally) be calculated with some precision. Insurance companies should provide the reduction in yield which will be produced by the charges they hide in premium and bonus rates of with profit policies. The actuary should provide a set of assumptions for investments in the scheme assets. All of these methods will produce contradictory, unsatisfactory and incorrect answers.

Probably the best way to deal with this matter is from the point of view of the member and their attitude to risk. All other things being equal, a range of risks can be placed before the member, and a range of past experience results achieved by taking these risks. A member can be invited to select the risk most consistent with their own philosophy. Inspection of the level of charges should be part of this process. If the employer has a subsidiary or owner in the USA contact could be made to see how they deal with this matter under their 401(k) (savings) plan. There is considerable experience available which can be imported with advantage.

Flexibility at retirement

Ability to take benefits other than at normal retirement [11.21]

Since 30 June 1999 there is no compulsion to take AVC or FSAVC benefits at the same time as the main scheme benefits. They can be taken at any time between ages 50 and 75 (or even before age 50 if retirement is due to serious ill-health). There may be restrictions written into the wording of some insurance contracts which may reduce this freedom.

If AVC benefits are taken early the member can still build up more AVC payments and take the value of these at a later date. Any benefits taken early must be by the 'draw down' method (see para [11.22]).

AVC benefits taken after the main scheme benefits are treated in the same way as early benefits.

Drawdown as opposed to taking at retirement [11.22]

The 'normal' way of taking AVC benefits is to convert the lump sum built up into a pension by purchasing an annuity. However, this is not compulsory. The member can elect for the 'drawdown' method. Under this system the assets are left invested with the main scheme (or perhaps the investment manager or insurer) and part of them withdrawn each year to provide an income. The amount withdrawn is based on tables provided by the Government Actuary's Department. The amount taken may, or may not, be payable until the death of the member, this depends on how well the investments perform compared with the assumptions in the table.

This method is sometimes seen as a way of avoiding the need to purchase an annuity at times when interest rates, and thus annuity rates, are very low.

There are limits on what can be taken as drawdown. All AVCs from one employer must be taken at the same time. All FSAVCs from one employment must be taken at the same time, but this can be a different date to the in-house AVCs.

Members wishing to consider drawdown should be encouraged to seek professional independent personal financial advice.

What if there is too much benefit? [11.23]

Because AVCs are additional to the normal benefits, are usually defined contribution and the member decides how much to contribute, the trustees do not have the usual level of control over the amount of benefit being built up. It is possible for members to over provide and end up with a benefit larger than that permitted by the PSO. In addition to the 'headroom' check (see para [11.4]) undertaken by the FSAVC provider, the trustees of the 'leading scheme' must check at 'relevant dates' to ensure there is no over provision.

The relevant dates are:

- leaving;
- death;
- retirement.

The 'leading scheme' is the one with which the member retires or (if only FSAVCs have been made) the one under which FSAVCs were made.

It should be noted that no check need be made if AVCs are taken early or late, only at the time main scheme benefits are taken.

Additional Voluntary Contributions [11.23]

The leading scheme works out the maximum permissible benefits (including spouse's, death and increasing benefits) and 'spends' the AVCs and FSAVCs up to this limit. Any excess is then refunded to the member less a tax charge (of 32% at 2001 rates). Higher-rate taxpayers will have an additional charge made, so there is no 'tax gain' in the equation.

Appendix A
List of Pensions Legislation

- 1908 (*Old Age Pensions Act 1908*) – The State introduced the first general old age pension paying a non-contributory amount of between 10p and 25p per week from age 70 on a means-tested basis.

- 1918 (*Income Tax Act 1918*) – Tax relief was limited on premiums paid to secure deferred annuities under a bona fide pension scheme.

- 1921 (*Finance Act 1921, s 32*) – Tax reliefs were granted to pension schemes satisfying certain conditions.

- 1922 (*Local Government and Other Officers' Superannuation Act 1922*) – Empowered local authorities to provide for the superannuation of their employees without requiring a separate Act of Parliament for each case.

- 1925 (*Contributory Pensions Act 1925*) – This built on the 1908 Act setting up a contributory State scheme for manual workers and others earning up to £250 p.a. The pension was 10 shillings (50p) per week from age 65. This was extended to others outside this category from 1937 on a voluntary basis.

- 1925 (*Trustee Act 1925*) – Defined the range of investments that could be used by trustees where no specific rules were laid down in the trust deed. Because this range was restrictive it became normal to have a comprehensive set of rules in the trust deed to ensure greater investment freedom.

- 1927 (*Superannuation and Other Trust Funds (Validation) Act 1927*) – There was a rule of law prohibiting perpetuities. This Act protected pension funds from this, provided they registered. To avoid registration most pension funds included a clause in the trust deed to ensure there was no perpetuity. It was not uncommon to state that the trust would end 'on the death of the last direct descendant of His Late Majesty King George Vth'.

- 1930 (*Finance Act, 1930*) – If a pension fund was approved under the *Finance Act 1921, s 32* (see above), the tax

Appendix A

payable on benefits other than death benefits was reduced from one-third to one-quarter of the standard rate.

- 1937 (*Local Government Superannuation Act 1937*) – Local government pensions were made mandatory on specified lines. The detail was contained in subsequent Acts and many regulations.

- 1946 (*National Insurance Act 1946*) – Introduced a contributory State pension for all amongst other benefits. Initially pensions were £1.6s (£1.30p) a week for a single person and £2.2s (£2.10p) per week for a married couple. They were paid from age 65 for a male and 60 for a female.

- 1947 (*Finance Act 1947*) – Limited the maximum amount of approvable pension and the proportion that could be taken as a tax-free cash sum.

- 1952 (*Income Tax Act 1952*) – This was a major Act of its time and set the style for many reforms in the future. It consolidated and amended the relevant sections of the *Income Tax Act 1918*, and the *Finance Acts of 1921* and *1947*.

    – *Section 219*: set out tax reliefs, life assurance and deferred annuity premiums.

    – *Section 225*: set out tax reliefs on premiums for widow's and orphan's benefits.

    – *Section 226*: set maximum limits on tax reliefs.

    – *Section 378*: granted tax relief on contributions to statutory pension schemes.

    – *Section 379*: gave full tax relief to employer and employee contributions paid to schemes approved under this Section. It set out the conditions for approval and gave tax relief to investment income.

    – *Section 386*: charged tax on all contributions to pension schemes *unless* they complied with *section 387*.

    – *Section 387*: set out the exceptions which allowed pension schemes to avoid taxation. Essentially the pension scheme had to comply with *sections 379, 388* or *390* of this Act.

    – *Section 388*: set out the basic requirements for approval under this section.

- *Section 389*: basically stated that all schemes of an employer must be approved as a whole, or approval for all would be rejected.
- *Section 390*: covered miscellania and schemes for employees earning under £2,000 p.a.
- *Section 391*: ensured the Act covered all employees including those of unincorporated bodies and associations, but not partnerships.

This Act brought certainty to pension schemes and their tax treatment but was also the beginning of the type of complexity we see today. Because of the way the different sections of the Act interacted it became common for pension schemes to seek approval under *section 379* for 75% of the benefit offered and *section 388* for the remaining 25%. This method maximised the tax reliefs available whilst maintaining the greatest flexibility.

- 1959 (*National Insurance Act 1959*) – Introduced an earnings related State pension (the 'graduated pension') in addition to the basic old age pension. The earnings band covered was from £9 to £15 per week. In addition the concept of contracting out was first introduced. An employer could decide to establish a private scheme providing comparable benefits and pay reduced 'graduated contributions'.

- 1963 (*National Insurance Act 1963*) – Extended the range of earnings covered by the graduated State scheme to £18 per week.

- 1963 (*Contracts of Employment Act 1963*) – Stated every employee was to have a written statement setting out the terms of their employment including, for the first time, details of pension schemes.

- 1970 (*Finance Act 1970*) – Set out a 'new code' of approval for pension schemes effectively eliminating the old distinction between the *Income Tax Act 1952, ss 379* and *388*. Exempt approved schemes were those which had proved to the Inland Revenue that they complied with all the relevant regulations and were granted tax relief on the contributions of employers and employees and on the returns from investment.

- 1975 (*Social Security Pensions Act 1975*) – A major Act setting up the State Earnings Related Pension Scheme with effect from April 1978, replacing the previous Graduated

Appendix A

Pension Scheme. Also introduced the rules for contracting out.

- 1986 (*Financial Services Act 1986*) – Set out terms and conditions under which investment business could be conducted and provided for the authorisation of persons to conduct the business. Obviously trustees and administrators are responsible for investment of the scheme assets and this Act had a major effect on how they could discharge this part of their responsibilities.

- 1988 (*Income and Corporation Taxes Act 1988*) – Sets out conditions for approval of retirement benefit schemes and personal pension schemes.

- 1989 (*Social Security Act 1989*) – Covers equal treatment of males and females.

- 1989 (*Finance Act 1989*) – Earnings cap introduced.

- 1990 (*Social Security Act 1990*) – Created the Office of the Pensions Ombudsman.

- 1992 (*Social Security Contributions and Benefits Act 1992*) – A consolidation Act bringing together various social security pension regulations and Acts.

- 1992 (*Social Security Administration Act 1992*).

- 1993 (*Pension Schemes Act 1993*) – Introduced equal access. Pensions arising after 6 April 1997 to be increased in line with limited price indexation. Consolidated previous legislation.

- 1994 (*Finance Act 1994*) – Covers taxation of unapproved schemes and annuities.

- 1995 (*Finance Act 1995*) – Permits 'income drawdown' from personal pensions.

- 1995 (*Pensions Act 1995*) – Major response to the Maxwell scandal. Set up Occupational Pensions Regulatory Authority and Pension Compensation Board. Fundamental changes to the way in which pensions are governed and regulated. Formalised the appointment of member nominated trustees and gave new responsibilities to trustees and advisers with penalties for non-compliance. Strengthened equal access. Changed contracting-out test to current (2001) system.

- 1996 (*Employment Rights Act 1996*) – Gave personal pension scheme trustees the right to time off work to train and discharge their duties, and protected them from unfair dismissal.

- 1997 (*Finance (No 2) Act 1997*) – Removed tax credits granted to pension funds on company dividends thus removing the wholly tax fee status and reputedly costing them billions of pounds.

- 1998 (*Finance (No 2) Act 1998*) – Removed tax benefits from pension schemes in relation to advance corporation tax.

- 1999 (*Welfare Reform and Pensions Act 1999*) – Set out system for dealing with pensions on divorce.

- 2000 (*Child Support, Pensions and Social Security Act 2000*) – Provisions due to come in from 6 April 2002 at the earliest covering new State Second Pension (S2P). It also removes the current right for employers to obtain an 'opt out' from the member nominated trustee regulations, but no date has yet been set for this.

Appendix B

The Disclosure Regulations – Key Duties and Timescales

This Appendix shows the most commonly encountered elements of the *Occupational Pension Schemes (Disclosure of Information) Regulations 1996 SI No 1655* (the *Disclosure Regulations*). It is not intended to be a complete list. The table sets out the information which must be provided automatically or on request, and any provision which allows the trustees of a scheme to refuse to supply information if the same or similar information has been requested recently.

Information to be provided automatically

Type	To whom	When
Scheme details	*Prospective members*	Immediately where practicable, otherwise within 2 months of joining the scheme.
Material changes in scheme details	*Members* and *beneficiaries*	If possible before the event, otherwise within 3 months of the change.
Details of benefits becoming payable	Individual *members* or *beneficiaries*	Before or within 1 month of becoming payable or within 2 months for early retirement (but in the case of a *money purchase scheme* a statement of all the options available must be provided at least 6 months before retirement date).
Change of benefits in payment (if not already advised)	Individual *members* or *beneficiaries*	Before or within 1 month after change made.

Basic Guide to Pensions

Benefits not yet payable (i.e. benefit statements) under *money purchase schemes*	*Members*	Within 12 months of end of each *scheme year*.
Benefits on death	Individual *beneficiaries*	As soon as possible within 2 months of notification of death.
Benefits on withdrawal	Individual withdrawing *members*	As soon as possible within 2 months once the date of leaving is known.
Refunds to employer	*Members* and *beneficiaries*	First notice – at least 5 months before refund. Second notice – at least 3 months before refund.
Details of contributions not paid within 60 days of due date under the schedule of contributions or schedule of payments	Affected *members*	Within a further 30 days.

Information to be provided on request

Type	To whom	When
Scheme documents	*Members*, spouses, prospective members & spouse, *beneficiaries*, recognised trade unions	Within 2 months of request; no limit on repeat *requests*.
Details of participating employers	*Members*, spouses, prospective members & spouse, *beneficiaries*, recognised trade unions	Within 2 months of *request*; no limit on repeat *requests*.
Scheme details	*Members*, spouses, prospective members & spouse, *beneficiaries*, recognised trade unions	Within 2 months of *request*; no repeat *requests* within 1 year.

Appendix B

Salary-related benefits not yet payable under defined benefit or hybrid schemes (i.e. a benefit statement)	Individual active *members* or deferred *members*	Within 2 months of *request*; no repeat *requests* within 1 year.
Benefits on death	Representative of the *member* or their *beneficiaries*	Within 2 months of *request*; no repeat *requests* within 3 years.
Benefits for transfer in	Individual *members* or *prospective members*	Within 2 months of *request*; no repeat *requests* within 1 year.
Withdrawal benefits including refunds	Individual *members*	Within 2 months of *request*; no repeat *requests* within 1 year.
Estimate of transfer value	Individual active *members*, or deferred *members* of a *money purchase scheme*	Within 3 months of *request*; no repeat *requests* within 1 year.
Guaranteed statement of transfer value	Individual deferred *members* of a *salary related scheme*	Within 3 months and 10 working days of *request*; no repeat *requests* within 1 year.
Latest actuarial valuation report plus minimum funding requirement statement, schedule of contributions or schedule of payments and statement of investment principles	*Members*, spouses, *prospective members* & spouse, *beneficiaries, recognised trade unions*	Within 2 months of *request*; no limit on repeat *requests*.
Trustees' reports*	*Members*, spouses, *prospective members* & spouse, *beneficiaries, recognised trade unions*	Within 2 months of *request*; only 1 copy of the latest report otherwise no limit on repeat *requests*.

All information must be provided as soon as practicable after it is requested and, in any event, within the timescale indicated.

* The trustees' report must include the accounts and auditor's statement, the latest actuarial statement, and the latest certificate on the schedule of contributions. It must be available within 7 months of the end of the *scheme year*.

Disclosure definitions

Beneficiary

A *beneficiary* of a scheme means a person (other than a member of the scheme) who is entitled to payment of benefits under the scheme.

Member

A *member* of a scheme is any active member, deferred member or pensioner member of the scheme.

Money purchase scheme

A *money purchase scheme* means a pension scheme under which all the benefits that may be provided, other than death benefits, are money purchase benefits.

Prospective member

A *prospective member* of a scheme is any person who may opt to join the scheme, or any person who, under the terms of their contract of service and scheme rules, will become able to opt to join the scheme if they continue in the same employment for a sufficiently long period, or who will be admitted automatically unless he opts otherwise, or who may be admitted subject to the consent of his employer.

Recognised trade union

A *recognised trade union* means an independent union which is recognised to any extent for the purposes of collective bargaining in relation to members and prospective members of the scheme. Any dispute over whether a trade union is recognised may be referred to an employment tribunal.

Appendix B

Request

A *request* means a request in writing.

Scheme year

A *scheme year* means whichever of the following the trustees decide:

- the scheme year specified in the scheme's documentation;
- the 12 months commencing on 1 April; or
- the 12 months commencing on a date chosen by the trustees.

If the trustees decide to change the basis of the *scheme year*, *scheme year* can also be a period of between 6 and 18 months following the commencement of the last *scheme year*. Similarly, the *scheme year* in which the scheme commences or terminates may be a period of between 6 and 18 months.

Salary related scheme

A *salary related scheme* means a pension scheme which is not a *money purchase scheme*.

Glossary

1% age addition
An extra rebate (1% of upper band earnings) of NI contributions paid for tax years 1993/94 to 1995/96 inclusive for **members** of personal pension schemes aged 30 or over at the beginning of the tax year who are contracted out. See also incentive payment.

2% incentive
See incentive payment.

20% director
Sometimes used to refer to a controlling director.

87-89 member
See Class B **member**.

Abatement
A rule by which a person who retires from the public service, and then resumes his/her former employment, has a reduction in pension in order to ensure that the total of the pay and pension does not exceed pay at the time of retirement.

ABI 1994 method
A test to determine whether benefits under a money purchase scheme which is not a SSAS are within Inland Revenue funding limits. See also SSAS 1996 method.

Accelerated accrual
Provision by a scheme of an accrual rate greater than one sixtieth of pensionable earnings for each year of pensionable service. See also uplifted 60ths/80ths.

Accounting bases
The methods developed for applying fundamental accounting concepts to financial transactions for determining both the accounting period in which income and expenditure should be recognised and the amounts of assets and liabilities in the balance sheet or net assets statement.

Accounting policies
The specific accounting bases adopted to present fairly the financial results and position of an organisation. For a typical larger occupational pension scheme, these might include decisions on accounting for conversion of foreign currency, the valuation of investments and recognition of dividend income, and the extent to which the cash basis is used.

Accounting Standards Board (ASB)
The successor organisation to the Accounting Standards Committee which is now responsible for producing accounting standards. Previously published as Statements of Standard Accounting Practice, accounting standards are now issued by the ASB as Financial Reporting Standards, though the ASB has adopted standards extant at the time it came into existence. Standards are preceded by discussion papers and exposure drafts (EDs).

Accounting Standards Committee (ASC)
The organisation responsible until July 1990 for the issue of Statements of Standard Accounting Practice which are mandatory and Statements of Recommended Practice which are non-mandatory. In August 1990, the Accounting Standards Committee was replaced by the Accounting Standards Board.

Accrual rate
The rate at which rights build up for each year of pensionable service in a defined benefit scheme.

Accruals concept
The accounting principle whereby revenues and costs are recognised as they are earned or incurred, rather than when money is received or paid.

Accrued benefits
The benefits for service up to a given point in time, whether vested rights or not. They may be calculated in relation to current earnings or projected earnings. Allowance may also be made for revaluation and/or pension increases required by the scheme rules or legislation.

Accrued benefits valuation method
A valuation method in which the actuarial liability at the valuation date relates to:
(a) the benefits for pensioners and deferred pensioners and their dependants, allowing where appropriate for future increases; and

(b) the accrued benefits for **members** in service on the valuation date.

Allowance may be made for earnings and service to be projected to the end of the control period and for revaluation thereafter in which case allowance may also be made for replacing **members** assumed to leave during that period.

Accrued rights
The benefits to which a **member** is entitled, as of right, under an occupational pension scheme. These include accrued benefits. Depending on the context, accrued rights for an active **member** can be based on benefits as if the **member** had left service or could include a right to have benefits linked to future salary changes. The term is given various specific definitions in *PSA 1993* for the purposes of preservation, contracting out and the *Disclosure Regulations*. It is also given a specific meaning in *PA 1995* e.g. in relation to scheme amendments.

Accrued rights premium (ARP)
A **State scheme premium** which could have been paid for **members** below **State pensionable age** when a scheme which was contracted out by reference to the provision of a GMP ceased to be contracted out before 6 April 1997. In return the **member** was reinstated in SERPS for the period covered by the ARP.

Accumulated contributions
The total of contributions paid by a **member** of a pension scheme during a given period, enhanced where appropriate by interest. In a money purchase scheme the term may also include the employer's contributions.

Active investment management
A style of **investment** management which is designed to achieve, over a period of time, out performance of a benchmark by being selective in the individual investments.

Active member
A **member** of an occupational pension scheme who is at present accruing benefits under that scheme in respect of current service.

Actuarial assumptions
The set of assumptions as to rates of return, inflation, increase in earnings, dividend increases, mortality etc. used by the actuary in an actuarial valuation or other actuarial calculations.

Glossary

Actuarial basis
Commonly used to mean valuation method and/or actuarial assumptions.

Actuarial certificate
A certificate given by an actuary arising out of actuarial work. Examples are:

(*a*) the certificate in respect of the solvency test which is required for some contracted out schemes.

(*b*) the certificate given to the PSO in connection with the rules for dealing with pension scheme surpluses under *ICTA 1988, ss 599A–602*.

(*c*) the MFR certificate required under *PA 1995, ss 56–60*.

(*d*) the bulk transfer certificate required under *Occupational Pension Schemes (Preservation of Benefit) Regulations 1991 SI No 167, reg 12*.

Actuarial deficiency
The excess of the **actuarial liability** over the actuarial value of assets, on the basis of the valuation method and actuarial assumptions used. If an actuarial report refers to a surplus or deficiency, it must be studied to ascertain precisely what assets and liabilities have been taken into account. In a stricter sense the terms surplus and deficiency might be used in relation to the results of a discontinuance valuation.

Actuarial increase
An enhancement of benefits to compensate for the deferment of pension beyond the normal pension date.

Actuarial liability
The value placed on the liability of a pension fund for outgoings due after the date to which the calculations relate.

Actuarial reduction
A reduction made to a **member's** accrued pension benefits in order to offset any additional cost arising from their payment in advance of the normal pension date.

Actuarial report
A report on an actuarial valuation, or actuarial advice on the financial effects of changes in a pension scheme. A report on an actuarial valuation should conform to actuarial guidance issued by the Institute and Faculty of Actuaries.

Actuarial statement
The statement required by the Disclosure Regulations to be included in the annual report. It must show in the prescribed form the security of the accrued and prospective rights of **members** and be signed by an actuary.

Actuarial surplus
The excess of the actuarial value of assets over the actuarial liability on the basis of the valuation method and actuarial assumptions used. See note under actuarial deficiency.

Actuarial undertaking
See employer's undertaking.

Actuarial valuation
An investigation by an actuary into the ability of a pension scheme to meet its liabilities. This is usually to assess the funding level and a recommended contribution rate based on comparing the actuarial value of assets and the actuarial liability.

Actuarial value of assets
The value placed on the assets by the actuary. This may be market value, present value of estimated income and proceeds of sales or redemptions, or some other value.

Actuarial value of future contributions
The present value of assumed future contributions and income therefrom.

Actuarial value of liabilities
See actuarial liability.

Actuary
An adviser on financial questions involving probabilities relating to mortality and other contingencies. For statutory purposes in the UK, the term automatically includes Fellows of the Institute of Actuaries and of the Faculty of Actuaries. Persons with other actuarial qualifications may be approved by the Secretary of State for a specific purpose. See also scheme actuary.

Added years
The provision of extra benefits by reference to an additional period of pensionable service in a defined benefit scheme, arising from the receipt of a transfer payment, the paying of AVCs or by way of augmentation.

Additional component
See additional pension.

Additional pension
The earnings related part of the State pension payable under SERPS, which is additional to the basic pension.

Additional voluntary contributions (AVCs)
Contributions over and above a **member's** normal contributions if any, which the **member** elects to pay to the scheme in order to secure additional benefits. See also FSAVCs.

Administrator
1. The person or persons notified to the PSO as being responsible for the management of a pension scheme. See *ICTA 1988, s 611AA*.

2. The person who is responsible for the day to day administration of the pension scheme. See *Personal and Occupational Pension Schemes (Pensions Ombudsman) Regulations 1996 SI No 2475*.

3. A type of insolvency practitioner in relation to companies under the *Insolvency Act 1986*.

Age related payment
Payments made by the NICO to an appropriate scheme, COMPS or COMBS from 6 April 1997 for **members** who have contracted out. These increase with the age of the member. See also **contracted-out** rebate.

Age related rebate
See age related payment.

Aggregate method
A prospective benefits valuation method in which the recommended contribution rate is calculated as that which, if paid over the expected period of membership of active **members**, would provide for the excess of the present value of all their benefits over the actuarial value of assets.

Allocation
1. The facility for a **member** to give up (or allocate) part of his/her pension in exchange for a pension payable to the member's spouse or dependant. Also known as surrender.
2. The process of the application of payments to the benefits of individuals under an insured scheme using controlled funding.

Allowable maximum
See earnings cap.

Alternative arrangements
Arrangements proposed by the employer for the selection of trustees (or directors of a corporate trustee) instead of appropriate rules proposed by the trustees or prescribed rules under the MNT Regulations.

Alternatives to short service benefit
Benefits or options permitted as a partial or complete substitute for short service benefit under the preservation requirements of *PSA 1993*.

Amortisation
1. The spreading of an actuarial surplus or deficiency over an appropriate period.
2. An accountancy term for the reduction in value of an asset, such as leasehold property, caused by the passage of time. If the cause is not solely related to time, the corresponding term is depreciation.

Annual premium method
See level annual premium method.

Annual report
The means by which the trustees of an occupational pension scheme communicate financial and other information about the scheme to **members**, employers and other interested parties. The term is used in particular to describe the specific information which is required to be made available by trustees in relation to each scheme year under the Disclosure Regulations, the detailed content being described in the **pension scheme SORP**. This must include a copy of the audited accounts and of the latest actuarial statement and other information specified including a financial review by the trustees and

an investment report. Trustees often publish a simplified annual report for members containing the above material suitably summarised and, perhaps, illustrated.

Annuity
A series of payments, which may be subject to increases, made at stated intervals until a particular event occurs. This event is most commonly the end of a specified period or the death of the person receiving the annuity. An annuity may take one of a number of different forms including compulsory purchase annuity, deferred annuity, purchased life annuity and reversionary annuity.

Annuity certain
An annuity payable for a fixed period irrespective of whether the annuitant is alive.

Anti franking requirements
The requirements which ban the practice of franking at one time followed by some schemes, whereby statutory increases in GMP e.g. between termination of **contracted-out** employment and **State pensionable age** were offset against other scheme benefits, rather than being added to a **member's** total benefits. The requirements are covered in Chapter III of Part IV **PSA 1993**.

Appointed representative
See tied agent.

Appropriate additions
Amounts to be added when calculating the minimum benefit for the purpose of the **anti-franking requirements** in respect of any further benefit accruing after **contracted-out** employment ceases or any enhancement of benefits in excess of the GMP due to postponed payment.

Appropriate rules
Rules proposed by trustees for the selection by **members** of **member** nominated trustees or **member** nominated directors instead of using the prescribed rules set out in the MNT Regulations.

Appropriate scheme
A personal pension scheme or FSAVC scheme granted an appropriate scheme certificate by the NICO, enabling its **members** to use it for contracting out.

Appropriate scheme certificate
The certificate issued by the NICO to a personal pension scheme or to an FSAVC scheme confirming that the scheme satisfies the conditions required for contracting out.

Approval
The process by which the PSO grants tax exempt status to pension arrangements providing they meet legislative requirements. Occupational pension schemes are approved under *Chapter I, Part XIV ICTA 1988*, retirement annuity contracts under *Chapter III, Part XIV ICTA 1988* and personal pension schemes under *Chapter IV, Part XIV ICTA 1988*. An approved occupational pension scheme may also be an exempt approved scheme. See also discretionary approval and mandatory approval.

Approved occupations list
A list published by the **PSO** of occupations from which **members** can take their benefits before age 60 for **retirement annuities** and 50 for **personal pension schemes**.

Approved scheme
A **retirement benefits scheme** which is approved by the Inland Revenue under *Chapter I, Part XIV ICTA 1988*, including an **FSAVC scheme**. The term may also be used to describe a **personal pension scheme** approved under *Chapter IV* of that Part. See also **exempt approved scheme**.

Article 119
Article 119 of the Treaty of Rome, providing that men and women are entitled to equal pay for equal work. See also **Barber judgment** and **Coloroll judgment**.

Asset allocation strategy
The splitting of the **assets** of a **pension scheme** between the various asset classes such as equities, fixed interest and cash. This will primarily reflect the long-term needs of the fund, the 'strategic view', but may be adjusted to favour particular **asset** classes or markets which look attractive in the short term, the 'tactical view'.

Asset and liability matching
A process of selecting **assets** which are likely to generate proceeds approximately equal to the cashflow needed to meet the **liabilities** as they occur under different economic scenarios. An example of this would be the matching of a level pension with fixed interest securities.

Asset and liability modelling
A technique used to test the effect of different economic scenarios on the **assets** and **liabilities** of an **occupational pension scheme**, the inter-relationship between them, the **funding ratio** and contribution rates.

Assets
The items such as investments, cash and **debtors**, to which the **trustees** of a **pension scheme** have title.

Associated employers
Companies where one directly or indirectly controls the other or where each is controlled by the same party. *ICTA 1988, s 590A* provides a precise definition. Practice Notes (IR12) allow associated employers to participate within the same **exempt approved scheme** without prejudice to its status.

Associated employments
Employment by **associated employers** where the employers have made arrangements with the same **occupational pension scheme**.

Attained age method
A **prospective benefits valuation method** in which the **actuarial liability** makes allowance for projected earnings. The **standard contribution rate** is that necessary to cover the cost of all benefits which will accrue to existing **members** after the **valuation date** by reference to total earnings throughout their future working lifetimes projected to the dates on which benefits become payable.

Audited Accounts Regulations
The *Occupational pension schemes (Requirement to Obtain Audited Accounts and a Statement from the Auditor) Regulations 1996 SI No 1975* made under *PA 1995, s 41* which deal with the content of **financial statements** and the **auditor's report** of an **occupational pension scheme**.

Auditor
An individual or firm appointed to report on the accounts of an entity. The results of their examination are incorporated within an **auditor's report**. See also **scheme auditor**.

Auditor's report
A report given by an **auditor** on a set of accounts. Under the **Audited Accounts Regulations**, the **scheme auditor** has to provide a report on whether the scheme accounts give a **true and fair view** and contain the information required by those Regulations.

Auditor's statement
A statement given by the **scheme auditor**, required by the **Audited Accounts Regulations**, on whether the contributions to the scheme have been paid in accordance with the **schedule of contributions** and/or **payment schedule**.

Augmentation
The provision of additional benefits in respect of particular **members** of an **occupational pension scheme**, normally where the cost is borne by the scheme and/or the **employer**.

Average earnings scheme
See **career average scheme**.

Average remaining service life
As defined by **SSAP 24**, a weighted average of the expected future **service** of the current **members** of the scheme up to their **normal pension dates** or expected dates of earlier withdrawal or death in service.

Balance sheet
A financial statement of the **assets** and **liabilities** of an entity at a particular date designed to give a true and fair view of the state of affairs. In **pension scheme** accounts, a **net assets statement** is required rather than a **balance sheet**.

Balanced management
A style of **investment** management where the **investment manager** is free to invest in all **asset** classes. This is in contrast to specialist management. Sometimes **trustees** will place some constraints on the manager such as not to invest in property or venture capital.

Band earnings
See **upper band earnings**.

Barber judgment
The judgment of the European Court of Justice in the case of *Barber v Guardian Royal Exchange* on 17 May 1990, which confirmed that pensions count as pay for the purposes of **Article 119**.

Basic component
See **basic pension**.

Basic pension
The flat rate (not earnings related) State pension paid to all who have met the minimum NI contribution requirements. The amount paid is increased if the recipient is married and a spouse or widow(er) may claim on the record of his/her spouse.

Benchmark
A yardstick against which performance is to be judged. Most commonly used to assess the investment performance of a fund or portfolio. See also **investment** performance measurement.

Beneficiary
A person entitled to benefit under a **pension scheme** or who will become entitled on the happening of a specified event.

Benefit statement
A statement or estimate of benefits payable in respect of an individual's membership of a scheme on the occurrence of specific events.

Benefits Agency (BA)
An executive agency of the DSS which administers the payment of State benefits.

Benefits in kind
Benefits other than cash provided as remuneration for an employment. In a pensions context only those which are taxable may be included for pension purposes. Also known as P11D benefits.

Block transfer
See **bulk transfer**.

Blowing the whistle
See **whistle blowing**.

Bonus sacrifice
A **salary sacrifice** arrangement whereby an employee agrees not to receive part or all of a bonus payment, in the expectation that a corresponding amount will be paid into a pension arrangement, by the **employer**, for the employee's benefit.

Book cost
The total purchase cost at which investments were acquired.

Book reserve scheme
An unfunded **occupational pension scheme** which is accounted for by a provision in the employer's accounts.

Book value
An ambiguous term which may be used to mean **book cost, historical cost, carrying value** or **net book value**.

Bridging pension
An additional pension paid from a scheme between retirement and **State pensionable age**, which is usually replaced by the State pension payable from that age.

Bulk transfer
The transfer of a group of **members** from one **occupational pension scheme** to another, usually with an enhanced **transfer payment** in comparison with an individual's **cash equivalent**. The **PSO** must be consulted about any such transfer payments.

Buy back
1. The payment of a **State scheme premium** to reinstate in **SERPS** the rights of a **member** who has been **contracted out**. Since 5 April 1997 only available in limited circumstances.
2. The purchase by a company of its own shares.

Buy out
The purchase by **trustees** of a **pension scheme** of an insurance policy in the name of a **member** or other **beneficiary**, in lieu of entitlement to benefit from the scheme, following termination of the member's **pensionable service**. Sometimes also used to refer to the purchase of an insurance policy in the name of the **trustees**. See also **section 32 policy**.

Cancellation notice
A document issued to an investor by the **pension provider** outlining the investor's legal right to cancel the contract within a specified period of receiving the notice.

Career average revalued scheme
A **career average scheme** where benefits are revalued by reference to an appropriate index during **pensionable service**.

Career average scheme
A scheme where the benefit for each year of membership is related to the **pensionable earnings** for that year.

Carry back
The election by a member of a **personal pension scheme** or a **retirement annuity** policyholder to have the **member's** contribution or part of it treated for tax purposes as having been paid in the tax year immediately before that in which it was paid, or, in the absence of **net relevant earnings** in that year, in the tax year before that. Carry back does not apply to **employer's** contributions.

Carry forward
The election by a member of a **personal pension scheme** or a **retirement annuity** policyholder to carry forward **unused relief** from previous tax years to the current tax year. Carry forward does not apply to employer's contributions.

Carrying value
The amount at which an **asset** is stated in the accounting records and **financial statements** of an entity. It may comprise cost less depreciation or may be a revalued amount.

Cash accumulation policy
See **deposit administration**.

Cash basis
A method of accounting under which the transactions are accounted for only at the time money is received or paid. This is in contrast to the **accruals concept**.

Cash equivalent
The amount which a **member** of a **pension scheme** may, under *PSA 1993, s 94*, require to be applied as a **transfer payment** to another permitted pension scheme or to a **buy-out** policy.

Cash option
See **commutation**.

Centralised scheme
An **occupational pension scheme** operated on behalf of several **employers**.

Certificate A
A statement required by the **OPB** from an **actuary** specifying that over the period covered by the certificate, the **assets** of a **contracted-out** scheme are expected to be adequate to meet **GMPs** and other **priority liabilities** in the event that the scheme winds up. Replaced from 6 April 1997 by **Certificate T**.

Certificate of eligibility
A certificate completed by an employee stating that he is eligible to contribute to a **personal pension**. It is required when joining a **personal pension scheme** and thereafter, whenever a self-employed **member** becomes employed, whenever an employed member changes **employer**, and when five years have elapsed since the completion of the previous certificate.

Certificate of existence
A document confirming that a person entitled to a pension is still alive.

Certificate T
A certificate signed by the **scheme actuary** after 5 April 1997, certifying for a **COSRS** whether certain **liabilities** are 100% funded in accordance with the **valuation method** specified for the **MFR**.

Certified amount (CA)
That part of a **contributions equivalent premium** which may be recovered out of any refund of scheme contributions to the **member**.

Class A (or B or C) members
Terms derived from specimen rules issued by the **PSO**, applying to **members** of **occupational pension schemes** who joined during specified periods. Differing **Inland Revenue limits** apply to each Class. Class A members of schemes established on or after 14 March 1989 and all new members of earlier schemes joining on or after 1 June 1989.

Glossary

Class B members of schemes established before 14 March 1989 who joined between 17 March 1987 and 31 May 1989. Class C members who joined schemes before 17 March 1987. A member may be exempt from treatment as a Class A or B member under transitional arrangements. Class B members or (where **scheme rules** permit) Class C members may elect to be treated as Class A members, but will then be subject to the **earnings cap**.

Closed scheme
A **pension scheme** which does not admit new **members**. Contributions may or may not continue and benefits may or may not be provided for future **service**.

Clustering
See **segmentation**.

Coloroll judgment
The judgment by the European Court of Justice on 28 September 1994 which clarified the temporal limitations of the **Barber judgment** and decided that **trustees** of **occupational pension schemes** bear joint responsibility with **employers** for equalisation. Receiving schemes are responsible for equalising benefits provided by transfers; **AVCs** are exempt from equalisation.

Commingled fund
Sometimes used to describe a **common investment fund** or an exempt unit trust.

Common investment fund (CIF)
An arrangement whereby **assets** of two or more **occupational pension schemes**, operated by a single **employer** or a group of **associated employers**, are added together for **investment**. This is not a **pooled fund** although pooled forms of investment can be used.

Commutation
The giving up of a part or all of the pension payable from retirement for an immediate lump sum.

Commutation factors
Factors used to determine the amount of pension which needs to be forgone in order to provide a given lump sum benefit.

Compensation Board
See **Pensions Compensation Board**.

Compliance audit
1. An audit at the instigation of the **PSO** to ensure compliance with Inland Revenue requirements.
2. An audit carried out to ensure compliance with the rules and regulations imposed by *FSA 1986*.

Compliance statement
A statement which the **Pension scheme SORP** suggests should be included in the **annual report** of an **occupational pension scheme** and which provides information which regulations require to be disclosed to **members** in that report. It may also be used to provide information which is disclosed voluntarily but which is not of such significance that it should be included in the **trustee report**.

Compulsory purchase annuity (CPA)
An **annuity** which must be purchased on retirement for a **member** of an insured **occupational pension scheme**. See also **open market option**.

Concentration of investment
Placing a significant proportion of the **assets** of a **pension scheme** in any single investment. The amounts requiring compulsory **disclosure** and reporting are laid down by *PA 1995*.

Connected scheme
A scheme operated by an **associated employer** which has provided benefits during periods of concurrent employment. Defined in *ICTA 1988, s 590A*.

Contingent annuity
An **annuity** payable to a person, if alive, on the death of another.

Contingent asset/liability
Assets and liabilities, the realisation of which is not certain but is dependent on the occurrence of a future event.

Continuation option
A facility offered by an insurance company which insures a scheme's death benefits, whereby a **member** leaving the scheme can effect a life assurance policy without evidence of health.

Glossary

Continued rights
Used in **Practice Notes (IR12)** to refer to the rights of scheme **members** who continue to be subject to pre-existing **Inland Revenue limits**, including both **pre-17 March 1987 continued rights** and **pre-1 June 1989 continued rights**.

Continuous service
Treatment by an **occupational pension scheme** of the **pensionable service** of a **member** as continuous with a previous period of pensionable service (within the same scheme or another scheme). Pensionable service can be treated as continuous where for example:

(*a*) a **member** moves from employment with one **participating employer** to another who also participates in the scheme;

(*b*) there is a gap in pensionable service e.g. for absence abroad or maternity leave;

(*c*) a member ceases to be in **pensionable service** in one scheme and enters service in another and there is a connection between the two schemes e.g. they relate to service with the same **employer** or an **associated employer**. See also **continued rights**.

Contract out
The use of a **pension scheme** which meets certain conditions to provide benefits (**GMPs, protected rights** or **section 9(2B) rights**) in place of **SERPS**. The conditions for contracting out are set out in *PSA 1993*.

Contracted out/contracted in
A **pension scheme** is contracted out where it provides benefits in place of **SERPS** and has been given a **contracting-out certificate** or **appropriate scheme certificate** by the **NICO**. Members are contracted out if they are in employment which is contracted out by reference to an **occupational pension scheme** or have elected to **contract out** via a **personal pension** or **FSAVC scheme**. A pension scheme is commonly called contracted in where it is not **contracted out** i.e. it provides benefits in addition to **SERPS**. The term 'contracted in' is not used in *PSA 1993* or *PA 1995*.

Contracted-out deduction
The amount deducted from a person's **SERPS** benefits for the period of being **contracted out**.

259

Basic Guide to Pensions

Contracted Out Employments Group (COEG)
The directorate of the **NICO** which deals principally with the administration of **contracted-out** employment and related matters.

Contracted out mixed benefit scheme (COMBS)
An **occupational pension scheme** which has separate defined benefit and **money purchase** sections and which contracts out on both bases (permitted by *PA 1995, s 149*).

Contracted out money purchase scheme (COMPS)
An **occupational pension scheme**, including a **defined benefit scheme**, which is **contracted out** on a **money purchase** basis i.e. where the **employer** pays **minimum payments** towards **protected rights**. Sometimes used more narrowly to refer to a **defined contribution scheme** which is contracted out on a money purchase basis.

Contracted out protected rights premium (COPRP)
A **State scheme premium** which could have been paid by a scheme which was **contracted out** by reference to the provision of **protected rights**, in order to purchase benefits in **SERPS** for a **member**, if the scheme ceased to **contract out** before 6 April 1997.

Contracted-out rebate
The amount by which the **employer's** and employee's NI contributions are reduced or **rebated** in respect of employees who are **contracted out** by virtue of their membership of an **appropriate scheme** or an **occupational pension scheme**. The contracted-out rebate consists of a flat rate rebate and (for appropriate schemes and **COMPS**) an **age related payment**.

Contracted out salary related scheme (COSRS)
An **occupational pension scheme** which is **contracted out** on a salary related basis i.e. by providing benefits (**section 9(2B) rights**) which are broadly equivalent to or better than those specified under the **reference scheme test**. Prior to 6 April 1997, COSRS were contracted out by reference to the provision of a **GMP**.

Contracting-out certificate
The certificate issued by the **NICO**, in respect of an **occupational pension scheme** which satisfies the conditions for contracting out, confirming that the employees in the employments named in the **Certificate** are to be treated as being in **contracted-out** employment.

Glossary

Contractual commitment
A legally binding obligation contained within a contract. The **Pension scheme SORP** requires disclosure of contractual commitments in scheme accounts.

Contribution holiday
A period during which **ordinary annual contributions** and/or **member's normal contributions** are temporarily suspended, normally when the fund is in **surplus**. Sometimes used loosely when contributions continue to be paid but at a reduced rate.

Contribution schedule
See **schedule of contributions**.

Contributions equivalent premium (CEP)
A **State scheme premium** which may be paid when a **member** leaves with less than two years **qualifying service**. In return, the member is reinstated in **SERPS** for the period covered by the CEP.

Contributory scheme
A scheme which requires contributions from **active members** (even if such contributions are temporarily suspended during a **contribution holiday**).

Control period
The period under an **accrued benefits valuation method** over which the **standard contribution rate** is calculated to remain constant assuming that at the beginning and end of the period the **funding ratio** is 100%.

Controlled funding
A **funding plan** which has regard to the **liabilities** of a **pension scheme** as a whole, rather than those for individual **members**. Most commonly used in connection with insured **final salary schemes**.

Controlling director
A director who, on his own or with associates, owns or controls 20% or more of the ordinary shares of the employing company or has done so at any time after 16 March 1987 and within ten years of retirement or leaving **service** or **pensionable service**. Special restrictions apply to controlling directors who are **members** of **approved schemes**. The full definition is set out in **Practice Notes (IR12)**(1991).

The term **20% director** is used in **Practice Notes (IR12)**(1979), which also contains references to former **controlling directors** as defined in earlier legislation.

Cooling off notice
See **cancellation notice**.

Cooling off period
A specified period during which an investor has a legal right to cancel a pension or **investment** related insurance policy without penalty. See also **cancellation notice**.

Corporate governance
The system whereby boards of directors are responsible for the governance of their companies upon appointment by shareholders, who ensure that an appropriate governance structure is in place.

Corporate trustee
A company which acts as a **trustee**. See also **trust corporation**.

Creditors
See **current liabilities**.

CREST
The computerised system for settling sales and purchases of shares. It enables shares to be held in electronic form as a computer record, rather than a paper certificate. CREST was introduced in stages starting in July 1996, and is became fully operational during 1997, applying only to UK equity investments.

Current assets
Assets which are not investments or fixed **assets** and which are essentially short term, such as debtors, payments in advance (**prepayments**), short-term deposits and cash.

Current funding level
The **funding level** at the present time, where the **actuarial liability** in respect of **active members** is taken as the **present value** of **accrued benefits** calculated in relation to current earnings, revalued as for preserved pensions on the statutory basis (or such higher basis as has been promised).

Glossary

Current liabilities
Creditors to be paid in the near future, such as amounts due to the suppliers of goods and services and sums to be paid in respect of benefits already due to **members** at the accounting date.

Current unit method
An **accrued benefits valuation method** in which the **actuarial liability** is based on earnings at the **valuation date**. The **standard contribution rate** is that necessary to cover the cost of benefits which will accrue in the **control period** following the valuation date by reference to earnings projected to the end of that period and non discretionary **revaluation** thereafter.

Custodian
An organisation which undertakes the role of holding and accounting for **assets** in a portfolio on behalf of an **investment manager** or **trustees**.

Custodian trustee
A **trustee** responsible for holding the **assets** of a **trust**, other trustees being responsible for the management of the trust including the **investment** decisions. See also **trust corporation**.

De minimis limit
1. The limit below which a pension is so small that it can be fully exchanged for cash.
   Currently £260 p.a. under contracting-out and **preservation** requirements, and **Inland Revenue limits**. See also **trivial pension**.
2. The limit below which maximum funding checks are not required by the **PSO** for insured **money purchase scheme**s and **SSASs**.

Debt on the employer
The statutory debt due from the **employer** to a **defined benefit scheme** (subject to exceptions) where, on **winding up** of the scheme or liquidation of an employer; the **assets** are insufficient to meet the **actuarial liabilities** calculated on a prescribed basis. The relevant statutory provisions are *PA 1995, s 75* and the *Occupational Pension Schemes (Deficiency on Winding up etc.) Regulations 1996 SI No 3128*.

Debtors
See **current assets**.

Declaration of trust
A formal document or part of a document establishing the **trusts** of a **pension scheme**.

Deed
A legal document which in England and Wales makes it clear that it is intended to be a deed and which, in the case of an individual, is signed in the presence of an attesting witness or, in the case of a corporation, is executed in accordance with company law (*Law of Property (Miscellaneous Provisions) Act 1989, s 1*).
In Scotland, deed has no technical legal meaning, although it is used in practice to describe some documents. These would normally then be executed in accordance with the *Requirements of Writing (Scotland) Act 1995*.

Deed of adherence
A **deed** admitting a new **employer** to an **occupational pension scheme** and containing an undertaking by the new **employer** to comply with the provisions of the scheme.

Deed of appointment
A **deed** by which a new **trustee** is appointed.

Deed of covenant
Sometimes used for **deed of adherence**.

Deed poll
A **deed** made by one party for the benefit of (and enforceable by) specified persons who are not parties to the deed.

Deferred annuity
An **annuity** which commences from a future date.

Deferred (delayed) annuity purchase
An option available to a **member** of a **SSAS, personal pension**, or **defined contribution scheme** under which the purchase of an **annuity** can be deferred to no later than age 75. In the meantime, income can be withdrawn from the fund.

Deferred maintenance order
See **earmarking**.

Deferred member
A **member** entitled to **preserved benefits**. Sometimes incorrectly used to mean a member who has **postponed retirement**.

Glossary

Deferred pensioner
A person entitled to **preserved benefits**. Sometimes referred to as a **deferred member**. Sometimes used confusingly to mean a **member** who has **postponed retirement**.

Deferred retirement
See **postponed retirement** and **late retirement**.

Deficiency
See **actuarial deficiency**.

Defined accrued benefits method
An **accrued benefits valuation method** in which the **actuarial liability** is based on the benefits that would arise if the scheme were to discontinue at the **valuation date**. The **standard contribution rate** is that necessary to cover both the cost of benefit payments in the ongoing scheme and the **accrued benefits** in the event of future **discontinuance**.

Defined benefit scheme
A scheme where the **scheme rules** define the benefits independently of the contributions payable, and benefits are not directly related to the investments of the scheme. The scheme may be funded or unfunded.

Defined contribution scheme
See **money purchase scheme**.

Definitive trust deed
The detailed **trust deed** which follows an **interim trust deed**.

Dependant
A person who is financially dependent on a **member** or **pensioner** or was so at the time of death or retirement of the member or pensioner. **Scheme rules** may define a dependant differently.
For **PSO** purposes, a spouse qualifies automatically as a dependant and a child of the member or pensioner may always be regarded as a **dependant** until attaining the age of 18 or ceasing to receive full-time educational or vocational training, if later.

Dependant's (pension) option
See definition 1 of **allocation**.

Deposit administration
An insurance policy under which contributions, net of expense charges, are accumulated in a pool to which interest and usually bonuses are added. The proceeds are applied to provide pensions and other benefits as they become due.

Derivatives
A generic term for financial instruments used in the management of portfolios, such as **futures contracts** and **options**.

Direct investment
The method of investment for a **self administered scheme** by which the securities are held directly by or on behalf of the **trustees** and do not involve any form of insurance contract.

Disability benefit
A benefit paid to an employee who is unable to work for medical reasons.

Disclosure
1. A requirement introduced by *PSA 1993* (formerly *SSPA 1975*) and strengthened by *PA 1995* for **pension scheme**s to disclose information about the scheme and benefits to interested parties.
2. Rules introduced by **PIA** and other regulatory bodies to disclose product and commission information to the purchasers of life assurance and insured pension products.

Disclosure Regulations
Regulations issued under *PSA 1993* and *PA 1995* requiring **disclosure** of information about **pension scheme**s and benefits to interested parties. The main regulations are the *Occupational Pension Schemes (Disclosure of Information) Regulations 1996 SI No 1655*.

Discontinuance
The cessation of contributions to a **pension scheme** leading either to **winding up** or to the scheme becoming a **paid up scheme**.

Discontinuance valuation
An **actuarial valuation** carried out to assess the position if the scheme were to be discontinued. The valuation may take into account the possible exercise of any discretion to augment benefits. See also **discontinuance**.

Discretionary approval
Approval by the **PSO** using its wide discretionary powers (under *ICTA 1988, s 591*) of **occupational pension schemes** which do not fully conform to the conditions set out in *ICTA 1988, s 590* (and so do not qualify for **mandatory approval**).

Discretionary increase
An increase in a pension in payment or in a **preserved benefit** arising on a discretionary basis i.e. other than from a system of **escalation** or **indexation**. Such an increase may be of a regular or an ad hoc nature.

Discretionary scheme
An **occupational pension scheme** in which the employees to be offered membership are selected by the **employer**. Often the benefits, or the contributions from which they are to be provided are also decided individually for each member.

Discretionary trust
A trust where the benefits are payable at someone's discretion (usually the **trustees**).

Disqualification order
An order made by **OPRA** under *PA 1995, s 29* disqualifying a person from being a **trustee** of any **occupational pension scheme**. See also **prohibition order** and **suspension order**.

Disregard
See **State pension disregard**.

Documentation certificate
A certificate used in lieu of submitting detailed scheme documentation, either in seeking or maintaining Inland Revenue **approval** in certain cases or to satisfy contracting-out requirements of the **OPB** before 6 April 1997.

Drawdown facility
See **income withdrawal**.

Dynamisation/dynamism
1. The **index linking** of earnings either for calculating scheme benefits or for determining **final remuneration** for the purpose of **Inland Revenue limits**.
2. Sometimes used to describe **escalation** or **indexation**.

Early leaver
A person who ceases to be an **active member** of a **pension scheme**, other than on death, without being granted an immediate retirement benefit.

Early leaver revaluation
See definition 1 of **revaluation**.

Early retirement
The retirement of a **member** with immediate retirement benefit before **normal pension date**. The benefit may be reduced because of early payment. See also **ill-health early retirement**.

Earmarked money purchase scheme
An **occupational pension scheme** providing **money purchase** benefits under which all the benefits are secured by one or more policies of insurance or **annuity** contracts, such policies or contracts being specifically allocated to the provision of benefits for individual **members** and/or their **dependants**.

Earmarked policy
Used in **Practice Notes (IR12)** to denote a policy held by a **pension scheme**, where each **annuity** or sum assured is earmarked to provide benefits for or in respect of an individual **member**.

Earmarking
An order of the court, made under amendments introduced by *PA 1995*, when a **member** of an **occupational pension scheme** or **personal pension scheme** divorces, directing the **trustees** or **managers** to pay some or all of the member's benefits to the ex-spouse at the time they become payable to the member. See also **pension splitting**.

Earnings cap
Limitation introduced by *FA 1989* on the amount of remuneration on which the benefits and contributions of a **member** who is subject to the Inland Revenue post-89 maximum benefit limits (i.e. a **member** without **continued rights**) may be based. This was set at £60,000 for tax year 1989/90, and is usually increased annually in line with prices. The same limitation applies to **net relevant earnings** for all members of **personal pension schemes** for tax years 1989/90 onwards. Also known as the **permitted maximum** (*ICTA 1988, s 590C*) or **allowable maximum** (*ICTA 1988, s 640A*).

Earnings factor
A notional amount of earnings used for the purpose of calculating state scheme benefits or **GMPs**.

Earnings limits
See **lower earnings limit** and **upper earnings limit**.

Eligibility
The conditions which must be met for a person to be a **member** of a scheme or to receive a particular benefit. These may, for example, relate to age, **service**, status and type of employment.

Employee trustees
Trustees of an **occupational pension scheme** who are employees of a **participating employer**. Employee trustees are given various protections under the *Employment Rights Act 1996* (formerly *PA 1995*). Employee trustees need not be **member nominated trustees**.

Employer
The person or body with whom the **member** of a **pension scheme** has a contract of employment relevant to that scheme. This term is to be preferred to 'company' as having more general application in the context of pension schemes. See also **principal employer** and **participating employer**.

Employer related investment (ERI)
Investment of the **assets** of the scheme in a **participating employer** or associate, by way of, for example, shares or other securities, land and property used by the employer and loans (*PA 1995, s 40*). See also **restricted employer related investment**.

Employer's normal contributions
See **ordinary annual contributions**.

Employer's undertaking
Commonly used for an undertaking given in a prescribed form by an **employer** to inform the **actuary** whether any of the specified events, which are likely to invalidate any certificate required for contracting-out purposes, have occurred. Continues after 6 April 1997 as long as a **Certificate A** is in place. Incorporated into the **trustees' undertaking** when a **Certificate T** is signed. Sometimes known as an **actuarial undertaking**.

Endowment assurance policy
A policy which provides a lump sum at a fixed future date or on earlier death.

Enhanced commutation factor
Used in **Practice Notes (IR12)** to denote a **commutation factor** that includes allowance for prospective **pension increases** for which provision is made in the **scheme rules**.

Entry age method
A **prospective benefits valuation method** in which the **new entrant contribution rate** is taken as the **standard contribution rate**.

Entry date
The date on which an employee is permitted to join, or actually joins a **pension scheme**.

Equal access
Identical entry conditions to **occupational pension schemes** for each sex. This is required by *PA 1995* strengthening earlier provisions in *PSA 1993*.

Equal treatment
The principle requiring one sex to be treated no less favourably than the other, as embodied in EC Council Directive 86/378. Now enacted in the UK under *PA 1995, ss 62–66*.

Equivalent pension benefit (EPB)
The benefit which must be provided for an employee who was contracted out of the former **graduated pension scheme**. See also **payment in lieu**.

Escalation
A system whereby pensions in payment and/or **preserved benefits** are automatically increased at regular intervals and at a fixed percentage rate. The percentage may be restricted to the increase in a specified index. See also **indexation**.

Ex gratia benefit
A benefit provided by the **employer** which he is not legally required to provide.

Glossary

Excess benefits/contributions
Benefits provided by/contributions to a **COMPS** or an **appropriate scheme** which are over and above the **protected rights** benefits/contributions. These benefits/contributions are not subject to the rules applying to protected rights benefits/contributions.

Exchange of letters
Used where a letter from an **employer** to an employee constitutes part or all of the documentation for an **individual arrangement**, and a copy is signed by the employee to signify acknowledgement of its terms. Where the letter does not itself incorporate a **declaration of trust**, it will usually be coupled with a formal **declaration of trust** to ensure that the arrangement is legally enforceable.

Executive scheme
An **occupational pension scheme** for selected directors and/or senior employees. See also **discretionary scheme**.

Exempt approved scheme
An **approved scheme** (other than a **personal pension scheme**) which is established under irrevocable **trust** (or exceptionally, subject to a formal direction under *ICTA 1988, s 592(1)(b)*) thus giving rise to the tax reliefs specified in *ICTA 1988*.

Exempt unit trust
A unitised form of investment, specifically designed for **pension funds** and charities, which enjoys the same tax advantages as a directly invested pension fund's **assets**. It is normally managed by an investment organisation.

Experience deficiency/surplus
An **actuarial deficiency** or **surplus** which arises because events have not coincided with the **actuarial assumptions** made for the last valuation.

Expression of wish
A means by which a **member** can indicate a preference as to who should receive any lump sum death benefit. The choice is not binding on the **trustees**, and as a result inheritance tax is normally avoided.

External investment manager
An **investment manager**, normally a third party, not employed solely by the **trustees** or by the **employer**.

FAS 87 & FAS 88
FAS 87 is the US Financial Accounting Standards Board's statement which deals with accounting for **pension costs** in **employers'** accounts. FAS 88 applies to **employers'** accounts when a scheme is wound up or if benefits are settled on termination of employment.

Final average earnings
See **final pensionable earnings**.

Final pay scheme
See **final salary scheme**.

Final pensionable earnings/pay/salary
The **pensionable earnings** on which the benefits are calculated in a **final salary scheme**. The earnings may be based on the average over a number of consecutive years prior to retirement, death or leaving **pensionable service**.

Final remuneration
The maximum amount of earnings which the **PSO** will permit to be used for the purpose of calculating **maximum approvable benefits**. The permissible alternatives are set out fully in **Practice Notes (IR12)**. See also **earnings cap**.

Final salary scheme
A **defined benefit scheme** where the benefit is calculated by reference to the **final pensionable earnings** of the **member**, usually also based on **pensionable service**.

Financial reporting standard (FRS)
An accounting standard issued by the **Accounting Standards Board**.

Financial statements
The formal presentation of accounting information in a structured manner, the objective of which is to provide information about the financial position, performance and financial adaptability of the reporting enterprise. The recommended contents of the financial statements of **occupational pension schemes** are contained within the **Pension scheme SORP**. The **Audited Accounts Regulations**, which specify the contents of statutory financial statements, use the term 'accounts' rather than 'financial statements'.

Fixed rate revaluation
A method used by a **COSRS** to revalue **GMP** between termination of **contracted-out** employment and age 65 (men), 60 (women) as one of the alternatives to applying **section 148 orders**. The rate changes periodically.

Flat rate scheme
A **defined benefit scheme** which provides a benefit for each year of **pensionable service** not related to earnings.

Fluctuating emoluments
That part of an employee's earnings which is not paid on a fixed basis but is additional to the basic wage or salary. It may include profit-related pay, bonuses and **benefits in kind**.

Forfeiture
The termination (or suspension) of all or part of the benefits under an **occupational pension scheme** because of some action of the **member** or **beneficiary**. The circumstances in which forfeiture can take place are limited by *PA 1995, ss 91–95* and regulations e.g. bankruptcy, assignment or exercise of **lien rule**.

FRAG 21/94 report
A report by those responsible for the custody of the **assets** of a scheme. It describes the control policies and procedures they have put in place to ensure the safe keeping of assets in their care. The report includes an opinion by an **auditor** on the appropriateness of the controls and whether they are functioning so as to achieve the control objectives set.

Franking
See **anti-franking requirements**.

Free cover
The maximum amount of death or **disability benefit** which an insurance company covering a group of lives is prepared to insure for each individual without production of evidence of health.

Free standing additional voluntary contribution scheme
A scheme established by a **pension provider** to accept **FSAVCs**.

Free standing additional voluntary contributions (FSAVCs)
Contributions to a pension contract separate from an **occupational pension scheme**, effected by an **active member** of that scheme.

Benefits are secured with a **pension provider** by contributions from the member only. It is possible to **contract out** by using an **FSAVC scheme** in which case **contracted-out rebates** will be received.

Frozen benefit
A **preserved benefit**, strictly one not subject to **revaluation**.

Frozen scheme
A **closed scheme** where no further contributions are payable, no further benefits accrue and **members** are entitled to **preserved benefits**. See also **paid up scheme**.

Fully insured scheme
A scheme where the **trustees** have effected an insurance contract in respect of each **member** which guarantees benefits corresponding at all times to those promised under the **rules**. Sometimes incorrectly used to mean insured scheme.

Fund account
A **financial statement** included in a scheme's annual accounts which gives details of the scheme's dealings with **members** and **investment income** and capital movements during the **scheme year**. The fund account is required by the **Audited Accounts Regulations** and is described in the **Pension scheme SORP**.

Fund manager
See **investment manager**. Sometimes used to mean the person at the **principal employer** who is responsible for the management and administration of the scheme.

Funded unapproved retirement benefits scheme (FURBS)
A funded **occupational pension scheme** which is not designed to be approved by the **PSO**. It is not subject to **Inland Revenue limits** and is thus unable to take advantage of the tax exemptions available to **exempt approved schemes**. Most FURBS are **top-up schemes** to provide retirement benefits in excess of those permitted from an exempt **approved scheme**.

Funding
The provision in advance for future **liabilities** by the accumulation of **assets**, normally external to the **employer's** business.

Funding level
The relationship at a specified date between the **actuarial value of assets** and the **actuarial liability**. Normally expressed as a

percentage. The funding level may be calculated separately in respect of different categories of liability, e.g. pensions in payment and **AVCs**.

Funding plan
The timing of payments of contributions with the aim of meeting the cost of a given set of benefits under a **defined benefit scheme**. Possible objectives of a **funding plan** might be that, if the **actuarial assumptions** are borne out:

(a) a specified **funding level** should be reached by a given date;

(b) the level of contributions should remain constant, or should after a planned period be the **standard contribution rate** required by the **valuation method** used in the **actuarial valuation**.

See also **schedule of contributions**.

Funding rate
Sometimes used to describe the **recommended contribution rate**.

Funding ratio
The ratio of the **actuarial value of assets** to the **actuarial liability**.

Futures contract
A contract which binds two parties to complete a sale or purchase at a specified future date at a price which is fixed at the time the contract is effected.

Generally accepted accounting principles (GAAP)
The canon of accounting methods, including accounting standards, which together constitute best practice in different accounting situations, especially where alternative methods are available. The term can be applied to distinguish between accounting methods used in different circumstances and locations, e.g. small company GAAP and UK GAAP, and is sometimes referred to as 'generally accepted accounting practice'.

Global custodian
A **custodian** with responsibility for custody of **assets** world wide

GN11 certificate
Issued by the **scheme actuary** to the **trustees** confirming that the **cash equivalent** has been calculated in accordance with legislative requirements and **guidance notes**. Prior to 6 April 1997 this included details of the **actuarial assumptions** used.

Graded scale scheme
See **salary grade scheme**.

Graduated pension scheme
The State earnings related scheme which commenced on 3 April 1961 and terminated on 5 April 1975.

Graduated retirement benefit
Pensions payable as a result of membership of the **graduated pension scheme**, the amount being dependent on the graduated NI contributions paid.

Group personal pension scheme
An arrangement made for the employees of a particular **employer**, or for a group of self-employed individuals, to participate in a **personal pension scheme** on a grouped basis. This is not a single scheme; merely a collecting arrangement.

Group policy
An insurance policy in respect of more than one individual.

Guaranteed annuity
An **annuity** payable for a guaranteed period of years and thereafter throughout life. On the death of the annuitant, payment may continue for any balance of the guaranteed period or may in certain circumstances be paid as a lump sum.

Guaranteed annuity option
The right to apply the proceeds of an insurance policy to buy an **annuity** at a rate guaranteed in the policy.

Guaranteed minimum pension (GMP)
The minimum pension which an **occupational pension scheme** must provide as one of the conditions of contracting out for pre-6 April 1997 **service** (unless it was **contracted out** through the provision of **protected rights**).

Glossary

Guaranteed pension
The **minimum benefit** available from an insurance policy. Sometimes used to denote **pension guarantee**, but not to be confused with **guaranteed minimum pension**.

Guidance notes (GN)
1. Notes published by professional bodies such as the Institute and Faculty of Actuaries, advising their members on the appropriate course of action in specified circumstances.
2. Notes published by the **PSO** describing the requirements for tax **approval** in respect of specified types of schemes, in particular those relating to **personal pension schemes** (IR76). See also **Practice Notes (IR12)**.

Hancock annuity
An **annuity** for an employee, ex employee or **dependant**, purchased by the **employer** at or after the time of the employee's retirement, death or leaving **service**.

Headroom check
A **funding** check to ensure **Inland Revenue limits** are not exceeded within an **FSAVC scheme**. This check is carried out prior to payment of contributions in certain circumstances, notably where the proposed gross contribution is £2,400 p.a. or more. Full requirements are set out in the Free Standing Additional Voluntary Contributions Supplement to **Practice Notes (IR12)**.

Historical cost
The basis of stating assets and **liabilities** in an entity's accounts as the cost of acquiring or producing them. According to the **Pension scheme SORP** and the **Audited Accounts Regulations**, the assets of an **occupational pension scheme** should be stated at **market value** in its audited accounts.

Home responsibilities protection (HRP)
Protection of entitlement to the **basic pension** for people unable to undertake regular employment because they are caring for children or a sick or disabled person at home.

Hybrid scheme
1. An **occupational pension scheme** in which the benefit is calculated as the better of two alternatives, for example on a final salary and a **money purchase** basis.

2. An occupational pension scheme which offers both final salary and money purchase benefits.

Hybrid small self administered scheme (hybrid SSAS)
A **SSAS** which includes insurance policies among its **assets**.

Ill-health early retirement
Retirement on medical grounds before **normal pension date**. The benefit may exceed that payable on **early retirement** in other circumstances.

Immediate annuity
An **annuity** which commences immediately or shortly after its purchase.

In-house AVC
An **AVC** facility provided by an **occupational pension scheme** (i.e. not an **FSAVC scheme**).

Incapacity
Inability to continue working due to ill health or disability. The precise meaning depends on the terms of the individual **pension scheme**. Specific restrictions are contained in **Practice Notes (IR12)**, the **preservation** legislation and (in relation to **personal pensions**) *ICTA 1988*.

Incentive payment
Payments equal to 2% of **upper band earnings** which SSA86 required the DSS to make in certain cases to an **appropriate scheme** or an **occupational pension scheme** which was newly **contracted out**. It ceased on 5 April 1993. See also **1% age addition**.

Income withdrawal
Withdrawal of income from a **SSAS**, **personal pension** or **defined contribution scheme**, while **annuity** purchase is deferred. See also **deferred annuity purchase**.

Independent financial adviser (IFA)
An intermediary not connected to a particular insurance or other financial product company (as opposed to a **tied agent**), who is required to choose suitable financial products for clients from the whole market place.

Independent trustee
An individual or corporate body with no direct or indirect involvement with the **pension scheme**, **employer** or **members**, other than performing the duties of the **trustee**. Under *PA 1995, ss 22–26,* an independent trustee is required, in some circumstances, to be appointed to an **occupational pension scheme**, where an **insolvency practitioner** has been appointed over an **employer**.

Index linking
An adjustment in line with an index (usually of prices or earnings). In relation to pensions, an alternative term for **indexation**.

Indexation
1. A system whereby pensions in payment and/or **preserved benefits** are automatically increased at regular intervals by reference to a specified index of prices or earnings. Occasionally used in relation to **index linking** of **final pensionable earnings** or **final remuneration**: see definition 1 of **dynamisation**.
2. An **investment strategy** designed to produce a **rate of return** in line with a particular index, either by replicating the constituents or by sufficient sampling to give a proxy.

Indirect discrimination
The unequal treatment of one sex in relation to the other by applying conditions which, while not expressly related to sex, are more likely to be met by one sex than the other.

Individual arrangement
An **occupational pension scheme** with only one **member** where the documentation, often an **exchange of letters**, relates only to that member. An **employer** may have several individual arrangements for different employees.

Industry wide scheme
A **centralised scheme** for non **associated employers** in a particular industry.

Inflation proofing
Commonly used to describe definition 1 of **indexation** and/or the purpose of a **discretionary increase**.

Basic Guide to Pensions

Inland Revenue limits
Limits which must be included in the **rules** of an approved **occupational pension scheme**, specifying the **maximum approvable benefits** and contributions for **members**. See also **Practice Notes (IR12)**.

Insolvency practitioner
The relevant officer appointed on the insolvency of a company or individual to take over the management of the affairs of the company and responsible for carrying out the purposes of the insolvency proceedings e.g. liquidation or bankruptcy. A person acting as an insolvency practitioner must normally be a qualified person in accordance with *Insolvency Act 1986, ss 230, 388*.

Insured scheme
A **pension scheme** where the sole long-term investment medium is an insurance policy (other than a **managed fund** policy).

Integration
The design of **pension scheme** benefits to take into account all or part of the State **pension scheme** benefits which the **member** is deemed to receive. One form of integration involves a **State pension offset**.

Interim trust deed
A form of **trust deed** commonly used to establish a **pension scheme** on broadly stated terms leaving the detailed provisions and the **scheme rules** to be provided later by a definitive **trust deed**. A scheme may be established by other methods, for example by a board resolution, **declaration of trust** or **exchange of letters**.

Internal dispute resolution procedure (IDR)
Occupational pension schemes (subject to exceptions) are required by *PA 1995, s 50* to have a procedure to deal with disputes between **trustees** and **members** and **beneficiaries**.

Investment
The process by which contributions and net income are used to increase the value of the **assets** of a **pension fund** by means of cash deposits, the purchase and sale of equities, fixed interest stocks, bonds, property and other assets as authorised by the trust deed or by law.

Investment income
The income derived from the **investment** of **assets**.

Glossary

Investment management agreement
The document agreed between an **investment manager** and the **trustees** of a scheme setting out the basis upon which the manager will manage a portfolio of investments for the trustees.

Investment Management Regulatory Organisation (IMRO)
An **SRO** set up under the supervision of **SIB** to protect investors. It is responsible for monitoring the way that UK investment management firms treat their customers, manage their funds and provide investment services.

Investment manager
An individual or body to which the **investment** of the whole or part of the **assets** is delegated by the **trustees** in accordance with the provisions of the scheme documentation.

Investment performance measurement
The comparison of the **rate of return** of a given **pension fund** and/or its constituent parts over a period with one or more of:

(a) the notional return of a model fund;

(b) the actual rates of return of other funds; or

(c) the movement in stock market indices, over the same period.

Investment policy/strategy
The periodic decisions regarding the types and proportions of **assets** in which a **pension fund** is invested.

Investment report
A document communicating details of the **assets** of a fund, their deployment and changes, together with reasons.

Investment trust
A limited liability company quoted on the London Stock Exchange, whose sole business is investing in securities. The value of its own shares tends to reflect the underlying value of its portfolio of investments.

Investors Compensation Scheme
A scheme set up under *FSA 1986* to compensate investors up to a maximum determined from time to time.

Joint life last survivor annuity
An **annuity** payable until the last of two annuitants dies. The amount of the annuity sometimes changes on the first death.

Joint Office
The Joint Office of the **OPB** and **SFO** which existed prior to 1 August 1991, when they shared the same premises.

Joint Office memoranda (JOM)
Explanatory memoranda issued by the **Joint Office** prior to its cessation on 31 July 1991.

Key features document
A compulsory document giving key information to prospective buyers of most life and pension investments, required by the regulators (e.g. **PIA**).

Late retirement
The retirement of a **member**, with immediate retirement benefit, after **normal pension date**. The benefit may be increased because of late payment.

Later earnings addition
An amount to be added when calculating the **minimum benefit** for the purpose of **anti-franking requirements** where a **member** continues in **pensionable service** after **contracted-out** employment ceases and the level of earnings is higher when he/she retires or leaves than on ceasing to be contracted out.

Leading scheme
The **pension scheme** responsible for checking compliance with **Inland Revenue limits** when a **member** is contributing to an **FSAVC scheme**. The term is used in the *Retirement Benefits Schemes (Restriction on Discretion to Approve)(Additional Voluntary Contributions) Regulations 1993 SI No 3016*.

Level annual premium method
A method of determining the premiums payable under an insurance contract so that the premium for each individual remains constant unless there is a change in benefits.

Levy
1. The general levy meets the expenditure of the **Pension Schemes Registry**, the **Pensions Ombudsman**, **OPRA** and grants made by OPRA (e.g. to **OPAS**). It is payable by

Glossary

registrable **occupational pension schemes** and **personal pension schemes**.

2. The compensation levy meets the expenditure of the **Pensions Compensation Board** including the costs of compensation payments, and is payable by occupational pension schemes which are eligible for compensation.

Liabilities
Amounts which a **pension scheme** has an obligation to pay now or in the future. The amounts may not be immediately ascertainable and some liabilities may be dependent on the occurrence of future events.

Lien rule
A rule in an occupational pension scheme under which an **employer** may recover from the scheme any money due to it through criminal, fraudulent or negligent act or omission by the employee. Restrictions on such a rule are contained in *PA 1995, ss 91–95*.

Life assurance scheme
A scheme which provides a benefit only on the death of a **member** (normally on death in service).

Limited Price Indexation (LPI)
The requirement under *PA 1995, ss 51–54* to increase pensions in payment under an **occupational pension scheme** (excluding **AVCs** and **FSAVCs**) and **protected rights** under an **appropriate personal pension scheme**, by 5% p.a. or RPI if less. It applies to pensions accrued in respect of service after 5 April 1997.

Limited revaluation
A method used by **COSRS** to revalue **GMP** by the lower of 5% per annum and **section 148 orders**, between termination of **contracted-out** employment and age 65 (men), 60 (women). It was withdrawn from 6 April 1997.

Limited revaluation premium (LRP)
A **State scheme premium** which could have been paid when a **member** of a **COSRS** ceased to be in **contracted-out** employment before 6 April 1997. In return for this premium any subsequent **revaluation** of **GMP** up to age 65 (men), 60 (women) above 5% per annum is provided by the State pension scheme instead of under the **occupational pension scheme**.

Linked qualifying service
Actual **service** in a previous scheme which gives rise to a **transfer credit**, which ranks as **qualifying service** (*PSA 1993, s 179*).

Long service benefit
Under the **preservation** requirements of *PSA 1993* the benefit payable at **normal pension age** with which **short service benefit** must be compared.

Long-term disability insurance (LTD)
An insurance policy, which pays an income while an individual is unable to work as a result of accident or illness. It can be purchased by an individual, or by a company for a group of its employees.

Lower earnings limit (LEL)
The minimum amount, approximately equivalent to the single person's **basic pension**, which must be earned in any pay period before NI contributions are payable.

Lump sum certificate
A certificate which must be provided by a transferring scheme in certain circumstances, described in **Practice Notes (IR12),** stating the maximum lump sum available from a **transfer payment**.

Managed fund
1. An investment contract by means of which an insurance company offers participation in one or more **pooled funds**.
2. An arrangement where the **assets** are invested on similar lines to **unit trusts** by an external **investment manager**.

Manager
Generally understood to mean the person who manages a **pension scheme**. Manager has various meanings in legislation; e.g. it is defined under *PA 1995* as the person responsible for management of a pension scheme which has not been established under trust.

Mandatory approval
Automatic approval by the **PSO** under *ICTA 1988, s 590* (formerly *FA 1970, s 19*) of **occupational pension schemes** which satisfy the statutory requirements. Such schemes cannot provide a pension of more than 1/60th of **final remuneration** for each year of **service** which cannot be exchanged for cash of more than 3/80ths.

Glossary

Market level adjustment
An adjustment applied to an **actuarial liability** to reflect the difference between the **market value** and **actuarial value of assets**.

Market level indicator (MLI)
An index giving a weighted comparison of values of equities and fixed interest securities. Market level indicators were used to adjust the amount of some **State scheme premiums** prior to 6 April 1997.

Market value
The price at which an **asset** might reasonably be expected to be sold in an open market. Although current market value should be defined by reference to actual current conditions of the market, for practical purposes other considerations may be postulated, e.g. adopting a 'willing buyer, willing seller' basis.

Market value adjustment
See **market level adjustment**.

Master policy
See **group policy**.

Matching
1. The policy of selecting **assets** of a nature, incidence or currency similar to that of the expected outgoings.
2. An accounting term, meaning that revenue and costs are matched with one another or 'hedged' so far as their relationship can be established or justifiably assumed. See also **accruals concept**.

Maximum approvable benefit
The maximum benefit for an individual which is allowable by the Inland Revenue under an **approved scheme** (other than a **personal pension scheme** or a **simplified defined contribution scheme**).

Member
A person who has been admitted to membership of a **pension scheme** and is entitled to benefit under the scheme. Sometimes narrowly used to refer only to an **active member**. The definition of **member** depends on its context as both **scheme rules** and

legislation may give a different meaning to the definition above, e.g. for some statutory purposes the term members may include employees who are **prospective members**.

Member nominated director (MND)
A person who becomes a director of a **corporate trustee** of an **occupational pension scheme** (under **appropriate rules** or **prescribed rules**) under arrangements required by *PA 1995, s 18(1)* for **members** of the scheme to select them. The statutory definition does not include directors elected or selected by members under **alternative arrangements** put forward by the **employer** and approved by members under *PA 1995, s 19*. See also **member nominated trustee**.

Member nominated trustee (MNT)
A person who becomes a **trustee** of an **occupational pension scheme** (under **appropriate rules** or **prescribed rules**) under arrangements required by *PA 1995, s 16(1)* for **members** of the scheme to select them. The statutory definition does not include **trustees** elected or selected by members under **alternative arrangements** put forward by the **employer** and approved by **members** under *PA 1995, s 17*. See also **member nominated director**.

Member participation
The active participation of **members** in the affairs of an **occupational pension scheme**. This may be directly through representation on the trustee body, or indirectly through joint consultative committees with an **employer**. See also **member nominated trustee**.

Member's normal contributions
The regular contributions required from an **active member** by the **scheme rules**.

Membership reconciliation
The agreement of membership numbers to source documentation, commonly used to identify the movement in **member** numbers over a defined period of time.

Middle tier/middle band earnings
See **upper band earnings**.

Minimum appropriate personal pension
See **rebate only personal pension**.

Minimum benefit
An amount of benefit which a scheme promises if the normal benefit for a particular **member** would be smaller.

Minimum contributions
Contributions payable to an **appropriate scheme** by the DSS in respect of a **member** who has elected to **contract out**. The contributions consist of the flat rate **rebate** and any **age related rebate** of NI contributions and basic rate tax relief on the employee's share of the **rebate** where it is paid to a **personal pension** arrangement.

Minimum funding requirement (MFR)
A requirement under *PA 1995, s 56* that, under a prescribed set of **actuarial assumptions**, the **actuarial value of assets** of a **defined benefit scheme** should not be less than its **actuarial liabilities**.

Minimum payments
The minimum amount which an **employer** must pay into a **COMPS**. This minimum amount consists of the flat rate **rebate** of NI contributions and corresponds to the reduction in NI contributions which applies in respect of employees who are **contracted out**. See also **age related payment**.

Minimum pension
See **minimum benefit**.

MNT Regulations
The *Occupational pension schemes (Member-nominated Trustees and Directors) Regulations 1996 SI No 1216* made under *PA 1995, ss 16–21* which deal with **member nominated trustees** and **member nominated directors**.

Model rules
Specimen rules produced by the **OPB** and or the **PSO** for certain categories of **pension scheme**s to facilitate **approval** and or the issue of a **contracting-out certificate** or an **appropriate scheme certificate**.

Modification order
An order by **OPRA** modifying an **occupational pension scheme** under *PA 1995, ss 69–72* (e.g. to allow payment of **surpluses** to an **employer**) overriding the terms of the scheme. Before 6 April 1997, the **OPB** had wider powers to make modification orders under *PSA 1993*.

Modified contribution rate
See **recommended contribution rate**.

Modified premium value
A **premium value** which excludes the loadings made by the insurer in premium rating for initial expenses, such as issue expenses, commission and stamp duty.

Money purchase
The determination of an individual **member's** benefits by reference to contributions paid into the scheme in respect of that member, usually increased by an amount based on the investment return on those contributions.

Money purchase scheme
A **pension scheme** providing benefits on a **money purchase** basis. For some statutory purposes, a **money purchase scheme** is one which provides only money purchase benefits, with the exception of death benefits.

Money purchase underpin
A **minimum benefit** calculated on a **money purchase** basis provided by a **hybrid scheme** (definition 1).

Money weighted return
An absolute measure of the **rate of return** earned by the **assets** in a fund which is affected by the timing of cash flows into or out of the fund. To be contrasted with **time weighted return**.

Movement of funds statement
A statement within the annual accounts of an **occupational pension scheme** which reconciles the changes in the net assets (**assets** less **liabilities**) with income and expenditure and changes in **market value**. For accounting periods ending on or after 6 April 1997, the **Pension scheme SORP** and the **Audited Accounts Regulations** require a **fund account** which replaces the income and expenditure account and the movement of funds statement.

Multiple benefit scheme
See definition 2 of **hybrid scheme**.

N/NS x P certificate
A certificate obtained by administrators of a **personal pension scheme** from **trustees** of an **occupational pension scheme** in respect of a **transfer payment** for a **controlling director** or an

individual who has earned over the **earnings cap**. It certifies that the **transfer value** covers the individual's total **accrued rights** and that these are within the limits specified in the *Personal Pension Schemes (Transfer Payments) Regulations 1988 SI No 1014*.

National Insurance Contributions Office (NICO)
An executive office of the Inland Revenue which administers the NI contributions system.

Net assets statement
A summary of the net assets (**assets** less **liabilities**) of an **occupational pension scheme** usually presented as part of the audited accounts in the **annual report**. This does not take account of the liabilities to pay benefits in future as this is dealt with in the **actuarial valuation**. According to the **Pension scheme SORP** and the **Audited Accounts Regulations**, the assets of an **occupational pension scheme** should be stated at **market value**.

Net book value (NBV)
The **historical cost** of a fixed asset less depreciation.

Net relevant earnings (NRE)
Relevant earnings after deducting losses and certain business charges on income, used in determining the maximum contributions to a **retirement annuity** or **personal pension scheme** which qualify for tax relief. From the tax year 1989/90 NRE for personal pension schemes have been restricted by the **earnings cap**.

New code
Used to distinguish pension arrangements approved under *FA 1970* from those approved under earlier legislation (**old code**).

New entrant contribution rate
A rate of contribution estimated as being sufficient to provide benefits for future entrants, including any contribution required from the **members**.

New money
The flow into a fund of contributions and **transfer payment**s less outgoings. Normally not considered to include income from existing **assets**.

NICO
See **National Insurance Contributions Office**.

Nil certificate
A certificate indicating that a **transfer value** is not to be used to provide retirement benefits in lump sum form, such as on a transfer from an **FSAVC scheme**.

Nomination
See **expression of wish**.

Non-approved scheme
See **unapproved scheme**.

Non-contributory scheme
A scheme which does not require contributions from its **active members**. Not to be confused with a **contributory scheme** where contributions are suspended during a **contribution holiday**.

Non-pensionable employment
1. For **personal pension** and **retirement annuity** purposes, employment where the individual is not or was not a **member** of an **occupational pension scheme**. Earnings from non-pensionable employment can be included in **net relevant earnings** (*ICTA 1988, s 654*).

2. Employment where there is no occupational pension scheme available for the individual to join.

Normal contributions
See **ordinary annual contributions** and **member's normal contributions**.

Normal pension age (NPA)
1. Commonly the age by reference to which the **normal pension date** is determined.

2. The statutory definition (relevant for **preservation** and contracting out purposes) is generally the earliest age at which a **member** is entitled to receive benefits (other than the **GMP**) on his/her retirement from employment to which the scheme relates ignoring any special provisions as to **early retirement** on grounds of ill health or otherwise (*PSA 1993, s 180*). This is commonly interpreted to mean the earliest age at which a member has a right to take benefits without reduction.
This may be different from definition 1 above or **normal retirement age**.

Glossary

Normal pension date (NPD)
The date at which a **member** of a **pension scheme** normally becomes entitled to receive his/her retirement benefits.

Normal retirement age (NRA)
1. For employment purposes the age at which the employees holding a particular position normally retire from **service**. This is often (but not always) the same as **normal pension age** or definition 2 below.
   The statutory term is "normal retiring age" used in *Employment Rights Act 1996*, *s 109* (unfair dismissal) and *s 156* (redundancy).
2. The age of a **member** of an **occupational pension scheme** at the **normal retirement date** as specified in the **scheme rules**.

Normal retirement date (NRD)
The date (usually the date of reaching a particular age) specified in the **rules** of an **occupational pension scheme** at which a **member** would normally retire. **Approved schemes** are required by the **PSO** to state a normal retirement date.

Occupational pension scheme
A scheme organised by an **employer** or on behalf of a group of employers to provide pensions and/or other benefits for or in respect of one or more employees on leaving **service** or on death or retirement. A more detailed definition is to be found in *PSA 1993, s 1*.

Occupational Pensions Board (OPB)
A statutory body set up under SSA73 with functions derived from that Act and SSPA75. The Board ceased in April 1997. Until then it was responsible for issuing **contracting out certificate**s or **appropriate scheme certificate**s for **pension scheme**s which met the statutory requirements, for supervising those schemes to ensure that **GMP**s and **protected rights** were secure and for ensuring that **equal access** and **preservation** requirements were satisfied.

Occupational Pensions Regulatory Authority (OPRA)
An independent body, set up under *PA 1995*, to regulate **occupational pension schemes** from 6 April 1997. OPRA's role is to protect **members**' interests if those who run occupational pension schemes do not meet their legal obligations under the Act. OPRA has the power to impose penalties for failure to comply with *PA*

1995 and *PSA 1993*, to prohibit or disqualify **trustees**, and to impose fines. OPRA does not deal with **personal pension schemes**.

Old code
Used to distinguish pension arrangements approved under legislation before *FA 1970* from those approved under later legislation (new code).

OPAS (the Pensions Advisory Service)
An independent organisation which gives free advice to members of the public who have a problem about an **occupational pension scheme** or **personal pension scheme**. It does not give financial advice or advice on state scheme benefits. Formerly known as the Occupational Pensions Advisory Service when its remit was restricted to occupational pensions.

Open market option (OMO)
The option to apply the proceeds of an insurance contract to buy an **annuity** at a current market rate from the same or another insurance company.

Opting out
A decision by an employee to leave or not to join an **occupational pension scheme** of the **employer**.

Option
A derivative financial instrument under which the payment of a sum of money gives a right, but not an obligation, to buy or sell something at an agreed price on or before a specified date.

Ordinary annual contributions
Used in **Practice Notes (IR12)** to denote the annual contributions payable to an **occupational pension scheme** by the **employer** on a common basis e.g. a fixed amount or fixed percentage of payroll. See also **special contributions**.

Overfunding
Where a pension arrangement has **assets** which exceed those required to meet **liabilities**. See also **actuarial surplus**.

Overfunding certificate
See **N/NS x P certificate**.

Glossary

Overlap
An arrangement whereby a pension for a **dependant** becomes payable in addition to the **pension guarantee** until the end of the guarantee period.

Overriding legislation
The application of statutory requirements to **pension schemes** by means of provisions which directly override **scheme rules**.

Paid up benefit
A preserved benefit which is fully secured for an individual **member** under a contract of insurance under which premiums have ceased to be payable in respect of that member.

Paid up pension (PUP)
See **paid up benefit**.

Paid up scheme
A scheme where all contributions have ceased but the **assets** of the scheme continue to be held by the **administrator** to be applied in accordance with the **scheme rules**. This definition is included in part 14 of **Practice Notes (IR12)**.

Partially approved scheme
An **occupational pension scheme** only partially approved by the **PSO** because it provides some benefits which are not approvable, for example for overseas employees. Not to be confused with partial loss of tax exemptions which occurs under *ICTA 1988, Sch 22* if an occupational pension scheme which is excessively overfunded fails to take action to reduce the **surplus**.

Participating employer
An **employer** whose employees have the right to become **members** of an **occupational pension scheme**. Usually applied where more than one employer participates in a single scheme.

Partly projected unit method
An **accrued benefits valuation method** similar to the **current unit method** but with only partial allowance for projected earnings.

Passive investment management
A style of managing a portfolio by linking the investments to a particular index so that the portfolio value moves with that index.

Past service
Service before a given date.

Past service benefit
A benefit granted for **past service** and/or **pre-scheme service**.

Past service reserve
Generally used to describe the **present value** of all benefits accrued at the date to which the calculations relate by reference to earnings projected to the dates on which **pensionable service** ceases.

Pay as you go (PAYG)
An arrangement under which benefits are paid out of revenue and no funding is made for future **liabilities**. The State pension scheme is pay as you go.

Payment in lieu (PIL)
A payment made to the DSS for a **member** who ceased to be contracted out of the former **graduated pension scheme**, where the equivalent pension benefit was not preserved within the **pension scheme**.

Payment schedule
A schedule specifying contribution rates to be paid and the due dates for such payments. Required for **money purchase schemes** under PA 1995, s 87.

Pension cost
Under **SSAP 24** the cost of providing pensions, which is charged to the profit and loss account of the **employer** over the expected service lives or **average remaining service life** of employees in the scheme. The amount may be more or less than the actual payments made to the scheme.

Pension earmarking
See **earmarking**.

Pension fraction
The fraction of **pensionable earnings** for each year of **pensionable service** which forms the basis of the pension in a **final salary scheme** or a **career average scheme**.

Pension fund
Strictly speaking the **assets** of a **pension scheme** but very often used to denote the pension scheme itself.

Glossary

Pension fund withdrawal
See **income withdrawal**.

Pension guarantee
An arrangement whereby on the early death of a **pensioner**, the **pension scheme** pays a further sum or sums to meet a guaranteed total. This total may be established by relation to, for instance, a multiple of the annual rate of pension or the accumulated contributions of the late **member**.

Pension increase
An increase in a pension in payment. Such an increase may arise as a result of **escalation** or **indexation** or may be a **discretionary increase**.

Pension provider
A body by which a **personal pension scheme** or **FSAVC scheme** must be established in order to be approved by the Inland Revenue.

Pension review
See **SIB review**.

Pension scheme
An **occupational pension scheme**, a **personal pension scheme** or an **FSAVC scheme**.

Pension scheme SORP
The **Statement of Recommended Practice** which applies to the accounts of **occupational pension schemes**. The Pension scheme SORP was updated and issued by the Pensions Research Accountants Group (PRAG) in September 1996 as 'Financial Reports of Pension Schemes'. Most of its recommendations were effectively made mandatory by the **Audited Accounts Regulations** and the SORP is effective for accounting periods ending on or after 6 April 1997.

Pension schemes Office (PSO)
The office of the Inland Revenue which deals with the approval of **pension scheme**s under the relevant tax legislation. Prior to 1 April 1992 known as the **Superannuation Funds Office (SFO)**.

Pension Schemes Registry
The register of **occupational pension schemes** and **personal pension schemes**, maintained by **OPRA**. The registry enables **members** to trace schemes with which they have lost touch and collects the **levy**.

Pension splitting
The splitting of a **member's** benefits under a **pension scheme** between the member and the divorced spouse, either within the scheme or by means of a **transfer payment**. The benefits belong to the member and divorced spouse separately and each can decide when to take their benefits (subject to any Inland Revenue restrictions). See also **earmarking**.

Pension tax relief at source (PTRAS)
The procedure whereby contributions to an **occupational pension scheme** are deducted from the **member's** pay before tax is calculated under PAYE, giving immediate tax relief at the highest applicable rate.

Pensionable age
Used in legislation (*Social Security Contributions and Benefits Act 1992, s 1*) to denote **State pensionable age**.

Pensionable earnings
The earnings on which benefits and/or contributions are calculated under the **scheme rules**.
One or more elements of earnings (e.g. overtime) may be excluded and/or there may be a **State pension offset**.

Pensionable employment
1. For **personal pension** and **retirement annuity** purposes, employment where the individual is or was a **member** of an **occupational pension scheme**. Earnings from pensionable employment cannot be included in **net relevant earnings** (*ICTA 1988, s 654*).

2. Employment where an individual is able to join an occupational pension scheme whether or not he she has actually done so.

Pensionable service
The period of **service** which is taken into account in calculating benefits. *PSA 1993* gives the term a statutory definition for the purposes of the **preservation, revaluation** and **transfer payment** requirements of the Act. *PA 1995* gives a further statutory definition.

Glossary

Pensioneer trustee
An individual or company with pensions experience appointed in accordance with the requirements relating to the approval of **SSASs** under *ICTA 1988* to act as a **trustee** of such a scheme.

Pensioner
A person who is currently receiving a pension from a **pension scheme**.

Pensioner member
A scheme **member** in receipt of, or entitled to, a pension.

Pensioner's rights premium (PRP)
A **State scheme premium** which could have been paid for a **member** or **pensioner** over **State pensionable age** when a scheme **contracted out** by the **GMP** test ceased to be contracted out before 6 April 1997. In return the member was reinstated in **SERPS** for the period covered by the PRP.

Pensions Compensation Board (PCB)
The Board administers the **pensions compensation scheme** for **occupational pension schemes**. It is able to provide compensation when an **employer** becomes insolvent and scheme **assets** have been dishonestly removed. It decides whether compensation can he paid and how much.

Pensions compensation scheme
A statutory arrangement, introduced by *PA 1995*, which protects **members** of **occupational pension schemes** from loss of benefit occurring as a result of a shortfall in **assets** due to dishonesty, where the **sponsoring employer** is insolvent. It covers funded, approved, occupational pension schemes except funded public **service pension scheme**s, one member schemes, death in service only schemes and **SSASs**. The pensions compensation scheme is administered by the **Pensions Compensation Board**.

Pensions Ombudsman (PO)
The Pensions Ombudsman deals with disputes about entitlement and complaints of maladministration from **members** of **occupational pension schemes** and **personal pension schemes**. The Ombudsman's role also includes investigating complaints or disputes between **trustees** of occupational pension schemes and **employers**, and between trustees of different occupational pension schemes.

Performance measurement
See **investment performance measurement**.

Permanent health insurance (PHI)
See **long-term disability insurance**.

Permitted investments
In general the types and classes of investment allowed to **trustees** under a **trust deed**. More specifically the investments stipulated by the Inland Revenue in connection with **SSASs** and **personal pension schemes**.

Permitted maximum
Used in legislation (*ICTA 1988, s 590*) to describe the **earnings cap**.

Perpetuities, rule against
A rule of law (in England, Wales and Northern Ireland) setting a maximum period within which benefits under a **trust** must vest absolutely. **Approved schemes** are exempted by *PSA 1993, s 163*.

Personal Investment Authority (PIA)
An SRO set up under the supervision of SIB with responsibility for regulating retail financial **services** business. The PIA was established in 1994, and its membership mainly consists of life assurance companies and independent financial advisers.

Personal pension
See **personal pension arrangement**. Also used to describe a **retirement annuity** effected under the tax legislation in force before July 1988.

Personal pension arrangement
An individual contract made under a **personal pension scheme**.

Personal pension contributions certificate (PPCC)
A certificate issued by a **personal pension scheme** provider to the **member** to enable that member to provide his/her Inspector of Taxes with evidence of membership and contributions.

Personal pension protected rights premium (PPPRP)
A **State scheme premium** which could have been paid by an **appropriate scheme** in order to purchase benefits in **SERPS** for a **member**, if the scheme ceased to **contract out** before 6 April 1997.

Personal pension scheme (PPS)
A scheme approved under *Chapter IV, Part XIV, ICTA 1988*, under which an individual who is self-employed, or in **non-pensionable employment**, or employed but not a **member** of an **occupational pension scheme** except a death in service only arrangement, can make pension provision. See also **self-invested personal pension** and **appropriate scheme**. *PSA 1993* and *PA 1995* use a slightly different definition which excludes a scheme open only to the self-employed but includes an **FSAVC scheme**.

Phased annuity
The bringing into payment of annuities under **personal pension arrangements** which have been subject to **segmentation**, at differing times.

Pivotal age
The age at which it is deemed more advantageous to cease to **contract out** and rejoin **SERPS**.

Pooled fund
A fund managed on behalf of different owners, in a common pool, e.g. **managed funds** and **unit trusts**. This contrasts with a **segregated fund**. The owners of **assets** in a pooled fund do not have to be associated, as opposed to investors in a **common investment fund**.

Post-89 member
See **Class A member**.

Post-89 regime
The package of **maximum approvable benefits** introduced by *FA 1989*, details of which appear in **Practice Notes (IR12)**. See also **Class A member**.

Postponed retirement
The situation where a **member** has reached **normal pension date** and pension payments have not commenced.

Practice note (auditors)
Guidance produced by the Auditing Practices Board in relation to the audit of particular types of entity, including the Practice Note on the audit of **pension schemes**.

Practice Notes (IR12) (PN)
Notes on the **discretionary approval** of **occupational pension schemes** by the **PSO**, currently issued as Practice Notes (IR12) (1991). Schemes approved before November 1991 continue to be subject to the earlier Practice Notes (IR 12) (1979), but may choose to adopt certain parts of the later Practice Notes.

Pre-1 June 1989 continued rights
The rights of a **member** of an **occupational pension scheme** who continues to be subject to the Inland Revenue maximum benefit limits which were generally applicable between 17 March 1987 and 31 May 1989. The full definition is set out in **Practice Notes (IR12)**.

Pre 17 March 1987 continued rights
The rights of a **member** of an **occupational pension scheme** who continues to be subject to the Inland Revenue maximum benefit limits which were generally applicable before 17 March 1987. The full definition is set out in **Practice Notes (IR12)**.

Pre 87 member
See **Class C member**.

Pre scheme service
Service before the start of the relevant **pension scheme** or before entry into membership.

Premium value
A basis of valuation of a long-term insurance policy for **occupational pension scheme** accounting purposes, based on an equivalent single premium. See paragraph 3.11 of the **Pension scheme SORP**.

Prepayment
In a pension context, an asset on the **balance sheet** of the **employer**'s accounts usually representing the excess of funding payments over the amount calculated by the **actuary** as being his/her best estimate under **SSAP 24** of the costs of providing pensions. It sometimes reflects or includes negative **pension cost** and/or a **surplus** included in the balance sheet under the transitional provisions of SSAP 24.

Prescribed rules
Rules in the **MNT Regulations** which must be used if the **employer's** proposals for **alternative arrangements** or the

trustee's proposals for **appropriate rules** (or both) have failed, or if it has been decided to adopt the default procedure for selecting **member nominated trustees** or **member nominated directors**.

Present value
The total of a series of future payments or receipts discounted to the date to which the calculation relates, allowing for the probabilities of payment or receipt.

Preservation
The granting by a scheme of **preserved benefits** to a **member** leaving **pensionable service** under an **occupational pension scheme** before **normal pension age**, in particular in accordance with minimum requirements specified by *PSA 1993*.

Preserved benefits
Benefits arising on an individual ceasing to be an **active member** of an **occupational pension scheme**, payable at a later date.

Preserved pensioner
See **deferred pensioner**.

Principal employer
Commonly used in scheme documentation for the particular **participating employer** in which is vested special powers or duties in relation to such matters as the appointment of the **trustees**, amendments and **winding up**. Usually this will be the employer which established the scheme or its successor in business.

Priority liabilities
Benefits and other **liabilities** which are given precedence in accordance with the **priority rule** when a scheme is wound up.

Priority rule
The provisions contained in the scheme documentation setting out the order of precedence of **liabilities** to be followed if the scheme is wound up. *PA 1995, s 73* introduced an overriding statutory order of priorities for a scheme which is subject to the **MFR** and starts to wind up after 5 April 1997. A transitional order of priority applies between 6 April 1997 and 5 April 2007 until the MFR is completely operational.

Proceeds of policy scheme
A **money purchase scheme** where the benefits promised to the **members** are those which can be provided from the proceeds of an insurance contract effected in respect of each member.

Professional adviser
An adviser required to be appointed by the **trustees** under *PA 1995, s 47*. This includes the **scheme actuary** and **scheme auditor**.

Prohibition order
An order made by **OPRA** under *PA 1995, s 3* prohibiting a person from being a trustee of a particular **occupational pension scheme**. See also **disqualification order** and **suspension order**.

Projected accrued benefit method
An **accrued benefits valuation method** which compares the accrued **actuarial liability** with the value placed on the scheme **assets** for valuation purposes. The actuarial liability is based on **service** up to the **valuation date** and makes allowance for projected earnings. Used only in the context of the *Pension Scheme Surpluses (Valuation) Regulations 1987 (SI 1987 No 412)*.

Projected unit method
An **accrued benefits valuation method** in which the **actuarial liability** makes allowance for projected earnings. The **standard contribution rate** is that necessary to cover the cost of all benefits which will accrue in the **control period** following the **valuation date** by reference to earnings projected to the dates on which benefits become payable. Known in the USA as the projected unit credit method.

Prospective benefits valuation method
A **valuation method** in which the **actuarial liability** at the **valuation date** is the **present value** of:

(a) the benefits for current and **deferred pensioners** and their **dependants**, allowing where appropriate for future increases, and

(b) the benefits which **active members** will receive in respect of both past and future **service**, allowing for projected earnings up to their assumed exit dates and, where appropriate, for increases thereafter, less the **present value** of future contributions payable in respect of current **members** at the **standard contribution rate**.

Prospective member
An individual, not currently a **member** of the **pension scheme** of his/her **employer**, who is either entitled to join or will become eligible to join in the future by virtue of continuing in employment with the employer. Given a wider meaning in the **Disclosure Regulations**.

Prospective service
The length of potential future **pensionable service** of a **member** up to a future date or age. Used in some cases in calculating **Inland Revenue limits** on early retirement and by some schemes in calculating some benefits (often **incapacity** pensions or spouse's pensions).

Protected rights
The benefits from a scheme **contracted out** on a **money purchase** basis deriving from at least the **minimum contributions** or **minimum payments**, which are provided in a specified form as a necessary condition of contracting out.

Protected rights annuity
The pension provided from **protected rights** by purchase from an insurance company or friendly society.

Protected rights premium
A **State scheme premium** which could have been paid by a scheme which was **contracted out** by reference to the provision of **protected rights**, in order to purchase benefits under the State scheme for a **member**, if the scheme ceased to contract out before 6 April 1997.

Provider
See **pension provider**.

Provision
1. An amount retained as reasonably necessary to provide for any liability or loss which is likely to be incurred but the amount or date of which is uncertain. (Sch 4, para 88, CA85).
2. An amount written off to provide for depreciation or diminution in the value of **assets**.
3. In a pensions context, the unfunded obligation to provide employees' pensions and/or the shortfall of funding payments over the amount calculated by the **actuary** as being his or

her estimate under **SSAP 24** of the costs of providing pensions.

Pension costs in **employers'** accounts should be actuarially assessed. If, as a result, there is a provision, the **balance sheet** formats of the Companies Act require it to be described under the heading 'Provisions for liabilities' as 'Pensions and similar obligations'.

Provisional approval
1. The allowing of tax relief on a provisional basis in respect of employee contributions where an **occupational pension scheme** is set up under interim documentation.
   Practice Notes (IR12) do not use the term. Strictly, Inland Revenue **approval** is not granted until definitive scheme documentation has been examined.
2. The granting of provisional approval in respect of a **personal pension scheme** under *ICTA 1988, s 655(5)* and the *Personal Pension Schemes (Provisional Approval) Regulations 1987 (SI No 1765)*.

Public sector pension scheme
An **occupational pension scheme** for employees of central or local government, a nationalised industry or other statutory body.

Public sector transfer arrangements
The arrangements of the **transfer club** to which certain schemes mainly in the public sector belong.

Public service pension scheme
A **public sector pension scheme** the particulars of which are defined by statute, Royal Prerogative or Royal Charter; for example the schemes for the civil service, local authorities, the police and fire services.

Purchased life annuity (PLA)
An **annuity** purchased privately by an individual. In accordance with *ICTA 1988, s 656*, instalments of the annuity are subject to tax only in part.

Qualifying period
See **waiting period**.

Qualifying service
The term defined in *PSA 1993, s 71(7)* denoting the **service** to be taken into account to entitle the **member** to **short service benefit**. The current condition is for at least two years' **qualifying service**. See also **linked qualifying service**.

Quantitative investment management
A method of selecting investments which relies exclusively upon screening of statistical data.

Quoted/unquoted investments
Quoted investments have their prices quoted on a recognised stock exchange. Unquoted investments do not.

Rate of return
The percentage change in the value of an investment over a period, taking into account both the income from it and the change in its **market value**. Often expressed as an equivalent annual rate. Rates of return are often quoted as **time weighted** or **money weighted**.

Real rate of return
The difference between the **rate of return** of an investment and a selected measure of inflation over the same period. The measure of inflation used should be specified, but will often be the index of retail prices or of national average earnings.

Rebate
See **contracted out rebate**.

Rebate only personal pension (ROPP)
An **appropriate scheme** which is funded solely by **contracted out rebates** payable by the DSS to the **pension provider**.

Recognised occupation
An occupation for which the **PSO** may be able to agree a pension age earlier than 50 under an **occupational pension scheme** or **personal pension scheme** or earlier than 60 under a **retirement annuity**.

Recognised professional body (RPB)
A professional body recognised by **SIB** as regulating and supervising for the purposes of *FSA 1986* those of its members who undertake investment business activities.

Recommended contribution rate
The contribution rate recommended by the **actuary**. It is usually obtained by adjusting the **standard contribution rate** for differences between the **actuarial liability** and the **actuarial value of assets** taking into account the objectives of the **funding plan**. See also **schedule of contributions**.

Recurrent single premium method
See **single premium method**.

Reference scheme
The standard scheme specified under *PSA 1993, s 12B* against which the benefits of a **COSRS** must be compared in order to remain **contracted out** after 5 April 1997 on that basis.

Reference scheme test
The comparison of the benefits provided by a **COSRS** with those under the **reference scheme** to ensure that they are at least equal, as required under *PSA 1993, s 12B*. The **scheme actuary** must certify that the scheme complies with the reference scheme test.

Register/registry
See **Pension Schemes Registry**.

Regular pension cost
An accounting term defined in **SSAP 24** as meaning the consistent ongoing cost recognised under the actuarial method and assumptions used.

Reinstatement
The acceptance into an **occupational pension scheme** of a **member** who has previously declined to join, or has opted-out in order to purchase a **personal pension arrangement**. Reinstatement can be solely for future service benefits or can also include **past service benefits**. See also **SIB review**.

Reinsurance
The practice whereby one insurer insures with another risks it has accepted in order to offset the impact of part or all of the expected claims. Used loosely to describe the insurance taken out by **trustees** to offset the effects of excessive death benefit claims.

Related party transactions
Financial transactions with related parties which **Financial Reporting Standard** 8 requires to be disclosed in an entity's

financial statements. The **Pension Scheme SORP** identifies the related parties of **occupational pension schemes** and the disclosures to be made in scheme accounts.

Relevant benefits
Used in *ICTA 1988* and **Practice Notes (IR12)** to describe the types of benefits which are within the tax regime governing **occupational pension schemes**. The full definition is set out in *ICTA 1988, s 612(1)* and covers any type of financial benefit given in connection with retirement, death or termination of service. The definition does not include benefits provided only in the event of accidental death or disablement during service.

Relevant earnings
Earnings from self-employment or non-pensionable employment. See also **net relevant earnings**.

Requisite benefits
The scale of benefits which an **occupational pension scheme** was originally required to provide as one of the conditions of contracting out. The requirement to provide requisite benefits was removed in November 1986.

Restricted employer related investment
The restriction under *PA 1995, s 40* of **employer related investment** to 5% of scheme **assets**. Certain exemptions exist e.g. for **SSASs**, and there are also transitional arrangements for schemes which exceed the limit. See also **self investment**.

Retained benefits
Retirement or death benefits in respect of an employee deriving from an earlier period of employment or self-employment. In some circumstances retained benefits must be taken into account in the **maximum approvable benefits**.

Retirement annuity
An **annuity** contract between an insurance company or friendly society and a self-employed individual or a person in **non-pensionable employment**, which was established before 1 July 1988 and is approved under *Chapter III, Part XIV, ICTA 1988*.

Retirement benefits scheme
An arrangement for the provision of benefits consisting of or including **relevant benefits**. The full definition is set out in *ICTA 1988, s 611*.

Revaluation
1. The application, particularly to **preserved benefits**, of **indexation**, **escalation** or the awarding of **discretionary increase**s. *PSA 1993* imposes a minimum level of **revaluation** in the calculation of **GMP** and of preserved benefits other than GMP.
2. An accounting term for the revision of the **carrying value** of an **asset**, usually having regard to its **market value**.

Revalued earnings
Used to describe **index linking** of earnings for calculating benefits.

Revalued earnings scheme
A scheme where the benefits are based on **revalued earnings** for a given period. A notable example is **SERPS**.

Revenue limits
See **Inland Revenue limits**.

Revenue undertaking
A written undertaking which was given by **administrators** of approved **occupational pension schemes** agreeing to notify the Inland Revenue of certain information or to refer to them before taking certain specified actions. The *Retirement Benefits Schemes (Information Powers) Regulations 1995 SI No 3103* cover most of the important items from the undertakings and they are no longer required for events which occur from 1 January 1996.

Reversionary annuity
An **annuity** which commences to be paid on the death of a specified person, normally to a spouse or a **dependant**.

Risk benefits
Benefits payable in the event of death or disability which are not pre-funded. Risk benefits are often insured annually.

Roll up fund
A fund where the income generated is reinvested in the fund, rather than being distributed to investors.

Rules
See **scheme rules**.

Salary grade scheme
A **career average scheme** in which the benefit for each year of **service** depends on the range into which the **member's** earnings fell during that year.

Salary related scheme
A **defined benefit scheme** in which benefits are related to earnings, i.e. a **final salary scheme** or a **career average scheme**.

Salary sacrifice
An agreement (which the Inland Revenue requires to be in writing) between the **employer** and employee whereby the employee forgoes part of his/her future earnings in return for a corresponding contribution by the **employer** to a **pension scheme**. This is not the same as an **AVC**.

Schedule 3 orders
Orders issued each year in accordance with *PSA 1993, Sch 3* specifying the rates of increase to be applied to **preserved benefits** over the period from the date of leaving to **normal pension date**. Formerly known as **section 52A orders**.

Schedule of contributions
A schedule specifying contribution rates and payment dates, (normally) agreed between the **employer** and the **trustees** and certified by the **scheme actuary** as being adequate to satisfy the **MFR** for the period concerned. Required for **defined benefit scheme**s subject to the MFR under *PA 1995, s 58*.

Schedule of payments
See **payment schedule**.

Scheme actuary
The named **actuary** appointed by the **trustees** or **managers** of an **occupational pension scheme** under *PA 1995, s 47*.

Scheme administrator
See definitions 1 and 2 of **administrator**.

Scheme auditor
The **auditor** appointed by the **trustees** or **managers** of an **occupational pension scheme** under *PA 1995, s 47*.

Scheme authorities
The persons regarded by the **NICO** as responsible for care of an **occupational pension scheme**. These are the **employer, scheme administrator, trustees, scheme actuary** and **scheme auditor**.

Scheme rules
The detailed provisions of a **pension scheme**, brought into operation by a **definitive trust deed** or in some other formal way, for example by a **trustees'** resolution.

Scheme year
The financial year of an **occupational pension scheme** for which the audited accounts and the annual report are prepared. The **Disclosure Regulations** permit the scheme year to be between 6 and 18 months when the scheme commences or winds up or when the scheme's financial year is changed.

Section 9(2B) rights
Rights to benefits (other than benefits from **AVCs**) under an **occupational pension scheme** which is **contracted out** on a salary related basis by virtue of *PSA 1993, s 9(2B)* and which are attributable to contracted out employment after 5 April 1997. Section 9(2B) rights are all benefits payable under the scheme, not just the minimum level of benefits required under the **reference scheme test**.

Section 19 scheme
See **section 590 scheme**.

Section 21 orders
See **section 148 orders**.

Section 32 policy
Used widely to describe an insurance policy used for **buy out** purposes. Came into use as a result of *FA 1981, s 32* (now contained in *ICTA 1988, s 591*), which gave prominence to the possibility of effecting such policies.

Section 32A policy
An insurance policy securing the **protected rights** of an **active member** or **deferred pensioner** upon the **winding up** of a **COMPS**. Introduced by *PA 1995*.

Glossary

Section 37A orders
See **section 109 orders**.

Section 49 scheme
See **section 53 scheme**.

Section 52A orders
See **Schedule 3 orders**.

Section 53 scheme
An **occupational pension scheme** which was formerly **contracted out** and by virtue of retaining **GMP**s or **protected rights** remains subject to supervision by the **NICO** under *PSA 1993, s 53* (*SSPA 1975, s 49*).

Section 109 orders
Orders issued each year in accordance with *PSA 1993, s 109* specifying the rates of increase to be applied to post-1988 **GMP**s in payment. Formerly known as **section 37A orders**.

Section 148 orders
Orders issued each year in accordance with *Social Security Administration Act 1992, s 148* specifying the rates of increase to be applied to the **earnings factors** on which the **additional pension** and **GMPs** are based. This revaluation is based on the increase in national average earnings. Formerly known as **section 21 orders**.

Section 226 annuity
See **retirement annuity**.

Section 590 scheme
An **occupational pension scheme** which has **mandatory approval** from the **PSO** under *ICTA 1988, s 590*.

Section 591 policy
See **section 32 policy**.

Section 608 scheme
An **occupational pension scheme** approved before 6 April 1980 under the **old code** which has not been re-approved under the **new code** and where no contributions have been paid since 6 April 1980.

Securities and Investments Board (SIB)
The chief regulator of financial services set up under *FSA 1986*. SIB is responsible for laying down the broad framework for investor regulation and is the supervisory body for specific regulatory organisations such as **IMRO** and the **PIA**.

Segmentation
A practice under which one or more arrangements are effected simultaneously to allow phased drawing of benefits by an individual who joins a **personal pension scheme**, or who prior to 1 July 1988 effected a **retirement annuity** contract. Also known as **clustering**.

Segregated fund
An arrangement whereby the investments of a particular **pension scheme** are managed by an **external investment manager** independently of other funds under its control. Often used to indicate an individual portfolio of stocks and shares in contrast to a **pooled fund**.

Self administered personal pension
See **self invested personal pension**.

Self administered scheme
An **occupational pension scheme** where the **assets** are invested, other than wholly by payment of insurance premiums, by the **trustees**, an in-house **investment manager** or an **external investment manager**. Although on the face of it the term self administered should refer to the method of administering contributions and benefits, in practice the term has become solely related to the way in which the investments are managed.

Self-employed annuity
See **retirement annuity**.

Self invested personal pension (SIPP)
A **personal pension** under which the **member** has some freedom to control investments.
The requirements governing self invested personal pensions are set out in **JOM** 101.

Self investment
The **investment** of the **assets** of an **occupational pension scheme** in **employer related investments**. A 5% limit is imposed on employer related investments by *PA 1995* (with certain exemptions).

Glossary

The **PSO** imposes separate restrictions on self investment by **SSASs**. Requirements as to disclosure and reporting of self investment are laid down by *PA 1995*.

Self regulating organisation (SRO)
A body authorised by **SIB** to regulate and supervise investment business or financial services activities.

Service
A period of employment with one or more connected **employers**. See also **continuous service**.

Short service benefit (SSB)
The benefit which must be provided for an **early leaver** under the **preservation** requirements of *PSA 1993*.

SIB review
A review, instigated by **SIB**, of **personal pension arrangements**, (including transfers to personal pensions and **section 32 policies**) sold between 29 April 1988 and 30 June 1994, to determine whether or not the purchasers had been given best advice in accordance with *FSA 1986*.

Simplified defined contribution scheme (SDCS)
A **money purchase scheme** subject to the simplified limits and **approval** procedure of the Inland Revenue described in part 22 of **Practice Notes (IR12)**.

Single premium method
A method of determining the premiums payable under an insurance contract with the object of meeting each year the cost of the benefit relating to that year.

Small self-administered scheme (SSAS)
A self administered **occupational pension scheme** with generally fewer than 12 **members** where at least one of those members is connected with another member or with a **trustee** or an **employer** in relation to the scheme. These schemes are subject to certain special conditions for **approval**, including the requirement for a **pensioneer trustee**. The statutory definition is contained in the *Retirement Benefits Schemes (Restriction on Discretion to Approve)(Small Self-administered Schemes) Regulations 1991 SI No 1614*.

Solvency test
An actuarial calculation to determine whether the **assets** of an **occupational pension scheme** are sufficient to meet the benefit obligations. There is a statutory minimum level of solvency known as the **minimum funding requirement**.

Special contributions
Used in **Practice Notes (IR12)** to denote contributions payable to an **occupational pension scheme** by the **employer** for a period of less than three years or as a single payment often to provide new benefits or to meet **deficiencies**. These are to be distinguished from **ordinary annual contributions**.

Specialist management
A style of investment management where individual **investment managers** concentrate on defined **asset** classes. An example would be to have separate UK equity, overseas equity and bond portfolios, with the allocation of monies between them determined elsewhere.

Sponsoring employer
See **principal employer**.

SSAS 1996 method
A test to determine whether benefits under a **SSAS** are within Inland Revenue funding limits. See also **ABI 1994 method**.

Standard contribution rate
The contribution rate required by a particular **valuation method** before taking into account any differences between the **actuarial liability** and the **actuarial value of assets**.

State Earnings Related Pension Scheme (SERPS)
The **additional pension** provisions of the State pension scheme.

State pension age
See **state pensionable age**.

State pension disregard
See **State pension offset**.

State pension offset
A reduction in pension or **pensionable earnings** to achieve **integration**.

State pensionable age (SPA)
The age from which pensions are normally payable by the State pension scheme as defined in *PA 1995, Sch 4*. *PA 1995* raised the State pensionable age for women to 65, bringing it in line with men and this is being phased in over a ten year period between 2010 and 2020.

State scheme premium
A payment made to the DSS in certain circumstances to reinstate all or part of an individual's **SERPS** benefits. Most State scheme premium**s** were abolished by *PA 1995* from 6 April 1997.

Statement of comfort
A statement confirming the validity of an existing **certificate A** issued by the **scheme actuary** for the purpose of re electing to **contract out** after 6 April 1997 and before a **certificate T** is signed.

Statement of investment principles (SIP)
A written statement of the principles governing decisions about **investment** for an **occupational pension scheme**, which **trustees** are required to prepare and maintain. Trustees must have regard to advice from a suitably qualified person and consult with the **employer**. See *PA 1995, s 35*.

Statement of recommended practice (SORP)
Guidance on best accounting practice for the presentation of financial information prepared by the particular industry to which the SORP relates. See also **Pension scheme SORP**.

Statement of standard accounting practice 24 (SSAP 24)
The accounting standard which deals with the accounting for and the disclosure of **pension costs** and commitments in the **financial statements** of **employers** in respect of arrangements for the provision of retirement benefits for their employees.

Statutory discharge
The discharge provided in respect of a **member** who exercises the statutory right to a **cash equivalent** under *PSA 1993, s 99*.

Statutory scheme
A scheme (usually in the public sector) established by Act of Parliament.

Stock lending
The process by which stock is released to a third party in return for security and a fee for so doing. This is normally undertaken on a short-term basis.

Stock selection
The continuous process of selecting which stocks are included in a portfolio.

Straight 60ths/80ths
Benefit scales of 1/60th and 3/80ths of **final remuneration** for pension and tax-free cash respectively. Usually, the **PSO** allows benefits to be provided up to these scales without reference to **retained benefits**.

Substituted annuity
An **annuity** under a **personal pension scheme** bought from a life assurance company or friendly society other than the original **pension provider**.

Superannuation Funds Office (SFO)
See **Pension schemes Office**.

Supplementary certificate A
An optional certificate that could have been issued if a **certificate A** was renewed shortly before 6 April 1997.

Supplementary scheme
See **top up pension scheme**.

Surplus
See **actuarial surplus**. Sometimes used incorrectly to describe an excess of income over expenditure in an occupational pension scheme's accounts.

Surrender
1. The cancellation of an insurance policy by the payment of a 'surrender value'.
2. Sometimes used to describe **allocation** or **commutation**.

Suspension order
An order made by **OPRA** under *PA 1995, s 4* suspending a person from exercising any functions as a **trustee** of any **occupational pension scheme** to which the order applies. See also **disqualification order** and **prohibition order**.

Targeted money purchase scheme
A **money purchase scheme** where there is a stated intention, but not a promise, to provide a particular level of benefit.

Tax approved scheme
Loosely used to mean a scheme approved by the **PSO**. See also **exempt approved scheme**.

Tax relief at source
See **pension tax relief at source**.

Temporary annuity
An **annuity** payable for a fixed period or until earlier death.

Term assurance policy
A policy which provides a lump sum on death only before a specified date. Sometimes referred to as a term insurance policy.

Tied agent
An agent, connected to a particular insurance or other financial product company, who must sell only the financial products of that company (as opposed to an **independent financial adviser**).

Tied annuity option
The option to apply the proceeds of an insurance contract to buy an **annuity** from the original insurer at its current market rate as an alternative to exercising a **guaranteed annuity option**.

Time weighted return
A relative measure of the **rate of return** earned by the **assets** in a fund, independent of the timing of cash flows into or out of the fund. To be contrasted with **money weighted return**.

Top hat scheme
See **executive scheme**.

Top up pension scheme
A scheme providing benefits which supplement those provided under another scheme. Used in **guidance notes** published by **PSO** to refer to an **unapproved scheme**.

Total earnings scheme
A type of **career average scheme** where the pension is a specified fraction of the **member's** aggregate earnings throughout the period of membership.

Tracing service
1. A service run by the **Pension Schemes Registry** to help individuals locate their past pension rights.
2. A service run by the DSS to help schemes trace their **deferred pensioners**.

Tracker/tracking fund
A fund which seeks to match investment performance to a particular stock market index. See also definition 2 of **indexation**.

Transfer club
A group of **employers** and **occupational pension schemes** which has agreed to a common basis of **transfer payments**.

Transfer credit
The benefit purchased by a **transfer payment** as defined in *PSA 1993, s 181* and *PA 1995, s 124*. The effect on **qualifying service** is to link that part of the previous **pensionable service** which gave rise to the transfer payment to the pensionable service in the receiving scheme. See also linked **qualifying service**.

Transfer payment
A payment made from a **pension scheme** to another **pension scheme**, or to purchase a **buy out** policy, in lieu of benefits which have accrued to the **member** or members concerned, to enable the receiving arrangement to provide alternative benefits. The transfer payment may be made in accordance with the **scheme rules** or in exercise of a member's statutory rights under *PSA 1993*. See also **cash equivalent**.

Transfer premium
A **State scheme premium** which could have been paid when **accrued benefits** in excess of **GMPs** were transferred to an **occupational pension scheme** which was not **contracted out**. Withdrawn from 6 April 1997.

Transfer value (TV)
The amount of the **transfer payment**.

Transfer value analysis
The investigation of whether it is likely to be more advantageous to transfer benefits to another pension arrangement based on stated **actuarial assumptions**.

Trivial pension
A pension which is so small that it can be fully exchanged for cash (commuted) without prejudicing the approval of the scheme by the **PSO**. The maximum amount of pension which may be commuted on account of triviality is also governed by **preservation** and contracting-out requirements.

True and fair view
Certain legislation requires accounts to show a true and fair view. This is generally understood as requiring accounts to contain information in sufficient quantity and quality as to satisfy the reasonable expectations of the readers. Compliance with accounting principles and standards is integral to this concept. According to the **Audited Accounts Regulations** and the **Pension Scheme SORP**, the accounts of an **occupational pension scheme** should present a true and fair view.

Trust
A legal concept whereby property is held by one or more persons (the **trustees**) for the benefit of others (the **beneficiaries**) for the purposes specified by the trust instrument. The trustees may also be beneficiaries.

Trust corporation
A company empowered under the *Public Trustee Act 1906* to act as **custodian** trustee and which is expected to provide professional expertise in managing **trusts**.

Trust deed
A legal document, executed in the form of a **deed**, which establishes, regulates or amends a **trust**. See also **interim trust deed** and **definitive trust deed**.

Trust instrument
A **trust deed** or other document or series of documents, by which a **trust** is created and the provisions governing the trust are prescribed.

Trustee
An individual or company appointed to carry out the purposes of a **trust** in accordance with the provisions of the **trust instrument** and general principles of trust law.

Trustee report
A report by the **trustees** describing various aspects of an **occupational pension scheme**. It may form part of the **annual report**.

Trustees' undertaking
The undertaking given by the **trustees** to the **scheme actuary**. The undertaking will require the trustees to provide such information as the scheme actuary determines and any items prescribed by regulations and professional guidance issued by the Institute and Faculty of Actuaries.

Unallocated assets
Assets of an **occupational pension scheme** providing **money purchase** benefits which have not been specifically allocated for the provision of benefits to or in respect of **members** (whether generally or individually).

Unallocated surplus
A **surplus** on the **winding up** of an **occupational pension scheme** which cannot be allocated under the terms of the **trust deed**. Now subject to statutory provision under *PA 1995, s 77*. Also called excess assets.

Unapproved scheme
An **occupational pension scheme** which is not designed for **approval** by the Inland Revenue. Following *FA 1989* an **employer** may provide benefits for an employee under an unapproved scheme without those benefits being taken into account in calculating **maximum approvable benefits** under an **approved scheme**. Such a scheme may be used to provide benefits on earnings in excess of

the **earnings cap**. The Inland Revenue has published **guidance notes** on the tax treatment of unapproved schemes. Also misleadingly used to refer to a scheme which is awaiting approval.

Underfunding
Where a pension arrangement has **assets** less than required to meet **liabilities**.

Underwriting
1. The analysis of the risk inherent in providing an insurance policy. It involves an investigation of the circumstances surrounding the subject to be insured. The policy may be written on special terms or insurance may be refused, if the risk is deemed to be higher than average.
2. Flotations of shares on the stock exchange are sometimes underwritten by financial institutions. They agree to purchase the shares, at a pre-determined price, if the shares are not all sold on the market, receiving a fee for doing so.

Unfunded scheme
A scheme where **assets** are not accumulated in advance of the benefits commencing to be paid.

Unfunded unapproved retirement benefits scheme (UURBS)
An unfunded **occupational pension scheme**, not designed to be approved by the **PSO**.

Uniform accrual
The treatment of retirement benefits as being earned equally over the period of potential **service** to **normal pension age**, especially for the purposes of the **preservation** requirements of *PSA 1993*.

Unisex annuity rates
Annuity rates which do not distinguish between gender.

Unistatus annuity rates
Annuity rates which do not distinguish between gender, marital status or the existence of **dependants**.

Unit linked pension scheme
A scheme, often an **individual arrangement**, where the amount of the retirement benefits is related to the performance of a specified **unitised fund**, usually through the medium of an insurance policy.

Unit linked policy
An insurance policy under which premiums paid by the policyholders purchase units. The price of the units fluctuates according to the value of the underlying investments.

Unit trust
A **trust** set up as a **pooled fund** usually under the supervision of **SIB**. Its portfolio of investments is unitised to enable investors to buy in to the trust or to redeem an earlier investment. The prices at which units may be bought or sold are determined by the **investment managers** based on the net asset value of the fund.

Unitised fund
A **pooled fund** which has been divided into units, such as a **unit trust**.

Unitised with profits
A **with profits policy** under which premiums paid by policyholders purchase units. The value of the policy may be increased by the addition of bonuses or bonus units. See also **unit linked policy**.

Unused relief
That portion of the tax relief available for **member** contributions to a **personal pension scheme** in any tax year which is in excess of that claimed by reference to the contributions already made. See also **carry forward** and **carry back**.

Uplifted 60ths/80ths
Scales set out in **Practice Notes (IR12)** expressed as more than one sixtieth or three eightieths of **final remuneration** for each year of **service** used for calculating **Inland Revenue limits** for pension and tax-free cash respectively. These apply to **members** of **occupational pension schemes** with **pre-17 March 1987 continued rights**.

Upper band earnings
Earnings between the **lower earnings limit** and **upper earnings limit** for NI contributions.

Upper earnings limit (UEL)
The maximum amount of earnings (equal to approximately seven times the **lower earnings limit** on which NI contributions are payable by employees.

Upper tier earnings
See **upper band earnings**.

Valuation balance sheet
A comparison of the **actuarial value of assets** with the **actuarial liability** showing the elements of these amounts in the form of a **balance sheet**, with an amount for **actuarial surplus** or **actuarial deficiency** as a balancing item. The results of an **actuarial valuation** may be presented in other ways.

Valuation basis
Commonly used by **actuaries** to mean **valuation method** and/or **actuarial assumptions**.

Valuation date
The date by reference to which the **actuarial valuation** is carried out.

Valuation method
An approach used by the **actuary** in an **actuarial valuation**. The main categories of approach are described under **accrued benefits valuation method** and **prospective benefits valuation method**. A variety of methods can be used but the method or methods used in a particular case should be adequately described in the **actuarial report**.

Valuation report
See **actuarial report**.

Value for money
A **minimum benefit** which is related to the **member's** contributions. SSA73 **preservation** requirements originally included such a minimum, but this was removed by amending regulations from 1 January 1986.

Variable pension
See **income withdrawal**.

Vested rights
(a) For **active members**, benefits to which they would unconditionally be entitled on leaving the scheme;

(b) for **deferred pensioners**, their **preserved benefits**;

(c) for **pensioners**, pensions to which they are entitled, including where appropriate the related benefits for spouses or other **dependants**.

Voluntary contributions certificate
A certificate issued by an **FSAVC scheme** to the **member**, to give evidence to his/her Inspector of Taxes of **members**hip and contributions.

Waiting period
A period of **service** specified in the **scheme rules** which an employee must serve before being entitled to join an **occupational pension scheme** or to receive a particular benefit. In some schemes the waiting period before being entitled to join may automatically count as **pensionable service**. Not to be confused with **qualifying service**.

Waiver of premium option
A benefit available under some **personal pension schemes** and **retirement annuity** contracts, whereby the **pension provider** undertakes to credit regular premiums to the individual's contract if he/she becomes unable to contribute because of lack of **relevant earnings** arising from **incapacity**.

Whistle blowing
The statutory duty imposed on the **scheme actuary** and **scheme auditor** by *PA 1995, s 48* to advise **OPRA** immediately in writing if they have reasonable cause to believe there is a material problem with an **occupational pension scheme**. Other persons may 'blow the whistle' but have no statutory duty to do so.

Widow's/widower's guaranteed minimum pension (WGMP)
The minimum pension which an **occupational pension scheme** must provide for the surviving spouse of a **member** as one of the conditions of contracting out (unless it is **contracted out** through the provision of **protected rights**) for **pensionable service** before 6 April 1997.

Widow's/widower's (pension) option
See definition 1 of **allocation**.

Winding up
The process of terminating an **occupational pension scheme**, usually by applying the **assets** to the purchase of **immediate annuities** and **deferred annuities** for the **beneficiaries**, or by transferring the assets and **liabilities** to another pension scheme, in accordance with the scheme documentation or statute (*PA 1995,*

s 74). There are statutory provisions to determine when winding up commences for statutory purposes, *Occupational Pension Schemes (Winding Up) Regulations 1996 SI No 3126, reg 2.*
See also **priority rule**.

With profits policy
An insurance policy under which a share of the **surpluses** disclosed by **actuarial valuations** of the insurance company's life and pensions business is payable as an addition to the guaranteed benefits or in reduction of future premiums.

With proportion
Describes an arrangement whereby on the death of a person receiving an **annuity** paid in arrears a proportionate payment becomes due from the date of the last full payment up to the date of death.

Table of Statutes

Banking Act 1987,	4.10
Child Support, Pensions and Social Security Act 2000,	3.3, 5.7, App. A
s 43,	5.7
Contracts of Employment Act 1963,	App. A
Contracts (Rights of Third Parties) Act 1999,	3.3
Contributory Pensions Act 1925,	App. A
Data Protection Act 1998,	3.3, 4.18, 4.45, 5.2, 6.6
Disability Discrimination Act 1995,	
s 17,	4.24
Disability Discrimination Act 1998,	3.3
Discrimination Act 1975,	
s 6(4),	4.26
Employment Rights Act 1996,	3.3, App. A
ss 58–60,	5.4
Equal Pay Act 1970,	
s 1,	4.26
s 6,	4.26
Finance Act 1921,	App. A
s 32,	App. A
Finance Act 1930,	App. A
Finance Act 1947,	App. A
Finance Act 1970,	App. A
Finance Act 1986,	
Sch 12,	9.14
Finance Act 1989,	App. A
Finance Act 1994,	App. A
Finance Act 1995,	App. A
Finance (No 2) Act 1997,	App. A
Finance (No 2) Act 1998,	App. A
Financial Services Act 1986,	3.3, 4.12, 5.16, 7.18, App. A
Financial Services and Markets Act 2000,	3.3
Income and Corporation Taxes Act 1988,	3.1, 3.7, 5.1, App. A
Part XIV, Chap I,	5.18
s 148,	3.9
s 416,	6.5
s 590,	
(2),	4.30
(3),	3.7, 5.18
s 590C,	3.9
s 591,	3.1, 3.7, 5.18
s 591B(2)	4.30
s 611AA,	5.14
s 615(6),	6.7
s 840,	6.5
Sch 22,	6.10, 9.6, 9.14
Income Tax Act 1918,	App. A
Income Tax Act 1952,	App. A
s 219,	App. A
s 225,	App. A
s 226,	App. A
s 378,	App. A
s 379,	App. A
s 386,	App. A
s 387,	App. A
s 388,	App. A
s 389,	App. A
s 390,	App. A
s 391,	App. A
Local Government and Other Officers' Superannuation Act 1922,	App. A
Local Government Superannuation Act 1937,	App. A
Matrimonial Causes Act 1973,	
ss 23–24,	4.20
ss 24B–24D	4.21
National Insurance Act 1946,	App. A
National Insurance Act 1959,	App. A
National Insurance Act 1963,	App. A
Old Age Pensions Act 1908,	App. A
Pension Schemes Act 1993,	3.3, 3.18, 3.19, 4.7, 4.33, App. A
s 6,	4.17
s 12B,	3.19
s 28,	3.20
s 29,	3.20
s 37,	4.30
s 72,	4.30
s 94,	
(1),	4.33
s 99,	4.33
s 111,	4.8
s 113,	4.15
s 168,	

Table of Statutes

(4),	4.46, 4.50	(6),	4.36
Pensions Act 1995,	3.2, 3.3, 3.4, 3.5,	(8),	4.8, 5.2
	3.17, 4.2, 4.16, 4.26,	(10),	4.36
	4.34, 4.35, 4.45, 5.1, 5.7, 5.19,	(12),	4.36
	6.3, 6.4, 6.6, 6.15, 9.6, App. A	s 50,	4.25, 4.36, 6.14
s 1,	5.19	s 56,	4.8
s 3,	5.5	s 57,	4.8, 6.10
s 6,	4.36	(7),	4.36
s 7,	5.5	s 58,	4.9, 5.2, 6.12
s 10,	4.46, 4.50, 5.5	(8),	4.36
s 11,	4.35	s 59,	
s 16,	5.7	(4),	4.36
ss 16–21,	4.23	s 60,	
s 17,	5.7	(8),	4.36
s 18,	5.7	ss 62–66,	4.26
s 21,		s 65,	4.26
(1),	4.36	s 67,	4.27, 4.30, 4.36, 6.4
(2),	4.36	(2),	4.27
s 23,		s 68,	4.30
(3),	5.8	s 69,	5.19
s 29,	5.4	ss 78–80,	5.21
s 30,	4.36	s 87,	5.2, 6.12
s 31,	4.46, 4.50	(5),	4.36
s 32,	4.54, 4.56	ss 87–89,	4.9
s 33,	4.46, 4.47	s 88,	
s 34,		(4),	4.36
(2),	4.12, 4.29	s 91,	4.7
(4),	4.12, 4.47	s 98,	4.16
(6),	4.47	s 101,	
s 35,	4.12, 6.7	(1),	4.36
(4),	4.12	s 166,	4.21
(6),	4.36	Public Trustee Act 1906,	5.11
s 36,	4.12, 4.47	Race Relations Act 1976,	4.26
(3),	4.12	Sex Discrimination Act 1975,	
(4),	4.12	s 6(4)	4.26
(6),	4.12	Social Security Act 1989,	App. A
(8),	4.36	s 23,	4.26
s 39,	4.4	Social Security Act 1990,	App. A
s 40,	3.17, 4.12, 6.11	Social Security Administration Act	
(4),	4.36	1992,	App. A
(5),	4.36	Social Security Contribtions and	
s 41,	4.15, 6.10	Benefits Act 1992,	App. A
(1),	6.11	Social Security Pensions Act	
(6),	6.11	1995,	App. A
s 47,	4.12, 4.13, 4.29, 4.36, 5.1,	Superannuation and Other Trust Funds	
	5.12, 5.13, 5.15, 5.16	(Validation) Act 1927,	App. A
(3),	4.36	Theft Act 1968,	4.45
(8),	4.36	Trustee Act 1925,	App. A
(9)(b),	4.16	s 14,	5.4
(11),	4.36	s 19,	4.51
s 48,	5.12, 5.13, 5.19	s 36,	5.5
s 49,		s 39,	5.5
(1),	4.10	s 40,	5.5

s 61,	4.46, 4.52
Trustee Act 2000,	3.3
s 11,	4.29
s 31,	4.4
s 34,	4.51
s 36,	4.29
Trustee Delegation Act 1995,	
s 5,	4.29
Unfair Contract Terms Act 1977,	4.47
s 2,	
(2),	4.47
Welfare Reform and Pensions Act 1999,	3.3, 4.22, App. A
s 11,	4.7

Table of Statutory Instruments

Disability Discrimination (Employment)
Regulations 1996 (SI 1996 No
1456),
  reg 4,   4.24
Occupational Pension Schemes
(Contracting-out) Regulations 1996
(SI 1996 No 1172),
  reg 3,   6.13
  reg 6,   6.13
Occupational Pension Schemes
(Disclosure of Information)
Regulations 1996 (SI 1996 No
1655),   4.15, 7.1, 7.2, 7.3, 7.4, 7.5,
7.7, 7.8, 7.15, App. B
  reg 3,   6.2
  reg 4,   6.6
    (1)   4.15
    (5)   4.30
  reg 6,   6.7, 6.11
  reg 11,   4.36
Occupational Pension Schemes
(Equal Treatment) Regulations 1995
(SI 1995 No 3183),   3.6, 4.26
Occupational Pension Schemes
(Independent Trustee) Regulations
1997 (SI 1997 No 252),
  reg 2,   5.8
Occupational Pension Schemes (Internal
Dispute Resolution Procedures)
Regulations 1996 (SI 1996 No
1270),   4.25, 6.14
Occupational Pension Schemes
(Member Nominated Trustee)
Regulations 1996 (SI 1996 No
1216),   5.7
Occupational Pension Schemes
(Minimum Funding Requirement
and Actuarial Valuations) Regulations
1996 (SI 1996 No 1536),
  Sch 6,   6.10

Occupational Pension Schemes
(Modification of Schemes)
Regulations 1996 (SI 1996 No
2517),
  reg 8,   4.36
Occupational Pension Schemes
(Requirement to Obtain Audited
Accounts and a Statement from the
Auditor) Regulations 1996 (SI 1996
No 1975),   4.11, 6.8, 5.13
  reg 2,
    (3),   4.36
  reg 6,   6.8
Occupational Pension Schemes
(Scheme Administration)
Regulations 1996
(SI 1996 No 1715),   4.10, 4.16, 4.57
  reg 9,   4.56
  reg 16,   5.2
Occupational Pension Schemes
(Transfer Values) Regulations 1996
(SI 1996 No 1847),   4.33, 6.11
Part-time Workers (Prevention of Less
Favourable Treatment) Regulations
2000 (SI 2000 No 1551),   3.6, 4.26
Pension Schemes Surpluses (Valuation)
Regulations 1987 (SI 1987 No
412),   5.12
Register of Occupational and Personal
Pension Schemes Regulations
1997(SI 1997 No 371),   4.17, 4.36
Rules of the Supreme Court 1965
(SI 1965 No 1776),
  Ord 85,
    r 2,   4.3
Stakeholder Pension Schemes
Regulations 2000 (SI 2000 No
1403),
  reg 22, 11.5
  reg 23, 11.5

Table of Cases

Armitage v Nurse [1997] 2 All ER 705, 4.47
Barber v GRE Assurance Group (1990) ECR I-1989, 3.6
Bartlett v Barclays Bank Trust Co Ltd (No 2) (1980) Ch 515, 4.40, 4.44
Brickenden v London and Loan Savings Co (1934) DLR 465, 4.40
Brooks v Brooks (1996) 1 AC 375, 4.20
CAS (Nominees) Ltd v Nottingham Forest plc (2000) AER (D) 1115, 3.2
Clough v Bond (1838) 3 My & Cr 490, 4.40
Coloroll Pension Trustees Ltd v Russell (1994) ECR I-4389; (1994) OPLR 179, 3.6
Cowan v Scargill (High Court) [1984] 2 All ER 750 at 760, 10.3
Defrenne v Sabena (No 2) (1976) ECR 455, 3.6
Fisscher v Vorhuis Hengelo BV (1994) ECR I-4583, 3.6
Hillsdown Holdings plc v Pensions Ombudsman (1996) PLR 427, 4.30, 5.2

Hole v Garnsey (1930) AC 472, 4.30
Imperial Group Pension Trust v Imperial Tobacco (1991) 2 AER 597, 5.2
Londonderry's Settlement (1965) Ch 918, 4.14
Marsh Mercer Pension Scheme v Pensions Ombudsman (2001) 16 PBLR (28), 3.18
National Grid (2001) 19 PBLR (21); (2001) UKHL 20, 3.5
Nestle v National Westminster Bank plc [1994] 1 All ER 118, 4.40
Preston v Wolverhampton Healthcare NHS Trust (2001) 09 PBLR (16); (2001) UKHL 5, 3.6
Target Holdings Ltd v Redfern (1994) 2 All ER 337, 4.40
Vestey's Settlement, Re (1950) 2 All ER 891, 4.30
Wilson v Law Debenture Trust Corporation plc (1995) Pensions Law Reports 141, 4.14

Table of European Legislation

Treaty of Rome,
 Article 119 (ex 141), 3.6, 3.18, 4.26

Index

A

Accounts,
  audited, 4.11, 6.8
  company, 6.9
  trustees, 7.5
Actuary,
  role, 9.6
  scheme, 5.12
  valuations,
    assets, 9.11
    assumptions, actuarial, 9.9
    benefits, 9.10
    discontinuance, 9.13
    generally, 9.4
    minimum funding requirement, 9.13
    ongoing, 9.8
    report, valuation, 9.15
    surplus test, 9.14
    timing, 9.5
  what actuary does not do, 9.7
Additional voluntary contributions (AVCs),
  advantages, 11.11
  benefits,
    added years, 11.10
    fixed pension, 11.9
    generally, 11.7
    money purchase, 11.8
  disadvantages, 11.11
  free-standing, 11.4
  investment,
    building society, 11.13
    generally, 11.12
    matching, 11.17
    with profits, 11.14
    scheme assets, 11.16
    unit-linked, 11.15
  matching, 11.17
  meaning, 11.1
  occupational pensions, 11.3
  personal pension, 11.6
  with profits, 11.14
  projections, 11.18–20
    range of assumptions, 11.20
    rough guide, 11.19
  reasons for making, 11.2
  retirement, flexibility at,
    drawdown as opposed to taking at retirement, 11.22
    taking benefits other than at normal retirement, 11.21
    too much benefit, where, 11.23
  stakeholder pensions, 11.5
  types,
    free-standing, 11.4
    occupational, 11.3
    personal pension, 11.6
    stakeholder, 11.5
Addresses, 3.23, 4.58, 5.23, 6.15
Administrator, 5.14
Advice,
  expert, 10.4
  investment, 10.4
Advisers, 5.15
Age,
  normal age of retirement, 2.18
  retirement, 1.7
    normal age of retirement, 2.18
Amendment of scheme rules,
  duties of trustees, 4.27
  powers of trustees, 4.30
Annual report,
  trustees', 6.11
Appointment,
  member-nominated trustees, 4.23, 5.7
  professional advisers, 4.13
  trustees, 5.5, 6.3
Assets,
  investment, 10.9
  valuation, 9.11
Assumptions, actuarial, 9.9
Audited accounts, 6.8
  duty of trustees to obtain, 4.11
Auditor, 5.13
Augmentation,
  powers of trustees, 4.31
AVCs. *See* **Additional voluntary contributions (AVCs)**

B

Bank accounts,
  duties of trustees, 4.10
Basic State pension, 2.1

Basic Guide to Pensions

Benefits,
  additional voluntary contributions
    (AVCs),
    added years, 11.10
    fixed pension, 11.9
    generally, 11.7
    money purchase, 11.8
  calculations. See Calculations, benefit
  death, on, 7.13
  limits, 3.15
  payment,
    trustees' duty, 4.7
  retirement, on, 7.12
  statements, 7.6, 7.9
  summary of limits, 3.16
  valuation, 9.10
  withdrawal, on, 7.14
Booklet, scheme, 6.6, 7.4
Breach of trust, 4.38
Building society, 11.13

C

Calculations, benefit,
  death in service, benefits on. See
    Death in service benefits
  defined benefit plan,
    early retirement lump sum, 8.11
    early retirement pension, 8.10
    late retirement pension and lump
      sum, 8.12
    lump sum, effect on normal
      retirement pension, 8.9
    member's details, 8.6
    model plans, structure of, 8.3
    normal retirement lump sum, 8.8
    normal retirement pension, 8.7
    retirement from, 8.5–12
  defined contribution plan, 8.4
    key factors, 8.14
    lump sum, 8.17
    pensions, 8.16
    retirement benefits, 8.15
    retirement from, 8.13–17
  disability, benefits on, 8.37, 8.38
  generally, 8.1
  increases to pensions in payment, 8.21
  Inland Revenue limits, 8.48
  leaving plan, 8.18–20
    death in service benefits, 8.29, 8.30
    generally, 8.18
    increases under defined benefit
      contribution plan between
      leaving and retirement, 8.20

    increases under defined benefit
      plan between leaving and
      retirement, 8.19
  model plans, structure of, 8.2
    defined benefit plan, 8.3
    defined contributions plan, 8.4
  pension splitting on divorce,
    defined benefit plan, 8.40
    defined contribution plan, 8.41
    generally, 8.39
  record keeping. See Record keeping
Combined pension forecasts, 7.10
Company accounts, 6.9
Consultants, pension, 5.17
Contract of employment, 5.2
Contracting in,
  occupational pensions, 2.14
Contracting out,
  certificate, 6.13
  legal framework, 3.17
  occupational pensions, 2.14
  stakeholder pensions, 2.26
  transfers from contracted-out
    schemes, 3.22
Contributions,
  collection by trustees, 4.8
  employer, 5.2
  limits, 3.14
  occupational pensions, 2.21
  personal pensions,
    limits, 2.23
  schedule, 6.12
    production by trustees, 4.9
  stakeholder pensions,
    employer, 2.26
    member, 2.26
  State pension, 2.6
Court orders relating to divorce,
  compliance with duties, 4.19
Custodian trustees, 5.11

D

Data Protection Act 1998,
  trustees' compliance with, 4.18
Death,
  benefits. See Death in service benefits
  retirement, 8.47
Death in service benefits, 7.13
  defined benefit plan,
    generally, 8.23
    leaving service, 8.29
    lump sum, calculation of, 8.24
    pension, calculation of, 8.25

Index

retirement, death in, 8.33–35
defined contribution plan,
  deferment, calculation of lump
    sum on death in, 8.31
  generally, 8.26
  leaving service, 8.30
  lump sum, calculation of, 8.27
  pension, calculation of, 8.28, 8.32
  retirement, death in, 8.36
generally, 8.22

Decision making,
powers of trustees, 4.53

Deeds,
adherence, 6.5
amendment, 6.4
appointment of trustees, 6.3
participation, 6.5
removal of trustees, 6.3
retirement of trustees, 6.3

Defined benefit plan, 2.11
calculations, benefit,
  early retirement lump sum, 8.11
  early retirement pension, 8.10
  late retirement pension and lump
    sum, 8.12
  lump sum, effect on normal
    retirement pension, 8.9
  member's details, 8.6
  model plans, structure of, 8.3
  normal retirement lump sum, 8.8
  normal retirement pension, 8.7
  retirement from, 8.5–12
death in service benefits,
  generally, 8.23
  leaving service, 8.29
  lump sum, calculation of, 8.24
  pension, calculation of, 8.25
  retirement, death in, 8.33–35
disability, benefits on,
  pension benefits, 8.38
model plans, 8.3
pension splitting on divorce, 8.40

Defined contribution plan, 8.4
calculations, benefit, 8.4
  key factors, 8.14
  lump sum, 8.17
  pensions, 8.16
  retirement benefits, 8.15
  retirement from plan, 8.13–17
death in service benefits,
  deferment, calculation of lump
    sum on death in, 8.31
  generally, 8.26

leaving service, 8.30
lump sum, calculation of, 8.27
pension, calculation of, 8.28, 8.32
retirement, death in, 8.36
pension splitting on divorce, 8.41

Delegation,
powers of trustees, 4.29

Dependant's benefits,
occupational pensions, 2.20

Disability, benefits on,
defined benefit plan,
  pension benefits, 8.38
  generally, 8.37
pension benefits,
  defined benefit plan, 8.38

Disability discrimination,
duties of trustees, 4.24

Disclosure of information,
members, 4.15
OPRA, 4.16
potential members, 4.15
professional advisers, 4.16

Discontinuance valuation, 9.12

Divorce,
pension sharing 4.22
pension splitting,
  defined benefit plan, 8.40
  defined contribution plan, 8.41
  generally, 8.39
trustees' duty to comply with orders
  relating to, 4.19–22
variations of settlements 4.20

Documents. *See* **Scheme documents**

Duties of trustees,
acting in accordance with trust deed
  and rules, 4.3
amendment of scheme rules, 4.27
audited accounts, duty to obtain, 4.11
bank accounts, 4.10
best interests of scheme members,
  acting in, 4.5, 10.3
collection of contributions, 4.8
court orders relating to divorce,
  compliance with duties, 4.19
earmarking 4.21
pension sharing 4.22
variations of settlements 4.20
Data Protection Act 1998,
  compliance with, 4.18
disability discrimination, 4.24
disclosure of information, 4.14–16
  members, 4.15
  OPRA, 4.16

potential members, 4.15
professional advisers, 4.16
equal treatment, provision to, 4.26
generally, 4.1, 4.2
impartiality, 4.6
internal dispute resolution procedure,
   implementation of, 4.25
investment of fund 4.12. *See also*
   Investment
member nominated trustees,
   appointment of, 4.23, 5.7
payment of benefits, 4.7
payment schedule, production of, 4.9
Pensions Act 1995, s 67, compliance
   with, 4.27
professional advisers, appointment of,
   4.13
prudently, conscientiously and
   honestly, duty to act, 4.4, 10.2
registration, 4.17
schedule of contributions, production
   of, 4.9
scheme records, 4.10
texts, useful, 4.59

E
Early retirement,
   payments, calculation of, 1.8
   without penalty, 1.10
Eligibility to join pension scheme,
   1.6
   sex discrimination, 1.6
Employer,
   contract of employment, 5.2
   contributions, 5.2
   duties, 5.2
   membership information from, 5.2
   occupational pension schemes, 5.2
   payroll systems, 5.2
   people in pensions, 5.2
   powers, 5.2
   trust deed, party to, 5.2
Equal treatment,
   trustees' duty to provide, 4.26
European law,
   legal framework, 3.6
Exclusion clauses,
   trust deed, 4.47

F
Fees,
   stakeholder pensions, 2.26
Final remuneration,
   definition, 3.10
Final salary schemes, 2.11
   information, 7.8
Forecasts,
   combined pension, 7.10
Fund managers, 5.16
Funding,
   actuarial valuations,
      assets, valuation of, 9.11
      assumptions, actuarial, 9.9
      benefits, valuation of, 9.10
      discontinuance, 9.12
      generally, 9.4
      ongoing, 9.8
      reports, valuation of, 9.15
      role of actuary, 9.6
      timing, 9.5
   assumptions, actuarial, 9.9
   discontinuance valuation, 9.12
   meaning, 9.1
   minimum funding requirement, 9.13
   money purchase schemes, 9.3
   reasons for funding pension scheme,
      9.2
   water tank analogy, 9.7

G
Group personal pensions, 2.9
Guaranteed minimum pensions,
   legal framework, 3.18

H
Historical background, 1.2
   legislation, overview of, 1.3

I
**Impartially between scheme
members, duty of trustees to act,**
   4.6
Indemnity clauses,
   employer, from, 4.49
   scheme, from, 4.50
Independent trustees, 5.8
Index-tracking, 10.20
Information,
   combined pension forecasts, 7.10
   disclosure. *See* Disclosure of
      information
   final salary schemes, 7.8
   membership, 5.2
   money purchase schemes, 7.7
   presentations, 7.16
   scheme booklet, 7.4

scheme documentation. *See* Scheme documentation	
scheme members, for,	
benefit statements,	7.6, 7.9
combined pension forecasts,	7.10
communication or information, whether,	7.1
communication material,	7.3
Disclosure Regulations,	7.2
final salary schemes,	7.8
forms of communications,	7.17
money purchase schemes,	7.7
presentations,	7.16
scheme booklet,	7.4
statements of entitlements,	7.11–15
strategies, effective communication,	7.18
trustees report and accounts,	7.5
statements of entitlements,	7.11–15
strategies, effective communication,	7.18

Inland Revenue,

address,	3.23
calculations, benefit,	8.48
defined terms used by,	3.8
final remuneration,	3.10
normal retirement date,	3.11
remuneration,	3.9
retained benefits,	3.12
limits,	3.7
people in pensions,	5.18
summary of limits on benefits,	3.16

Insurance,

trustees,	4.51

Insured schemes, 10.15

Internal dispute resolution procedure,

scheme documents,	6.14
trustees' implementation of,	4.25

Investment,

additional voluntary contributions (AVCs),	
building society,	11.13
generally,	11.12
matching,	11.17
with profits,	11.14
scheme assets,	11.16
unit-linked,	11.15
advice,	10.4
assets,	10.9
balanced management,	10.18
Cowan v NUM,	10.3
diversification,	10.5
index-tracking,	10.20
insured schemes,	10.15
management approaches,	
alternatives,	10.21
balanced management,	10.18
index-tracking,	10.20
passive management,	10.20
scheme-specific,	10.19
selection of manager,	10.22
specialist managers,	10.19
manager,	10.22
monitoring,	10.26
past performance,	10.23
performance targets,	10.25
selection,	10.22–24
money purchase schemes,	10.12
monitoring investment manager,	10.26
passive management,	10.20
performance targets,	10.25
pooled funds,	10.16
segregated management,	10.17
selection of manager,	10.22
self investment,	10.7
specialist managers,	10.19
statement of investment principles,	6.7, 10.8
strategy,	10.10–12
final salary scheme,	10.11
money purchase scheme,	10.12
segregated management,	10.17
structure,	
generally,	10.13
insured schemes,	10.15
pooled funds,	10.16
suitability,	10.6
trustees' duties,	
best interests of scheme member,	10.3
diversification,	10.5
expert advice,	10.4
generally,	4.12, 10.1
prudent man,	10.2
self investment,	10.7
statement of investment principles,	6.7, 10.8
suitability of investments,	10.6
UK pension fund investments,	10.11

J

Joining pension schemes, 1.6

Basic Guide to Pensions

L
Leaving plan,
  calculations, benefit, 8.18–20
  death in service benefits, 8.29, 8.30
  generally, 8.18
  increases under defined benefit contribution plan between leaving and retirement, 8.20
  increases under defined benefit plan between leaving and retirement, 8.19
  record keeping, 8.45
Legal advisers, 5.15
Legal framework,
  cases, decided, 3.5
  contracting out, 3.17
  European law, 3.6
  generally, 3.1
  guaranteed minimum pensions, 3.18
  Inland Revenue limits, 3.7
  limits on benefits, 3.15
  limits on contributions, 3.14
  mixed benefit schemes, 3.21
  money purchase schemes, 3.20
  reference scheme test, 3.19
  secondary legislation, 3.4
  statutes governing pensions, 3.3
  transfers from contracted-out schemes, 3.22
  trust law, 3.2
Liabilities,
  trustees,
    accounting for profit, 4.41
    breach of trust, 4.38
    choice of remedy, 4.42
    compensation for loss suffered, 4.40
    costs, 4.44
    extent, 4.39
    generally, 4.1
    invalidity of acts, 4.43
    penalties, 4.35, 4.36
    statutory liability, 4.45
    trust law, 4.37
Lump sum,
  distribution by trustees on death, 4.32

M
Matching, 11.17
Meetings,
  minutes, 4.57
  notice, 4.56
Member-nominated trustees, 5.8
  appointment, 4.23, 5.7

MFR, 9.13
Minimum funding requirement, 9.13
Minutes of meetings, 4.57
Mixed benefit schemes,
  legal framework, 3.21
Money purchase schemes, 2.12
  funding, 9.3
  information, 7.7
  investment, 10.12
  legal framework, 3.20
  lifestyle, 10.12

N
Notice of meetings, 4.56

O
Occupational pensions,
  additional voluntary contributions (AVCs), 11.3
  age of retirement, 2.18
  contracting in, 2.14
  contracting out, 2.14
  contributions, 2.21
  defined benefit schemes, 2.11
  dependant's benefits, 2.20
  design methods,
    defined benefit schemes, 2.11
    final salary schemes, 2.11
    generally, 2.10
    hybrid schemes, 2.13
    money purchase schemes, 2.12
  employer, 5.2
  final salary schemes, 2.11
  group personal pensions, 2.9
  hybrid schemes, 2.13
  large, 2.7
  money purchase schemes, 2.12
  normal retirement age, 2.18
  pensionable salary, 2.16
  pensionable service, 2.17
  Small Self-Administered Schemes (SSAS), 2.8
  taxation of benefits, 2.19
  types,
    group personal pensions, 2.9
    large, 2.7
    Small Self-Administered Schemes (SSAS), 2.8
Occupational Pensions Advisory Service (OPAS), 5.20
Occupational Pensions Regulatory Authority. *See* **OPRA**
OPAS, 5.20

Index

OPRA,
  disclosure of information, 4.16
  offences, 5.19
  penalties, 5.19
  powers, 5.19

P

Payment of benefits,
  trustees' duty, 4.7
Payment schedule,
  trustees, production by, 4.9
Payroll systems, 5.2
Penalties,
  table, 4.36
  trustees, 4.35, 4.36
Pension schemes,
  concept, 1.5
  eligibility, 1.6
  generally, 1.1
  history, 1.2
  joining, 1.6
  present position, 1.4
  purpose, 1.5
  reasons for having, 1.11
  types of provision. *See* Types of provision
Pension splitting on divorce, 8.39
  defined benefit plan, 8.40
  defined contribution plan, 8.41
Pensionable salary,
  occupational pensions, 2.16
Pensionable service,
  occupational pensions, 2.17
Pensioneer trustees, 5.10
Pensions Compensation Board, 5.21
Pensions Ombudsman, 5.22
People in pensions,
  administrator, 5.14
  advisers, 5.15
  auditor, 5.13
  employer, 5.2
  fund managers, 5.16
  generally, 5.1
  Inland Revenue, 5.18
  legal advisers, 5.15
  pension consultants, 5.17
  scheme actuary, 5.12
  trustees. *See* Trustees
Personal pensions,
  additional voluntary contributions (AVCs), 11.6
  contributions,
    limits, 2.23
  income drawdown, 2.24
  meaning, 2.22
  self-invested personal pensions, 2.25
Pooled funds, 10.16
Powers of trustees,
  addresses, 4.58
  amendment of scheme rules, 4.30
  augmentation, 4.31
  decision making, 4.54
  delegation, 4.29
  distribution of lump sum on death, 4.32
  exercise,
    decision making, 4.54
    minutes of meetings, 4.57
    notice of meetings, 4.56
    trust deed and rules, 4.55
  generally, 4.1, 4.28
  notice of meetings, 4.56
  texts, useful, 4.59
  transfers, 4.33
Presentations, 7.16
Professional advisers,
  appointment by trustees, 4.13
  disclosure of information, 4.16
Professional trustees, 5.9

R

Record keeping,
  annual, 8.44
  general requirement, 8.42
  joining plan, member, 8.43
  leaving service, 8.45
  ongoing, 8.44
  retirement, 8.46
Reference scheme test,
  legal framework, 3.19
Registration,
  duties of trustees, 4.17
Removal,
  remuneration, 5.6
  trustees, 5.5, 5.6, 6.3
Remuneration,
  definition, 3.9
  final,
    definition, 3.10
  trustees, 5.6
Retained benefits,
  definition, 3.12
Retirement,
  age, 1.7
    normal age of retirement, 2.18
  benefits on, 7.12

death, 8.47
early retirement,
  payments, calculation of, 1.8
  without penalty, 1.10
late retirement payments, calculation
  of, 1.9
normal age of retirement, 2.18
normal retirement date, 3.11
record keeping, 8.46
trustees, 6.3

S
Schedule of contributions, 6.12
Scheme actuary, 5.12
Scheme booklet, 6.6, 7.4
Scheme documents,
  actuarial valuation report, 6.10
  addresses, 6.15
  annual report, trustees', 6.11
  audited accounts, 6.8
  booklet, scheme, 6.6
  company accounts, 6.9
  contracting-out certificate, 6.13
  deeds,
    adherence, 6.5
    amendment, 6.4
    appointment of trustees, 6.3
    participation, 6.5
    removal of trustees, 6.3
    retirement of trustees, 6.3
  establishing scheme, 6.2
  generally, 6.1
  internal dispute resolution procedure,
    6.14
  schedule of contributions, 6.12
  statement of investment principles, 6.7
Scheme members,
  best interests of scheme members,
    trustee's duty to act in, 4.6, 10.3
  disclosure of information to, 4.15
  impartially between scheme members
    duty of trustees to act, 4.6
Self investment, 10.7
Self-invested personal pensions, 2.25
SERPS, 2.4
Service,
  limits,
    benefits, 3.15
    contributions, 3.14
    meaning, 3.13
Sex discrimination,
  eligibility to join pension scheme,
    1.6

**Small-Self Administered Schemes
  (SSAS),** 2.8
Stakeholder pensions,
  additional voluntary contributions
    (AVCs), 11.5
  background, 2.26
  benefits, 2.26
  concurrency, 2.26
  contract based, 2.27
  contracting out, 2.26
  contributions,
    employer, 2.26
    member, 2.26
  fees, 2.26
  group personal pension, 2.26
  provision for others, 2.26
  relevant employees, 2.26
  set up, 2.26
**State Earnings Related Pension
  (SERPS),** 2.4
State pension,
  basic, 2.3
  contributions, 2.6
  generally, 2.1, 2.2
  provision, 2.2
  State Earnings Related Pension
    (SERPS), 2.4
  State Second Pension (S2P), 2.5
State Second Pension (S2P), 2.5
Statement of investment principles,
    6.7, 10.8
Statements of entitlements, 7.11–15
  death, benefits on, 7.13
  retirement, benefits on, 7.12
  transfer values, 7.15
  withdrawal, on, 7.14
Strategy,
  effective communication, 7.18
  investment, 10.10–12
    final salary scheme, 10.11
    money purchase scheme, 10.12

T
Taxation of benefits,
  occupational pensions, 2.19
Transfer values,
  statements of entitlements, 7.15
Transfers,
  acceptance, 4.33
  contracted-out schemes, from, 3.22
  making, 4.33
  powers of trustees, 4.33
Trust law, 3.2

Index

Trustees,
accounts, 7.5
acting in accordance with trust deed and rules, 4.3
annual report, 6.11
appointment, 5.5, 6.3
best interests of scheme members, acting in, 4.5
breach of trust, 4.38
collection of contributions, 4.8
court orders relating to divorce, compliance with duties, 4.19
custodian, 5.11
Data Protection Act 1998, compliance with, 4.18
deeds of removal, retirement and appointment, 6.3
delegation by, 4.29
disability discrimination, compliance with law on, 4.24
distribution of lump sum on death by, 4.32
duties. *See* Duties of trustees
eligibility to be, 5.4
exclusion clauses, 4.47
generally, 5.3
impartially between scheme members, duty of trustees to act, 4.6
indemnity clauses. *See* Indemnity clauses
independent, 5.8
insurance, 4.51
internal dispute resolution procedure, implementation of, 4.25
investment of fund by, 4.12
liabilities, 4.34
  accounting for profit, 4.41
  breach of trust, 4.38
  choice of remedy, 4.42
  compensation for loss suffered, 4.40
  costs, 4.44
  extent, 4.39
  generally, 4.1
  invalidity of acts, 4.43
  penalties, 4.35, 4.36
  statutory liability, 4.45
  trust law, 4.37
  Trustee Act 1925, s 61, 4.52
member-nominated, 4.23, 5.7
payment of benefits, 4.7
payment schedule, production of, 4.9
penalties, 4.35, 4.36

pensioneer, 5.10
powers. *See* Powers of trustees
professional, 5.9
professional advisers, appointment of, 4.13
protection, 4.46–52
  exclusion clauses, 4.47
  indemnity clauses. *See* Indemnity clauses
  insurance, 4.51
prudently, conscientiously and honestly, duty to act, 4.4
removal, 5.5, 5.6, 6.3
remuneration, 5.6
reports, 7.5
retirement, 6.3
schedule of contributions, production of, 4.9

Types of provision,
generally, 2.1
occupational pensions. *See* Occupational pensions
personal pensions. *See* Personal pensions
SERPS, 2.4
stakeholder pensions 2.26–2.28. *See also* Stakeholder pensions
State Earnings Related Pension (SERPS), 2.4
State pension,
  basic, 2.3
  contributions, 2.6
  generally, 2.1, 2.2
  provision, 2.2
  SERPS, 2.4
  State Earnings Related Pension (SERPS), 2.4
  State Second Pension (S2P), 2.5
State Second Pension (S2P), 2.5
unapproved pensions,
  background, 2.29
  funded, 2.30
  unfunded, 2.31
  use, 2.32

U
Unapproved pensions,
background, 2.29
funded, 2.30
unfunded, 2.31
use, 2.32

V
Valuations,
  actuary,
    assets, valuation of, 9.11
    assumptions, actuarial, 9.9
    benefits, valuation of, 9.10
    generally, 9.4
    ongoing, 9.8
    reports, 6.10, 9.15
  timing, 9.5
  assets, 9.11
  benefits, 9.10
  discontinuance, 9.12
  methods, 9.8
  minimum funding requirement, 9.13
  reports, actuarial, 6.10, 9.15
  sample result, 9.11